~ REVIEWS ~

"This book is short on philosophy and long on pragmatic advice."
— Harvey Mackay, author of *Swim with the Sharks* and *Pushing the Envelope*

"This is the only book on CRM that has made it to my credenza."
— Stan Davis, author of *Blur* and *Lessons from the Future*

"*CRM Automation* is a blueprint for a successful CRM implementation."
— Ken Blanchard, co-author, *The One Minute Manager*®

"Barton Goldenberg's bottom-line approach to CRM makes this book a necessity to any company concerned with ROI."
— Beth Struckell, VP, division of PepsiCo

"*CRM Automation* gets to the heart of what a successful CRM implementation is all about—people, process, and technology. You can save hundreds of hours and thousands of dollars by reading this book before launching a CRM initiative."
— Bob McLaughlin, former VP, McGraw-Hill

"I would not consider embarking on a CRM project unless I read this book."
— Jonathan Allen, managing director, WorldMail (DHL/Deutsche Post)

"In *CRM Automation* Barton Goldenberg shares his real-world experience and pragmatism, the same approach that led us to the success of our global CRM initiative."
— Rosalie Duong, VP of sales and marketing/general manager, North America, QIAGEN

"If you have anything to do with CRM, buy this book."
— Tim Bajarin, president, Creative Strategies, Inc.

CRM
Automation

ISBN 0-13-008851-X

90000

CRM Automation

BARTON J. GOLDENBERG

Prentice Hall PTR
Upper Saddle River, NJ 07458
www.phptr.com

Library of Congress Cataloging-in-Publication Data

Goldenberg, Barton.
   CRM automation / Barton Goldenberg.
     p. cm.
   Includes index.
   ISBN: 0-13-008851-X
     1. Customer relations--Marketing. 2. Customer relations--Data processing. I. Title.

   HF5415.5 .G65 2002
   658.8'12--dc21

                                                                    2001059140

Editorial/Production Supervisor: *Vanessa Moore*
Acqusition Editor: *Paul Petralia*
Editorial Assistant: *Richard Winkler*
Marketing Manager: *Debby vanDijk*
Manufacturing Manager: *Alexis Heydt-Long*
Cover Design: *John Christiana* and *Talar Agasyan-Boorujy*
Cover Design Director: *Jerry Votta*
Series Design: *Gail Cocker-Bogusz*
Project Coordinator: *Anne R. Garcia*
ISM, Director of Public Relations: *Jennifer Aleknavage*

© 2002 Barton Goldenberg
Published by Prentice Hall PTR, a division of Pearson Education, Inc.
Upper Saddle River, NJ 07458

The publisher offers discounts on this book when ordered in bulk quantities.
For more information, contact
Corporate Sales Department,
Prentice Hall PTR
One Lake Street
Upper Saddle River, NJ 07458
Phone: 800-382-3419; FAX: 201-236-7141
E-mail: corpsales@prenhall.com

Printed in the United States of America

10 9 8 7 6 5 4 3 2 1

ISBN 0-13-008851-X

Pearson Education Ltd.
Pearson Education Australia PTY, Limited
Pearson Education Singapore, Pte. Ltd
Pearson Education North Asia Ltd
Pearson Education Canada, Ltd.
Pearson Educación de Mexico, S.A. de C.V.
Pearson Education — Japan
Pearson Education Malaysia, Pte. Ltd

This book is dedicated to:
My ISM colleagues, whose support has made this book a reality.
My beautiful wife Marina, whose love has never wavered.
Daniel and Nina, whom I love so much; always make time to learn!

Contents

CHAPTER 3
Successful CRM: Getting the
People, Process, and Technology Mix Right   13

CHAPTER 4
CRM Strategy Formulation   23

CHAPTER 5
Determining CRM Business Processes   33

CHAPTER 6
CRM Business Application Trends   39

CHAPTER 20
Ensuring Consistent Customer Service Across Channels   157

CHAPTER 21
E-Marketing and CRM   165

CHAPTER 22
Knowledge Management and CRM   171

CHAPTER 23
Application Service Providers (ASP): An Overview   175

CHAPTER 24
Addressing CRM System Security Risks   189

CHAPTER 25
The Importance of Data Integrity   199

CHAPTER 26
CRM: An International Perspective   207

CHAPTER 27
The Future Direction of CRM   213

Preface

It is with great pleasure that I introduce the first edition of *CRM Automation*. Over the past 18 years, I have had the pleasure of working with more than 300 enterprise-class customer relationship management (CRM) deployments. This book attempts to share the lessons learned.

The book contains 27 chapters that include:

- A definition of CRM;

- A description of the people, process, and technology issues that impact CRM;

- "How-to" chapters on creating CRM strategy, putting together your CRM value proposition and Business Case, writing your CRM system specification document, selecting your CRM software vendor, and addressing CRM security risks;

- Discussions on the significance of data integrity, the role of e-business, e-marketing, e-service, knowledge management, and international CRM issues;

- A 10-step blueprint for effective CRM; and

- A list of ISM's Top 30 CRM software selections for 2002.

Many individuals who purchase this book are also considering buying a CRM software package. To obtain comparative, extensive reviews of ISM's Top 30 winners, each of which has been evaluated against 166 business functions, technical features, and user friendliness/support criteria, I strongly encourage you to follow the simple instructions listed on the tearout card at the back of this book. You will be instructed to log onto ISM's Web site, *http://www.ismguide.com/ph2*, put in an access code PH2, which will provide you direct access to purchase a paper or electronic version of our 2002 CRM Software Reviews product. You will be able to purchase one, three, the Top 15, or all Top 30 review(s).

Please note that ISM's Top 30 software selections have been chosen as a result of testing dozens of CRM software packages currently sold worldwide. Each Top 30 software evaluation, which tests the vendor's latest commercially available release, lasts between one to three days in ISM's Software Testing Laboratory in Bethesda, Maryland. Fifteen of the Top 30 packages get designated to ISM's "Top 15" list. When you purchase a paper or electronic version of our 2002 CRM Software Reviews product, you also will receive full contact information for the winners.

Here are my best wishes that *CRM Automation* assists you in your CRM automation efforts.

Barton Goldenberg
President & Founder
ISM, Inc.
Bethesda, MD

About the Author

Barton Goldenberg, president of ISM, Inc., has established his Bethesda, Maryland-based company as the premier Customer Relationship Management (CRM) research, market analysis, and consulting firm. He founded ISM in 1985.

Goldenberg's foresight and vision to integrate sales, marketing, customer service, e-business, and business intelligence has been central to today's CRM industry success. He has reinvented the industry and is now poised to pioneer another business model for the 21st century, which he speaks about in his new presentation, *Creating the Real-Time Enterprise.*

His bottom-line, results-oriented style has made him popular with chief executives around the world and has helped to make him a sought after speaker and writer. In the United States, Europe, and Asia, Mr. Goldenberg conducts executive development programs on information technology and its impact on corporate productivity and business strategy. ISM's services include CRM software selection and implementation roadmap, CRM readiness assessments, CRM Business Case formulation, CRM strategy creation, CRM management briefings, and CRM company, vendor and investment community research. Clients include Abbey National, IBM, Lucent Technologies, New York Stock Exchange, McGraw-Hill, Roche and Xerox.

Mr. Goldenberg is the author of *CRM Automation* (Prentice Hall, 2002), which provides a step-by-step process for successfully implementing a CRM program; and the benchmark *Guide to CRM Automation* (now in its 10th anniversary edition), which features ISM's selection of the Top 30 software packages, inclusive of the Top 15 leaders.

Mr. Goldenberg is co-chairman and co-founder of the CRM conferences and expositions sponsored by DCI, Inc. worldwide. He has presented keynote addresses at conferences including Sales and Marketing Executives International and The Conference Board. He also speaks at executive seminars sponsored by *Business Week, CIO* magazine and *Inc.* magazine.

Mr. Goldenberg is a columnist for *CRM* magazine, *e-Week*, and *Sales & Marketing Management*, for which he serves on the publication's Editorial Advisory Board. As a CRM industry spokesperson, he is often quoted in trade and general media, including *CIO*, *The Industry Standard*, *Information Week*, and PlanetIT.com, and he conducts broadcast interviews including CNBC's "Minding Your Business."

He was recognized by *CRM* magazine as one of the "Ten Most Influential People in Customer Relationship Management" for his leadership in galvanizing the CRM industry and his role in co-founding and co-chairing DCI's CRM conferences.

Prior to founding ISM, Mr. Goldenberg held senior management positions at the U.S. Department of State and Monsanto Europe S.A. He holds a B.Sc. (Economics) degree with honors from the Wharton School of Business and a M.Sc. (Economics) degree from the London School of Economics.

Customer Relationship Management (CRM)—An Overview

Understanding the CRM industry has become increasingly complex. The overall CRM industry grew in excess of 40 percent per year from 1995 to 2000. This rapid growth attracted many new players to the industry, which led to numerous new vendor offerings. In an effort to achieve differentiation, many new business functional modules have been developed along with new and complex technology alternatives. It has become difficult to answer the simple question "What type of CRM program is best for me?"

Despite the negative impact of the current economic slowdown on overall CRM industry growth, which decreased in 2001 to between 15–20 percent, ISM and other leading CRM analysts forecast that starting in 2002, the CRM industry will return to an annual growth rate of 20–30 percent through 2005. Recent forecasts call for worldwide CRM software spending alone to reach $76 billion by 2005, up from $23 billion in 2000.

Nonetheless, all the new players, new business functional modules, and the new and complex technology alternatives mean that making sense of today's CRM marketplace has become an increasingly daunting task, even for companies like ISM that have been actively involved in the CRM industry since the mid-1980s.

There are two critical issues that will impact the future direction of the CRM industry: resolution of butting life cycles and overcoming the current doom and gloom.

Butting Life Cycles

There is a tension resulting from the dynamics of today's CRM marketplace, where one CRM life cycle (client/server technology) is butting heads with a newer CRM life cycle (Web-based, e-customer). The life cycle based on client/server technology largely supports employee-facing CRM systems (aimed at helping internal sales, marketing, and customer service personnel), whereas the newer Web-based, e-customer life cycle supports more customer-facing CRM systems (where customers use Web browsers to access company-specific information and services). Moreover, the increasing availability of new Web-based tools has helped to accelerate the impressive growth of the Web-based, e-customer life cycle.

What, you may ask, is likely to happen with these two butting life cycles, and what will this mean for the future of the CRM industry? These two butting life cycles are likely to co-exist over the next five years. Here's why.

The Client/Server Life Cycle

The client/server life cycle has a large installed client base that has seen the benefits of CRM firsthand. In other words, the clients trust their CRM client/server vendor. Moreover, most, if not all, CRM client/server vendors are in the process of adopting a more Web-based, e-customer centric approach. While their CRM automation software may not be Web-based from the ground up, they are taking necessary steps to become Web-compatible and they are promoting this to their large client/server installed base. Some of these vendors (e.g., Onyx) have rewritten their software to become entirely Web-based.

The result: The large client/server installed base trusts their CRM client/server vendor and continues to work with them as these vendors continue to support their client/server architecture while moving towards a new Web-based, e-customer centric approach. This trust, along with a very significant sum of promotional money by the CRM client/server vendors, keeps the client/server life cycle alive and kicking despite this technology becoming increasingly dated.

The Web-Based, E-Customer Life Cycle

On the other hand, the new Web-based, e-customer CRM vendors are in the process of building their own customer base. Needless to say, Web-based, e-customer CRM software is several years younger than client/server CRM software and thus Web-based, e-customer CRM software vendors have had less time to build their client base. In this regard, the Web-based, e-customer life cycle is at this time in the introduction/growth phase, whereas the client/ server life cycle is at this time in the growth/maturity phase. Despite having a smaller installed client base, the Web-based, e-customer CRM automation vendors are offering very impressive CRM software. In fact, one could argue that their entire Web-based software offers functionality (e.g., customer self-service, click-stream analysis, content management, etc.) that many of today's customers desire.

The result: Their business continues to grow rapidly. Moreover, given the very large market capitalization of the existing and emerging Web-based, e-customer CRM automation vendors (e.g., BroadVision, KANA, E.piphany, Vignette, etc.), there is plenty of money to promote this new and exciting class of CRM automation software.

Learning to Live with Butting Life Cycles

In summary, there are two life cycles that exist within today's CRM automation industry. The client/server life cycle is made up of hundreds of solid CRM automation vendors that are moving into the Web world. The Web-based, e-customer life cycle is made up of dozens of respectable CRM automation vendors that are growing their customer base. ISM feels strongly that both life cycles will co-exist over the next five or so years, and that slowly the client/server life cycle will give way to the Web-based, e-customer life cycle.

If you are a CRM automation software buyer, expect to be pulled in two directions during this butting period, which could well last another few years. To maintain control of this situation over the next few years, be sure to ask the client/server CRM automation software vendors to explain their short-, medium-, and long-term development strategy vis-à-vis Web-based, e-customer business functionality. When dealing with Web-based, e-customer CRM software vendors, be sure to ask how these vendors currently integrate with existing client-server applications and how they expect to manage integration in the future. I humbly submit that over the long-term, the CRM industry will indeed move to a Web-based world.

Why the Current Doom and Gloom?

Another critical issue that will impact the future direction of the CRM industry is overcoming the industry's current doom and gloom. The dot-com demise along with a deteriorating global economy has, without doubt, negatively impacted the CRM industry's current stability and growth. On the one hand, most executives acknowledge that they need to stay close to their customers during this unprecedented business cycle. On the other hand, executives need to keep costs down; if they do spend on CRM initiatives, they need to see measurable success early on.

The IT Analyst Dilemma

It does not help matters that a number of leading IT analysts (Gartner Group, META Group and others), continue to claim that greater than 50 percent of all CRM projects fail to meet user expectations. I've been in this business for 17 years and have helped more than 300 companies worldwide to implement their global CRM initiatives. To the contrary, my customers claim a success rate for their CRM initiatives well in excess of 50 percent. That is why the doom and gloom figures of leading IT analysts have always troubled me. As explained below, CRM initiatives, if properly implemented, can deliver measurable benefit.

I'm not knocking the leading IT analysts. After all, it is their business to provide general reports of interest to their paying client base. What concerns me is the way that they measure success rates. Let's take an example.

A Mini Case Study

I had the pleasure of working with one of America's leading telecommunications manufacturers. This company decided to implement a global CRM initiative to approximately 4,500 employees worldwide. When the project was completed, I asked the VP of sales and marketing (the sponsor of the CRM initiative) whether the initiative was a success. He put his thumb up, said "yes," and explained that because of the system, he now had a fairly complete customer profile of his key accounts that could be used by all customer-facing personnel when dealing with the customer. Yet when I went to the CIO of this company and asked whether the initiative was a success, he placed his thumb down and said "no." He explained that the system was to have integrated several dozen internal legacy and external information sources into the CRM system and that this had not happened due to integration complexity. So, how would leading analysts categorize this implementation, a success or a failure?

Here is where I have my biggest problem with the leading IT analyst figures of 50 percent or more failures. In the majority of implementations that I have been a part of, the company sets clear and measurable metrics prior to implementing the CRM system and then uses these metrics to measure success or failure of the system. This requires discipline but then again, as Peter Drucker, a renown author and advisor on corporate management, reminds us, if you can't measure it you can't manage it.

Getting to Success

For me, success or failure of a CRM initiative does require the company to create a powerful CRM Business Case (see Chapter 10, "Creating Your CRM Business Case") that:

1. Sets baseline metrics for those business functions that will be automated (e.g., how much time per week a sales rep spends creating difficult reports, the number of customer service calls that are successfully resolved during the initial customer call).

2. Sets measurable objectives ("success criteria") for each of the proposed business functional areas that will be impacted by the system (e.g., reps will save *x* hours per week by not having to create difficult reports since the system will automatically deliver needed reports to the rep; resolution of customer service calls resolved during the initial call will increase by *x* percent because the system provides customer service personnel with needed information at the touch of a button).

3. Measures and reports on the accomplishment of each objective on a regular basis (preferably quarterly and not less than every six months) to the top management team responsible for the ultimate success of the CRM initiative.

While this simple three-step approach seems quite logical, you would be surprised how few companies get this measurement part of their CRM initiative right, or how few companies create a CRM Business Case that incorporates these measurements along with ROI information. By acknowledging that measuring success will differ for each CRM initiative depending on the metrics agreed to by the company, perhaps leading IT vendors would be in a position to refine their current 50 percent failure rate suggestion.

Summary

The CRM industry is in transition. On the one hand, rapid CRM industry growth has slowed considerably. On the other hand, CRM still remains a very healthy industry as well as the fastest growing application in the software industry. The industry will migrate from client/server architectures to Web-based, e-customer offerings. New players will enter the industry and there will be more consolidations. More companies will set and measure CRM-related metrics in support of their respective CRM Business Case.

It is my hope that in the following chapters, which cover topics ranging from how to build a CRM implementation blueprint, to a description of the latest business, technical, and future CRM industry trends, you will better understand how to drive your CRM initiative's success, and gain insight into how other companies have achieved their CRM value proposition.

CRM:
A Working
Definition

2

Defining Customer Relationship Management (CRM) is not an easy task. Coined in the mid-1990s and heavily promoted during in the late-1990s, the term *CRM* still means different things to different people. While ISM is convinced that there is no one correct definition of CRM, and that the definition of CRM will evolve and change over time, here is our definition for this year's Guide:

"CRM" integrates people, process, and technology to maximize relationships with all customers. CRM is a comprehensive approach that provides seamless coordination between all customer-facing functions. CRM increasingly leverages the Internet.

ISM can't stress enough the importance of the people, process, and technology integration for a successful CRM initiative. While important, all too often the technology component takes on a disproportionate emphasis within a CRM initiative to the detriment of the overall success of the initiative. Keeping this warning in mind, let us now turn to the possible components of a CRM automation system.

ISM feels that through December 2002, CRM automation will consist of 10 components as described below. Each of these 10 components consists of subcomponents (with each subcomponent equating to specific software modules offered by CRM software vendors). This means that your initial CRM automation system is likely to consist of one or more of these components—based on your prioritized CRM business functional needs—and is likely to grow over time to include additional components from this list, as well as new components that will emerge as the CRM industry matures. A word of caution: it is unreasonable to assume that any initial CRM automation system would consist of all 10 of these components, as this would be the equivalent of swallowing an elephant. As you review the 10 components of CRM, and their subcomponents, ask yourself which of these components seem to make sense for your company's CRM initiative and in what order you would incorporate these components.

Components of CRM

Time Management

This component includes single user and group calendar/scheduling as well as e-mail. Microsoft Outlook (as well as Lotus Notes) has become the calendar/scheduling standard within the CRM software industry. Moreover, bidirectional integration with MS Outlook is also becoming a de facto standard such that you can enter a date-specific activity or a contact from within MS Outlook and the activity or date is automatically input within the CRM software application, or vice versa. In addition to single user and group calendar/scheduling, the time management component also includes the creation and management of task lists as well as e-mail.

Sales/Sales Management

This component includes management of contact profiles and history, management of account information including activities, and order entry. Increasingly, this category includes proposal generators, which permit sales personnel to easily and quickly create a comprehensive and good-looking proposal that draws upon "boiler-plate" templates, as well as configurators that allow sales personnel (or increasingly the customer) to easily and quickly configure products and services based on specific customer needs. Pipeline analysis (forecasting, sales cycle analysis), sales metrics (e.g., win rates, loss rates), territory alignment and assignment, and roll-up/drill-down reporting functionality are also important considerations.

Telemarketing/Telesales

This component includes classical functionality such as call list assembly, auto dialing, scripting, call tracking and order taking. While traditionally this had been an outbound function, increasingly telemarketing/telesales handles inbound calls as well.

Customer Contact Center

This component includes customer service functions such as incident assignment/escalation/tracking/reporting, problem management/resolution, order management/promising, and warranty/contract management. Increasingly, customer service and support software includes a Web-based, self-service capability that customers can easily access using a browser. Improvements in customer self-service and support have been significantly enhanced by the use of knowledge management engines, along with the ability to apply the principles of one to one customer service. Assisted (e.g., interactive chat, assisted Web browsing) and self-service options coincide in the Customer Contact Center environment.

E-Marketing

The marketing component continues to receive considerable attention within the CRM software industry. Increased attention continues to be given to Web-centric encyclopedias and knowledge management, to market segmentation complemented by comprehensive campaign management life cycle tools, to lead generation/enhancement/tracking, and increasingly to partner relationship management (i.e., offering information links within the differing distribution channel layers). E-marketing facilitates one-to-one, permission-based marketing efforts. These marketing subcomponents often depend on customer data received from Web sites, and/or from a data warehouse enhanced by data warehouse tools such as data mining engines.

Business Intelligence

This component includes extensive and easy-to-use reporting capabilities. Fixed and ad-hoc reports are the norm, and to ensure the highest quality of reporting functionality many CRM software vendors are opting to integrate with leading third-party report writing tools (e.g., Crystal Reports, Actuate), which provide comprehensive report writing and graphical tools. Increasingly, CRM software vendors also are offering executive dashboards and personalized portals to facilitate and enhance the business intelligence (i.e., executive information) component within CRM automation.

Field Service Support

While field service support has not received a lot of attention in the past, increasingly CRM software vendors acknowledge that this is a large and growing market segment. The field service support component includes work order dispatching, part order/reservation, preventative maintenance schedules, and real-time information transfer via mobile technologies.

These first seven components constitute what is commonly referred to as the *front office* or *customer-facing* functions. The remaining three components comprise both business and technology issues. They deserve close attention given their impact on tomorrow's CRM industry.

E-Business

This component, which is primarily focused on functionality for the exchange of products/services via the Web, has become increasingly important given the growth of Web-based business-to-business (B2B) and business-to-consumer (B2C) e-commerce applications. It is unlikely that CRM automation software will include every e-commerce component. What has become clear, however, is that CRM software will include a Web-based, front-end interface into commercially available, third-party e-commerce engines, which include shopping carts and storefront applications. This front-end interface will in turn support increasingly complex B2B and B2C e-business applications leveraging new technological advances in such areas as intelligence routing/click stream monitoring, content management/personalization, customer self service and cross selling/up-selling.

Multimodal Access

This component allows customers to reach your company via mail, phone (including leaving messages), fax, e-mail (including attachments), and the Web (including chat forums). This means that your CRM system must support multiple modes of access from your customers while simultaneously giving the impression that regardless of which mode or modes a customer uses, you maintain one holistic view of the customer at all times.

Data Sharing Tools

Although integration to legacy systems, the Web, and third-party external information sources has become increasingly important for an effective CRM system, this component is somewhat of a technical component. Sales personnel, customer service personnel, maybe even customers, may want to know the status of their orders, or whether an invoice has been received. Production-line and inventory managers may want to know the latest sales forecast. CRM automation software vendors either build native ERP hooks directly into their software, or seamlessly integrate into ERP systems via third-party "hook" software from companies like CrossWorlds, web-Methods, and others. Data synchronization is also very important for data sharing. This includes mobile data synchronization from multiple field devices (wired or increasingly wireless), as well as enterprise synchronization with multiple databases/application servers. Many CRM software vendors have built their own data synchronization functionality, although we also see integration with third-party synchronization engines such as Synchrologic.

Unfortunately, there still are no data synchronization standards within the CRM industry, and all too often it becomes the onus of the customer to ensure the quality of a CRM automation software vendor's data synchronization capability, including whether or not the software synchronization process is scalable. There are now data synchronization testing facilities that can test scalability of a CRM software vendor's product (e.g., at Compaq, Microsoft, and elsewhere), so be sure to ask your CRM software vendor to show you their scalability test results if this is germane to your CRM implementation.

Summary

To summarize, the CRM definition is an umbrella concept that currently consists of the following 10 components:

- Time management
- Sales/sales management
- Telemarketing/telesales
- Customer contact center
- E-marketing
- Business intelligence (executive information)

- Field service support
- E-business
- Multimodal access
- Data sharing tools

At the beginning of this chapter, we suggested that the above 10-component definition would be valid through the end of year 2002. Given the dynamic nature of the CRM marketplace, we expect this list of 10 components to evolve and change to reflect developments in the marketplace.

Successful CRM: Getting the People, Process, and Technology Mix Right

CRM success requires the seamless integration of every aspect of business that touches the customer—including people, process, and technology—revolutionized by the Internet. Each component presents significant challenges, but it is the ability to integrate all three that makes or breaks a CRM system.

People

The people component is the most difficult component given the sensitivity of users to change. CRM systems, which support and/or automate integrated customer processes, often imply changes in the way users do their day-to-day jobs. Users who have not properly understood the reasons for the change, who did not participate in formulation of the change, who did not receive sufficient information about the change, or who did not get sufficiently trained on the change will often be adverse to that change. The story of "the rotten apple spoiling the lot" is relevant here since negative feedback can substantially harm a CRM system's success.

Here are a few examples of companies that have been substantially impacted by the people component within their CRM initiative.

Example 1

A globally respected telecommunications company launched a global CRM initiative. The launch included the formation of a superuser group (consisting of 12–16 user representatives from sales, marketing, customer service, e-business, and other customer-facing functions). The superuser group, which is formed at the outset of the CRM initiative, is responsible for providing user needs input throughout implementation of the CRM initiative.

Senior management had some doubts about the company's ability to meet the initiative's deadlines, and therefore decided not to communicate or promote the initiative too loudly to potential internal and external users until the initiative was near completion. Needless to say, as with all CRM initiatives, a number of minor glitches occurred. All of these glitches were successfully resolved. Yet through the company's internal rumor mill, these minor glitches became major problems, even system killers. By the time the company was ready to invite internal and external users for training on the application, approximately 50 percent of the users said they knew little about the initiative, were not interested in participating in the initiative, and declined training for the initiative. The initiative struggled along for another four months, and the company then pulled the plug and absorbed a loss in excess of $800,000.

Lesson learned: the company should have launched a full-fledged communications program around the CRM initiative, thereby ensuring that key personnel and users were kept up to date on how the initiative was coming along and how the initiative would impact their day-to-day work lives.

Example 2

In another example, a leading service organization launched a global CRM initiative. It formed a "core team" consisting of senior managers from technical, business, and training functions. Business users were not involved from the outset since the business manager (who was a part of the CRM "core" team, and not too highly respected by business management) felt that he could speak on their behalf. What a mistake! It became evident early on that the business manager was out of touch with the needs of the business users. More important, the business manager foolishly saw the business users as a threat to his next promotion and refused, despite putting up multiple smokescreens, to collaborate closely with the users. After 12 months and in excess of $10 million spent, the organization placed the CRM initiative on hold until a reorganization could take place (which fortunately replaced the business manager).

Lessons learned: Don't be afraid to let the users drive the system's specifications and implementation.

Example 3

In a third example, a global publishing company launched their CRM initiative again using a superuser group. This superuser group remained very active throughout implementation of the initiative (e.g., they helped select the CRM software vendor, they reviewed software screen customizations, and many of them became trainers during the system launch). Moreover, the company launched a comprehensive communications program that included a Friday "paper" memo that updated all potential internal and external users on the status of the initiative, an intranet, and regularly scheduled question and answer sessions at all key company meetings (e.g., the annual company meeting, regional sales meetings, customer service gettogethers). When it came time for CRM system applications training, there actually was an internal argument between users and the training coordinator as to which users would get trained first—almost all users wanted to be a part of the first training session! This CRM initiative went on to deliver an average productivity gain of 22 person-days per user in the first year alone.

Lesson learned: Get users involved early on, and help them to manage their own change.

Process

The process component of CRM is the most delicate because inappropriate automation of the CRM business process will only speed up the errant process. While most companies do have customer-facing business processes in place (i.e., processes that directly interface with the customer during the purchase, payment, and usage of the company's products and services), many times these business processes need to be updated or even replaced.

To realize effective process change, a company needs first to examine how well existing customer-facing business processes are working. Then the company needs to redesign or replace broken or nonoptimal process with ones that have been created and/or agreed upon internally. In other words, while it is not wrong from an educational perspective to look at built-in processes within a CRM software package, new processes tend to stick better when the process had been internally driven. Companies pursuing a CRM initiative often make the dangerous mistake of trying to correct their own customer-facing process deficiencies not by agreeing internally on how users would like a process to be done, but rather by purchasing CRM software that contains one or more business processes that have been prebuilt by the CRM vendor and then forcing the "not-built-here" process upon system users.

When reviewing your customer-facing business processes, use a structured approach. For example, does each customer-facing business process have clear ownership, goals, and measures? Does each process have proper departmental interfaces that ensure that needed customer information flows across multiple departments? Does each process have documented procedures? Does each process have integrity (i.e., the process gets implemented the same regardless of who implements it and where)?

Here are a few examples of companies that have been substantially impacted by the process component within their CRM initiative.

Example 1

A global life sciences company decided to revamp its lead management business process prior to implementing their CRM initiative. Why? Prior to the new process, leads would come in from a variety of sources including the company's Web site, trade shows, magazine ads, and word of mouth. All leads were quickly screened by the marketing department prior to being assigned to field sales personnel based on zip code and/or area of specialization. There were two kinks in this approach. First, during busy periods, the marketing department did not have sufficient time to qualify leads and the department was hesitant to send out unqualified leads to field sales personnel. The result was that leads often remained in the marketing department until they could be qualified, which might mean days or even weeks later, by which time the lead had become cold. Second, the field sales personnel were often overwhelmed by the number of leads received from marketing, and had difficulty knowing which ones to pursue first.

To correct this situation, the company brought together sales, marketing, and top management to create an "ideal" customer leads process. Leads were designated as "A" (ultra-hot), "B" (hot), "C" (warm), or "D" (cold). Designations were made based on a number of agreed-on weighted criteria (e.g., contact method, product interest, type of application). The result was a new lead-management process that was agreed upon and promoted effectively throughout the company. Next, all marketing and sales personnel received training on the new process. Last, the new process was automated using CRM software workflow tools. Today, lead screening takes place in an automated manner and sales reps are sent prioritized leads immediately after the company has received the lead.

Result: Improved lead close from 10 to 15 percent, which equates to millions of dollars of new and ongoing business for the company.

Example 2

In a second example, a global consumer goods company embarked upon its CRM initiative. A critical component of the initiative was the creation and automation of a key-account management process, yet the company made a blunder right out of the gates. Rather than mapping out an appropriate key-account management process, the manufacturing company decided to look for a CRM software vendor who incorporated a key-account management process within their software. They did find a vendor who offered a generic key-account management capability. The manufacturing company purchased the software, and then trained their personnel on use of the software's key-account management process.

During the software application training, personnel became increasingly uncomfortable with the depth and value of the software's key-account management capabilities. Personnel felt that the software's key-account management process failed to address key internal issues such as their criteria for choosing a key account, guidelines for determining which personnel join a key-account management team, and policies for customizing service level agreements for each key account. After much debate, the manufacturing company placed the CRM initiative on hold, created their own key-account management process internally with full backing from potential users, and then went back out with a revised Request For Proposal based on the internally generated process specification.

Lesson learned: To maximize the effectiveness of your customer-facing processes, rely first on internally generated processes (preferably with customer participation), document and train on new or modified processes, and only then look into CRM technology as a tool to help make your customer-facing processes work more efficiently.

Example 3

In a third example, a global manufacturing company proposed to streamline their sales process using CRM automation software. They mapped out their existing sales process using a Visio flowchart as follows:

By mapping out their sales process, this manufacturing company determined that the process currently had seven steps, and they knew it took, on average, six months to close. The VP of sales suggested that by using CRM, a sales close could easily be cut by two months or from six to four months. By mapping out the sales process, however, the company also learned that delays in the sales process were not necessarily the result of delays within the sales department, but often were brought on by inefficiencies in other departmental processes that impacted the sales process. For example, to complete the fourth step of the sales process, namely the work scope and definition step, sales personnel were dependent on receiving timely drawing ("takeoffs") and preliminary pricing, which it turns out were always late to arrive. To complete the fifth step of the sales process, namely the proposal submittal step, sales personnel were dependent on both corporate and legal departmental approval of the bid, which also were regularly late in arriving. In other words, the ability to decrease the sales process from six to four months was as much dependent on streamlining how other departments conducted their own processes and interfaced with the sales process as it was on helping sales personnel to sell more efficiently.

Lesson learned: CRM software will not create or replace a business process, fix an ineffective or broken process, create or maintain customer relationships, make decisions, or produce products/services. Take the time to review your customer-facing processes in detail, and make necessary corrections prior to implementing your CRM initiative.

Technology

The technology component is the most overwhelming given the ever-expanding number of technology offerings and alternatives. There are two issues related to technology: dealing with CRM software vendors and staying on top of CRM technology trends.

CRM Software Vendors

Let's start with dealing with CRM software vendors. Today's CRM technology will address most, if not all, CRM user requirements. Moreover, there are dozens of competent, financially sound CRM vendors to choose from. Nonetheless, can the CRM vendor's offering deliver what it promises to deliver? The response to this question is not always evident. Here are a few examples. In one case, a leading CRM software vendor claimed its software seamlessly integrated with all back-office systems. Only after the software had been purchased did the purchasing company realize that the integration was not so seamless and required a fairly expensive ($200,000) piece of Enterprise Application Integration middleware to seamlessly connect to its SAP back-office system.

In another case, a leading CRM software vendor claimed that all CRM system users needed to purchase their customer service base module if users expected to exchange data between the sales, marketing, and customer service functions. Fortunately the purchasing company learned that this was not necessary since all functions could easily draw and share information from the common database regardless of the base module used. The purchasing company came very close to paying $150,000 for unnecessary software.

In a third case, one of the largest database software vendors claimed that their emerging CRM software offering would contain the most comprehensive CRM functionality available in the industry. They actually fooled quite a few potential buyers who waited months and months for promised functionality to arrive. Promised functionality never did arrive and finally, under pressure from a variety of sides including analysts like ISM, the database vendor was forced to admit that they would be unable to offer promised functionality. Shortly thereafter, they opened their emerging yet incomplete CRM software's API to third-party software vendors!

Lessons learned: When dealing with CRM software vendors, remember that these vendors face incredible competition (and analyst/venture capital pressure) that may force them to stretch the truth from time to time. Understand this and then make them demonstrate their promises in real time.

Keeping Up with CRM Technology Trends

As concerns the second issue related to technology, namely staying on top of CRM technology trends, this has become increasingly difficult as a result of the proliferation of CRM technologies available in the marketplace. Rather than making the error of trying to keep up with each new technology, companies are well advised to track those technologies that are most likely to impact the CRM industry's future as well as their own company's CRM efforts (Chapter 6 attempts to make sense of the latest technology trends).

This may include, for example, customer self-service applications built on top of an effective knowledge base, e-marketing applications such as permission-based direct marketing, wireless and voice recognition capabilities, or the use of major framework tools to consolidate and enhance n-tiered architectures within a CRM implementation. While it is unreasonable to even imagine learning about every new technology trend that is likely to impact CRM, try to keep up to date on the big ones.

Integrating People, Process, and Technology

Personnel responsible for delivering successful CRM initiatives acknowledge the above people, process, and technology issues. More importantly, though, these personnel understand that during the life of the CRM initiative, the integration mix of people, process, and technology will change. Table 3.1 provides a generic model for understanding how the people, process, and technology mix changes for key CRM implementation activities. This generic model needs to be adjusted for your company, taking into account that different companies will realize key CRM implementation activities at different speeds.

TABLE 3.1
Developing the right mix of people, process, and technology.

Key CRM Implementation Activities	Most Relevant Components
Determining business requirements	People, some process
Setting up the project management team	People, some process
Integrating legacy and other needed systems	Technology
Customizing the CRM software	People, process, technology
CRM system pilot	People, technology
CRM system roll-out	People, technology
CRM system support	People, some process
Growing your CRM system	People, process, technology

Let's look at a few of the CRM implementation activities in Table 3.1 to better understand the dynamics of getting the mix right. To determine business requirements, a company will want to apply a structured *process* to ensure that user needs are properly identified and prioritized. Most of the effort for determining business requirements, however, will deal with *people* issues, namely working with potential users to help them think through their existing and potential business requirements, and to help them manage their expectations concerning how the CRM initiative is likely to impact these requirements. *Technology* plays a minor role at best in determining business requirements.

Similarly, when a company is ready to set up their CRM project management team, the *people* component plays a critical role (e.g., agreeing on who is responsible for which CRM implementation activities). *Process* (how to optimally set up the project management team and subteams) is also important. *Technology*, however, plays a minor role at best in setting up the CRM project management team.

Yet when the company is ready to begin integrating legacy and other needed systems, *technology* plays the critical role. The selection of an appropriate Enterprise Application Architecture (EAA), agreement on appropriate frameworks or the use of middleware toolsets, etc., will greatly impact the effectiveness and efficiency of systems integration. *People* may insist that their system needs to be integrated first, and there should be a *process* for determining which systems to integrate and in which order, but overall *technology* drives this activity's success.

As a last example, when performing CRM software customization, all three components play critical roles. *Technology* is key for developing, modifying, and deleting screens and for navigating between screens. *Process* is important for driving workflow development (which, in turn, gets built by *technology*). *People* are critical for ultimately judging how well the customizations meet their needs as well as for commenting on how the workflow impacts the overall user friendliness of the system.

Summary

In summary, to achieve CRM success, companies are well advised to take the time to understand the issues impacting people, process, and technology components individually, but also to proactively manage the integration of all three components to ensure that the people, process, and technology mix is right during all phases of the CRM initiative.

CRM Strategy Formulation 4

Companies too often embark upon their CRM initiative without having a clear vision of where they want to go, and how they intend to get there. Needless to say, these companies are the ones that end up reporting CRM implementation results "below user expectation." Any surprise?

There also is a minority of companies that take their time to properly set CRM vision and utilize a structured methodology to create and realize their CRM strategy. These companies tend to be ones that report CRM implementation results that "exceed user expectation."

What follows is a 10-step approach to formulate CRM strategy. Some companies may already have embarked on or even accomplished one or more of these steps, and thus may not need to implement all the steps. Nonetheless, because these steps are meant to fit together like a well-coordinated jigsaw puzzle, use the 10 steps as a checklist and be sure that each step has been properly addressed prior to moving forward with your CRM initiative.

The 10-Step Approach to
Formulating a Successful CRM Strategy _____

Step 1: Prepare an Executive CRM Vision

In this first step, it is critical to gain the support of the top management team who will ultimately drive the CRM initiative. The way to accomplish this is to spend 30–60 minutes with each of the business heads of customer-facing departments to obtain their CRM vision, as well as with the CEO and potentially other executives (e.g., CIO, CFO).

I'll never forget helping one of the world's leading pharmaceutical companies to formulate their CRM vision. I met first with the CEO and he clearly had thought about what CRM would mean for his company. He was keen that regardless of how a customer contacted the company, that customer would receive outstanding service and that CRM would provide the tools to make this happen. When pressed to discuss how e-business fit into his CRM vision, the CEO felt uncomfortable. This troubled me since the vast majority of the company's customers were computer literate and already certain customer segments were demanding e-functionality, such as customer self-service, e-marketing, and e-procurement.

I next met with the business heads of their customer-facing departments; there were seven in total. To my surprise, each of these executives had a different view of what CRM was, and what its primary objective would be for this company. One executive said that CRM was really salesforce automation. Another said that CRM was a cost-cutting toolset. Another said that CRM would help identify product weaknesses and make recommendations to research and development internal personnel. Another said that CRM would once and for all tie together sales and customer service efforts. Not a single one of them came up with anything even close to what the CEO had said!

After formulating a CRM vision statement based on input received from all of the interviewees, I next facilitated a CRM vision meeting attended by the CEO, business heads of customer-facing departments, and other executives including the CIO and the CFO. The objective of this session was to describe to all participants the wide range of CRM visions that I had received during my interviews and to get to a common, agreed-to CRM vision. After considerable discussion, the objective was obtained and the following CRM vision was agreed to:

Our goal is to provide customers and partners with a coherent, easy-to-use, error-free way to enhance the customer experience. In order to meet this goal, we must implement exceptional customer-facing processes and provide customer-facing personnel with CRM tools (e.g., feedback mechanisms, customer knowledge databases, information repositories) that help enhance job performance and drive cost efficiencies. Regardless of the media channel, we will fully understand the value and satisfy the needs of each customer, ultimately driving customer satisfaction, loyalty, service differentiation and long-term profitability.

While still a bit too long for my liking, at last the company had a common view of why CRM would be implemented. Moreover, the significance of this CRM vision was reinforced when the top management team decided to published its CRM vision statement and distribute it to all company personnel.

Step 2: Determine "Burning" Business Issues

On the other hand, if you are doing a "how to" book then you should develop a set of products and materials customers can purchase in support of the "how to." For example, a fill in the blanks computer template for determining organizational structure and arranging interviews.

"Burning" business issues are those that impact the current day-to-day running of the business. These issues may concern product or service problems (e.g., the product is too often on back-order), competitiveness (e.g., our service is good but the competitor's is better), personnel issues (e.g., we've had three open sales territories for the past six months but our hiring freeze prohibits us from filling the openings), marketing or customer service frustrations (e.g., we are not able to easily identify our high-value customers), or lack of information sharing dilemmas (e.g., the customer had to call our company seven times, and each time was connected to a different department since departments do not share common customer information).

To uncover these burning business issues, set up additional 30–60 minute interviews with the same business heads of customer-facing departments as well as potentially with the CEO and other executives that were interviewed in Step 1. (Steps 1 and 2 interviews can be combined if feasible.) Write up an "Interim" Burning Issues Report, which summarizes and groups the interview findings to date by business functional areas, e.g., sales, marketing, and customer service. Next, in a continued effort to build user support for the CRM initiative, share the Interim Burning Issues Report with the next level of customer-facing departmental personnel, and obtain their feedback. Do the findings address their burning issues? Are there additional issues that need to be added? Once needed alterations have been made, the Interim Burning Issues Report now becomes the "final" version.

Successful CRM strategies acknowledge that while the long-term objective may be realization of the CRM vision, unless burning issues are addressed along the way users tend not to support the initiative. Burning issues impact the day-to-day lives of potential CRM system users and this is where users feel they need help most. Respect these feelings. In fact, it is imperative that burning issues be addressed early on in a CRM initiative to build support from the bottom up.

To better understand this point, consider an average CRM initiative that typically has three to five phases, with phases usually being realized three to six months apart, and with each phase consisting of the implementation of up to five business functions. A reasonable CRM strategy would look as follows:

TABLE 4.1
CRM strategy example.

	Phase 1	Phase 2	Phase 3	Phase 4
Burning Issues Emphasis	80%	60%	40%	20%
CRM Vision Emphasis	20%	40%	60%	80%

In other words, in the first phase of implementing the initiative, 80 percent of the emphasis would be placed on addressing burning issues and 20 percent of the emphasis on achieving the company's agreed-on CRM vision. In the second phase of the initiative, implemented three to six months after completion of the first phase, the emphasis would be 60 percent on burning issues and 40 percent on CRM vision. In the third phase, the emphasis would be 40 percent burning issues and 60 percent vision. The fourth phase would be 20 percent burning issues and 80 percent vision.

Step 3: Identify CRM Technology Opportunities

In Chapter 3, "Successful CRM: Getting the People, Process, and Technology Mix Right," I am careful to state that successful CRM occurs when people, process and technology are carefully mixed throughout the CRM initiative. Furthermore, I state that people account for at least 50 percent, process accounts for at least 30 percent, and technology accounts for not more than 20 percent of a CRM initiative's success. So why make the identification of CRM technology opportunities a separate step when formulating CRM strategy?

Because CRM technology may offer new business opportunities that may not be apparent at first. For example, sophisticated CRM technology has allowed Amazon.com to create an entirely new business model as compared to the traditional bookstore model. CRM technology also has allowed Cisco to offer self-service to its customers, which has saved Cisco hundreds of millions of dollars since 1999 and which has enhanced customer satisfaction rating among the 83 percent of customers who have opted to use Cisco's self-service capability over alternative options such as telephone support.

In Step 3, review CRM technology trends and prepare for a meeting with the business heads of customer-facing units (invite the CEO and other executives as appropriate) to discuss these trends. The purpose of the meeting is to identify CRM technology opportunities and to have customer-facing personnel determine whether these trends would have little, medium, or large impact on their business. Document the results of the meeting.

Steps 1, 2, and 3 of CRM strategy formulation—namely the creation of a CRM vision, determination of burning business issues, and identification of CRM technology opportunities—need to be carefully coordinated to ensure that the CRM strategy formulation gets off on the right footing. While an agreed upon long-term vision is critical, it needs to be balanced, pragmatically, with burning business issues. Moreover, unless CRM technology trends are known, their potential impact may never be realized in the CRM vision or as a way to address burning business issues. In other words, take the time to stop after completion of Step 3 to ensure that each of the first three steps has been accomplished with excellence and that these steps have been carefully integrated.

Step 4: Determine Key People Issues

This step identifies the likely people issues that will impact your CRM initiative. The issues tend to emerge from the interviews held in Steps 1 and 2. Some people issues include skepticism driven by prior CRM efforts that failed, lack of training for other IT systems, a corporate culture that does not promote information sharing across customer-facing departments, and so forth.

Once identified, the CRM strategy should include recommendations about how to overcome each of the people issues. They may include, for example, a comprehensive CRM communications program to overcome initial skepticism, a comprehensive CRM training program to address the need for multiple types of training (e.g., computer literacy training, CRM application software training, remedial training, remote training), or a revised information sharing approach that actively encourages people to share information across customer-facing departments.

Step 5: Develop Multiyear Technical Architecture Plan

It is necessary to review what technology the company currently has in place, and what technology will be needed over time to address the company's CRM vision and burning business issues. There are many ways to determine an appropriate multiyear technical architecture plan, including conducting one or more technical architecture "grease board" sessions that result in an emerging technical roadmap. Then it is necessary to research potential technical tools (e.g., EAI tools) that may be useful for you to accomplish your emerging technical architecture plan. Lastly, write up the findings, including recommendations.

Step 6: Identify Business Process Similarities, Differences, and Issues

For each customer-facing business area, develop key business process outlines that highlight the key steps in each process. As discussed on Chapter 5, "Determining CRM Business Processes," assess each process in terms of ownership, goals, measures, interfaces, procedures, integrity, and fit with vision. Then conduct cross-functional business process meetings to identify process interfaces and shared process areas. Lastly, write up the findings.

For each customer-facing business area, outline the milestone business process steps and key interfaces. At the same time obtain a general sense of the key business drivers and similarities and differences between the processes. For example, are the sales processes opportunity-driven or account-driven? Is customer service primarily inbound and incident driven or is it both inbound and outbound? As you work with key representatives from each business area also identify any major issues relevant to ownership, goals, measures, interfaces, procedure, integrity, and fit with vision. During this step also evaluate key metrics (e.g., number and type of customers and personnel).

The intent of this step is not to perform a detailed business review as discussed in Chapter 5. Instead, it is to "understand" the similarities and differences between the processes so their impact to strategy can be assessed (e.g., highly complex processes with significant issues are inherently more difficult to change than simpler processes).

Step 7: Determine Customer Desires and Likely CRM Impact to the Customer

All too often, companies undertaking CRM initiatives leave their customers out of the initial stages. The feeling is that the company knows what customers need. Most companies set the rules as to how a customer is expected to interface with the company. The danger of creating a CRM initiative in a vacuum away from customers seems obvious. What if the customers don't see value in the proposed CRM business functions being proposed? What if they wouldn't use the CRM functionality offered to them.

Not too long ago, we devised the CRM strategy for a global biotechnology company. The company was convinced that e-business was of tremendous value and made it one of their top priorities for the CRM initiative. The company was convinced that because their buyers were researchers who were extremely computer literate, these same customers would welcome the opportunity to gather information, buy, and service themselves electronically using e-business functionality. Well, the company was in for a real surprise. They held three focus groups for three different customer segments only to learn that the customer's desire to move from the current state to an e-business mode was weak at best. I remember one focus group participant saying that if she could no longer call her friends at the company's customer service by phone, she would be pleased to take her business elsewhere!

To overcome the danger of creating an inward-facing CRM initiative, several steps can be taken. First, review existing customer information held within business/functional areas. Second, work with business heads of customer-facing departments to determine the most appropriate manner to obtain needed customer information in view of emerging CRM business functional prioritization. Third, work with your customers to obtain their CRM needs. Focus groups, customer questionnaires, and customer service interviews are effective ways to gather customer input. Lastly, write up your findings.

Lesson learned: take the time to gather valuable customer input, preferably from the outset of your CRM initiative and not as a last-minute sanity check.

Step 8: Provide CRM Program Observations and Recommendations

This step prepares and delivers a CRM program observations document that is based on the CRM vision, identified burning business issues, customer input, as well as people, process, and technology issues. These observations and recommendations in turn get presented back to the business heads of customer-facing departments, the CEO and other executives as appropriate.

Step 9: Recommend a CRM Program Management Approach

This step lays out recommendations for how to implement the recommended CRM strategy. It often includes project management office (PMO) recommendations including organization, job descriptions, policies and procedures.

Step 10: Prepare the CRM Program Business Case

This Business Case is the document that most companies use to approve the CRM investment. Chapter 10, "Creating Your CRM Business Case," details the steps for preparing a solid business case, and thus these steps are only briefly mentioned below.

- Executive summary (includes an overview of what happens when, to whom, and at what cost)
- Financials (includes specific value proposition and ROI information)
- Key risks and mitigating factors
- Operational/organizational impact
- Appendices (details the basis of the value proposition)

Summary

The 10-step CRM strategy formulation can be summarized in the following Figure 4.1. As mentioned at the beginning of this chapter, think of the 10 steps as a checklist of requirements to get to a successful CRM strategy formulation.

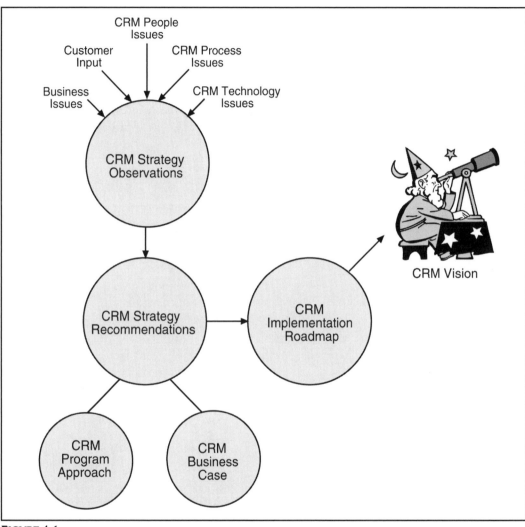

FIGURE 4.1
The CRM Strategy Formulation Process

Determining CRM Business Processes

5

CRM solutions promise an "ideal" customer relationship process via instantaneous sharing of detailed customer information across multiple interfaces. But "ideal" is not always optimal or even feasible. CRM is built upon and acts as an enabler to your individual business processes (e.g., sales, marketing, customer service) and also the more holistic, integrated total customer process.

Therefore, the degree of success realized with CRM is dependent on the functionality of your existing or future business processes.

It is important to note that all organizations have business processes, even though many may claim a lack of process. Processes are the natural business activities performed that produce value, serve customers, and generate income. Therefore, all organizations have business processes, they just may not be documented, fully understood, or functional.

CRM applications do not replace your business processes or fix a broken or ineffective process. They don't create or maintain relationship, or produce a product or service. In fact, automating an ineffective or broken process can be a very costly mistake leading not only to CRM system failure, but also diversion of key personnel time and financial resources.

CRM does provide the opportunity to enhance your existing processes as well as create new, more integrated and customer-centric processes. To maximize the value of these opportunities for your company, you must understand the key business processes that lead to the purchase, payment, and usage of your products and services with special emphasis on the processes targeted for automation. This understanding must be developed from both a company and customer perspective.

Detailed below are a number of areas that you will want to consider when reviewing and potentially modifying your business processes. Because ISM has helped many organizations with business process assessments, we describe the steps that we would use. Nonetheless, you will likely find the information presented here to be invaluable to your efforts, whether you perform the CRM business process evaluation in-house or seek outside assistance.

At ISM, we use a stepwise procedure that has proven highly effective in identifying "gaps" in existing business processes and determining corrective action(s) needed prior to or during CRM implementation. There are two basic approaches to this procedure dependent on the perceived state of readiness of your organization.

In the abbreviated Business Process Review approach, ISM performs an initial assessment of your business process functionality as part of the ISM software selection and implementation process. In this approach, ISM typically spends a limited number of days with key process owners in direct interviews and meetings to obtain an overview of current business process functionality as well as make preliminary recommendations for business process enhancement.

The full business process review is typically utilized in the following circumstances:

- The findings of the CRM business process assessment previously described warrant a more in-depth evaluation or redesign of business processes.
- Your current business processes are dysfunctional to the extent you feel it is imperative to obtain a detailed process review and recommendations prior to beginning the CRM system design and implementation process. This approach may also be warranted if you are planning significant process redesign in conjunction with the implementation of CRM.

Irrespective of the approach utilized, it is imperative that you:

1. Create a visual model of your key processes.
2. Develop an understanding of business process needs from the perspective of customer-interfacing personnel and customers.
3. Identify "gaps" in process functionality.
4. Determine actions needed to position your business processes for effective CRM implementation.

In determining functionality, you should, at a minimum, evaluate the following key business process elements.

- Ownership: Is there clear responsibility, authority and accountability for the success of the process invested within a functional group or groups?
- Integrity: Is the process consistent across time and within all units that use the process within the organization?
- Interfaces: Are critical interfaces between groups (internal), partners (external), and with the customer understood and functional?
- Procedures: Have key process steps been documented and agreed upon by process owners and customer-interfacing personnel?
- Measures: Are performance standards and measures routinely used to determine the success of the process from both a company and customer viewpoint?

Each of these elements should be evaluated for both the individual processes and the total process targeted for the CRM system. Not all elements will have the same level of functionality. For example, the sales process within your organization may have exceptionally clear and authoritative ownership but the interfaces between sales and marketing or customer service may be highly dysfunctional. The more dysfunctional elements create gaps that must be corrected prior to or during CRM implementation.

The Eight-Step Process Review Procedure _____

Following is a brief discussion of ISM's full eight-step business process review procedure. The outlined steps provide general guidelines for the activities that must take place for you to understand your current and desired business processes relative to CRM.

CRM Business Application Trends

6

Over the past year, there have been a number of new CRM business application trends that have made a significant impact among users. Here are eight major trends that currently are affecting the business functional evolution of CRM systems:

1. Increased consolidation and mergers among CRM vendors.
2. Increasing product and marketing focus on the small to mid-market niche.
3. Movement toward CRM solutions with Web-based architectures.
4. Increased use of analytical tools (e.g., predictive modeling) in CRM solutions.
5. Increased integration with Geographical Information Systems in CRM solutions.
6. Increased availability of customer lifetime value tools.
7. Increased capability for lead management (e.g., incubation, qualification, etc.).

8. Increased availability of supply chain management functionality (e.g., e-procurement, logistics management, etc.).

When evaluating a vendor, make sure that you compare their current business application offering against this trend list. Below is a detailed description for each of the eight trends.

Increased Consolidation and Mergers Among CRM Vendors

With the current economic downturn and pressure from customers to provide comprehensive applications, consolidation of CRM vendors into a handfull of dominant major players will increase. Analysts do predict that some small CRM vendors, particularly those in niche markets will survive. Some of the key acquisitions over the past few years within the CRM industry include:

- Avaya's acquisition of Quintus
- Broadbase's acquisition of Servicesoft and KANA's acquisition of Broadbase
- J.D. Edwards's acquisition of YOUcentric
- Microsoft's acquisition of Great Plains
- Nortel's purchase of Clarify and subsequent sale of same to Amdocs
- PeopleSoft's purchase of Vantive
- Peregrine's purchase of Remedy
- Sage's acquisition of Interact Commerce
- Siebel's acquisition of Janna

The significance of these acquisitions is still to be determined. Some of the resulting organizations have already effectively integrated their offering (e.g., PeopleSoft appears to have effectively integrated Vantive software). Others have not (e.g., Nortel's acquisition of Clarify). Many are still in the integration phase.

Likely impact of this trend: More comprehensive CRM software offerings to chose from.

Increasing Product and Marketing Focus on the Small to Mid-Market Niche_____

Anecdotal evidence along with recent studies (e.g., a recent D&B [formerly Dun & Bradstreet] study) point to a steady stream of CRM software adoption by small and mid-sized businesses in the near term. In contrast, larger companies are scaling back their IT purchases for the short term due to the current economic downturn. The opportunities within the small and mid-sized business niche are therefore increasing, leading to additional CRM products that target the small to mid-market niche. Recently, PeopleSoft introduced the PeopleSoft Accelerated CRM product, a fixed-price CRM package aimed at companies with less than $500 million in revenue. Oracle and J.D. Edwards also have announced their intent to target this niche in their future marketing efforts. Sage purchased Interact Commerce to secure its place in the small to mid-size market segment.

Likely impact of this trend: Better CRM software offerings in tune with the needs of small to mid-sized companies.

Movement Toward CRM Solutions with Web-Based Architectures_____

As an example, PeopleSoft's PeopleSoft 8 CRM solution is built on a Web-based architecture. The solution is accessible via an Internet connection and has no requirements for code from the client. The PeopleSoft 8 CRM architecture has the additional advantages of the ability to support the components of the PeopleSoft enterprise suite (e.g., human resources, financials, supply chain) and the ability to integrate with other applications, including those from other vendors (e.g., SAP, Oracle). PeopleSoft has also embedded XML messages into the system, which allow PeopleSoft 8 CRM applications to work seamlessly with either legacy or new applications. PeopleSoft's major competitors—Siebel, Oracle, SAP—are currently moving toward introducing products with a Web-based architecture in the foreseeable future. Several other CRM software vendors already are built on Web-based architectures, e.g., Onyx, J.D. Edwards.

Likely impact of this trend: New Web service offerings, and improved customer-centric software functionality (e.g., self-service).

Increased Use of Analytical Tools in CRM Solutions

Analytical tools now exist for predicting the monetary value and profitability of a particular customer, profiling customers based on their behavior, segmenting markets, predicting customer purchases based on past purchase information and psychographic/demographic data, and determining cross-selling opportunities. The annual growth rate for analytical tools within the CRM marketplace from 2001–2005 is projected to be 27.3 percent. CRM vendors are thereby increasingly integrating analytical tools and functionality into their overall CRM offering. Examples of CRM companies that provide predictive modeling tools within their product offerings include the Matrix Technology Group which specializes in marketing campaign software with analytical tools for market segmentation and SPSS which recently announced an alliance with Siebel to integrate SPSS data mining and statistical tools with the Siebel e-business suite. Examples of CRM companies offering comprehensive analytical toolsets include Applix's iEnterprise v8.3 application, and E.piphany's E.5 System application.

Likely impact of this trend: Better, quicker analysis of what is happening within your business, allowing a better determination of how best to respond.

Increased Integration with GIS in CRM Solutions

There is a trend among CRM vendors to integrate their software offering with Geographical Information Systems (GIS), which provide, for example, a demographic map with an overlay of where the company's customers are located. The GIS can show an overlay of actual customers to potential customers on a map for market analysis. For example, if a user is a coffee buyer, he/she can use the GIS software to determine where all the cafes are located within a certain area. Alternatively, a user can place a red dot on all of his/her current customers. The cafes without red dots may signal potential sales opportunities. Alternatively, the GIS can also show prospects based on user-defined criteria, e.g., prospects with sales of over $60K within a certain area. A good example of this trend is Firstwave eCRM v.6.1, which integrates with MapInfo and MapLink for GIS functionality.

Likely impact of this trend: New capabilities to identify opportunities for territory management.

Increasing Availability of Customer Lifetime Value Tools

CRM vendors are now providing the ability to calculate a customer lifetime value of a customer based on various criteria. One model offered by Worldtrak determines the customer lifetime value on a formula based on the recency, frequency, and monetary values for a customer.

- Recency—amount of recent purchases by the customer.
- Frequency—the frequency of purchases by a customer.
- Monetary values—the monetary values of purchases by a customer.

Likely impact of this trend: The ability to track customer lifetime value and to segment customers more precisely for eventual offering of unique services and products depending on their current and perceived value.

Increased Capability for Lead Management

For example, deuxo's software product, Intelligent Optimization, offers lead incubation capabilities within the software. Lead incubation refers to the ability to develop leads for future qualification. If a lead is currently unqualified, it can be placed in hibernation for a specific time period, such as six months, to be examined again for lead qualification.

Additional lead qualification features in CRM software packages (e.g., MarketSoft, Cognicase) enable users to qualify leads, classify qualified leads as opportunities, and easily assign the opportunities to sales reps.

Likely impact of this trend: Less time spent by sales reps qualifying leads leaving them more time to sell.

Increasing Availability of Supply Chain Management Functionality

Supply chain management functionality is increasingly being offered within CRM solutions either within the package or via EAI integration. For example, Siebel offers inventory management and logistics management functionality within its Siebel Service Inventory and Siebel Field Service applications. The Siebel CRM package can additionally be configured to provide links to other B2B exchanges and software packages using Enterprise Application Integration. Additional offerings from companies like SeeCommerce or i2 Technologies' impressive Web-centric applications greatly enhance the performance of supply chain operations.

Likely impact of this trend: Direct integration between CRM applications (including customer-centric applications) and supply chains that allow either near or real-time product availability product status.

Summary

There are new business application trends annually. It is always difficult to determine which trends will stick and which trends will pass. Based on observations from our software testing laboratory, along with market input from customers and leading authorities, I believe the above eight trends will indeed continue to stick and mature over time. In this regard, buyers would be well advised to understand these trends and to ask potential vendors their current and planned intentions for each of the trends.

CRM Technology Trends 7

In the last three years, there have been significant changes in CRM software and industry direction with regards to technology. Here are 15 major trends that are currently affecting the technical evolution of CRM systems:

1. CRM vendors are moving their architecture from client/server, Web-enabled, and 3-tier architectures to full N-tiered architected applications.
2. CRM vendors are including more portal architecture.
3. CRM vendors are incorporating field force automation modules.
4. Many CRM vendors are beginning to offer product configuration tools.
5. Wireless components are increasingly common in CRM platforms.
6. XML is playing a major role in all areas of CRM.
7. Web services are the new software infrastructure that will facilitate a whole new generation of super-charged business interactions in CRM; another emerging standard is DOM.

8. Enterprise Application Integration (EAI) is now being offered by many vendors.

9. Many vendors are beginning to align and develop new products with framework architecture.

10. Vendors are re-architecting products to service the requirements of ASPs.

11. Enterprise/satellite server architecture is being offered by more vendors.

12. CRM vendors are increasingly providing CIC (customer interaction center) solutions.

13. More CRM vendors are beginning to address multilingual/multicurrency at the core of the architecture.

14. More CRM vendors are offering graphical workflow mapping tools.

15. Numerous CRM vendors are incorporating Business Intelligence through ETLs or connecting to data warehouses.

When evaluating a vendor, make sure that you compare their technical directions against this list. Below is a detailed description for each of the 15 CRM technology trends.

Client/Server to N-Tiered

Over the last few years, vendors that have driven the growth of the Web have come up with new architectures to accommodate increased Internet traffic and other demands. Several CRM vendors have embraced new technologies such as N-tiered, Web centric, XML enabled, etc. and used this as a marketing message. Many other vendors have remained back in the client/server era, but bolted a few Web interfaces onto their product in order to remain competitive.

Some vendors have adopted 100 percent Web-centric architectures and have totally forgotten about the requirements of the occasionally connected users. Other vendors still have both products (client/server and N-tiered) and force customers to develop in two different architectures; this raises the costs of systems integration and customization. Make sure that you do a thorough analysis and really understand the vendor's architectures before you leap into a new system.

Portal Architecture

Portals provide the ability to put a customized face onto your company's CRM platform. Several CRM vendors are beginning to get into the portal space that has been led by companies such as BroadVision, Vignette, IONA, Plumtree, and others.

Personalization, within a portal environment, comes in many different flavors:

- Customer personalization (MyCompany.com)
- Partner hub personalization
- Sales rep personalization (summary page including forecasts, hot leads, relevant customer news, etc.)
- Management personalization (today's sales, forecast, customized almost real-time reports, etc.)
- Employee personalization (401k, paycheck information, company news, etc.)—an area that most CRM vendors will not become involved in

Whatever your requirements, you can be assured that more vendors will be offering some of these features. In addition, many vendors have the flexibility to customize portals because they have chosen to develop with enterprise software vendor frameworks and utilize application server engines used by application service vendors.

Within the area of portals, there is growing interest in the enterprise information portal (EIP). EIPs combine the best of the consumer portal with a platform to put mission-critical enterprise data, applications, and processes at the fingertips of Web-enabled employees and partners. EIPs can be viewed as an enabling platform for information dissemination and collaboration. EIPs are a very important enabling technology for CRM and every variety (B2B, B2C, and B2E) of e-commerce. EIPs acts as a single point of access to internal and external information. Other functions include:

- Control of user access to information
- Search across all organizational information sources
- Allowing users to publish and share information
- Enterprise application integration
- Workflow business process support and collaboration

Field Force Automation

In 2000, more CRM vendors began to offer some version of mobile field force automation (FFA). Nonetheless, a majority of these offerings contained some smoke and mirrors. Some vendors merely WAP-enabled a few fields on one of the CRM modules and claimed a field force or field service application. FFA is much more involved than WAP enabling an application. FFA involves synchronization (with and without wireless), a wireless component, inventory management, work orders, dispatch components, history, limited access to a knowledge base, skill and location based routing, SLA management, and other multiple features.

During this next year, we will see more CRM vendor offerings in this area; we suggest that you pay attention to the level of integration between FFA and other CRM modules.

Configuration Tools

The expansion of Web and e-business has driven the visibility of product configurator tools. While configuration vendors have been around for several years, the market for configuration tools has grown much more over the last year.

Implementation of product configuration is not easy. Rules must be built. Possible integration choices must be configured and ongoing maintenance of the configurations must be planned for and executed.

For the most part, product configuration tools will remain Web based or client/server architecture. The main reason for this is that the amount of data required to support complex configurations is tough to keep updated on field force systems. A few things to consider when looking at vendors that offer product configuration tools include:

- Do the products seamlessly integrate with you CRM package of choice?

- Do the systems have easy-to-use tools for building configurations?

- Does the product have a dynamic pricing toolset?

- Can the configuration finished by the customer be maintained as an object for future reference or use by other CRM components?
- Is the capability available to produce quotes and conversions in the appropriate currency?
- Can the product scale to meet your needs?

Wireless Components _____

Wireless devices do not automatically communicate with back-end systems, particularly when there are a variety of products—PDAs (with various operating systems), WAP-enabled phones (that do not all follow the same WAP standards), a combination of wireless infrastructure technologies like CDMA, GSM, TDMA, upcoming G3, CDPD, SMS (short messaging services), and packet radio networks—to exchange information with diverse databases and systems like SAP, Oracle, PeopleSoft, Siebel, Onyx, Pivotal, etc.

Thus, the latest in middleware solutions must be part of your mobile enterprise project if you hope to untangle the myriad front-end and back-end technologies. In addition to these issues, there are other things to consider such as reduced bandwidth caused by wireless latency and anomalies. Add to this the nonwireless-friendly network protocol called TCP/IP, and vendors have a lot of work to do.

While all of this does seem a little overwhelming, vendors such as Microsoft, OracleMobile, Sun Microsystems, Palm, Ericsson, AvantGo, Thin-AirApps, Openwave, and Broadbeam, among others, are investing large amounts of R&D funds to bring wireless application architectures to market. In 2001, Handspring using Palm OS integrated the cellular telephone with the PDA. This technology is already being used as part of a field/sales force automation solution. Also, Microsoft announced that its Pocket PC will have a module that allows it to function as a mobile phone.

When choosing a wireless-enabled product, make sure that the application or interface is user friendly and responsive. Too many vendors have not mastered the small user interface or the wireless technology. Also make sure that the vendors have options for users that are not always located in wireless coverage areas.

XML Is Playing a Major Role

The leading CRM vendors have not hesitated to add XML functionality to their platforms. Nonetheless, just as many client/server vendors Web enabled their applications and took a long time to re-architect them to Web-centric architecture, the same holds true for XML. XML is very flexible in that it provides a data standard that can encode the content, semantics, and schemata for a wide variety of cases. The functionality can be as simple as a document definition or as complex as a stand-alone applet that operates in a disconnected mode. Some examples of where XML can be used in CRM are:

- An ordinary document such as a word processing document, spreadsheet, etc. In the near future many vendors will allow users to save these types of documents in XML, thereby allowing the document to be viewed by a variety of devices.

- A structured record, such as a customer record, appointment record, or purchase order. The XML architecture allows these items to be contained as individual objects.

- An object with data and methods, such as the persistent form of a Java object or ActiveX control. This allows for even more information on customers and their transactional history to be contained.

- A data record, such as the result set of a query can be saved and viewed at a later time or distributed. In the future, data warehouses will store these types of XML objects.

- Meta-content about a Web site, such as Channel Definition Format (CDF). This allows viewers to become subscribers to a particular organizations site and have their object updated as changes are made. This architecture works well for partner relationship management applications where information that needs to be shared with partners is held behind the firewall.

- Graphical presentation, such as an application's user interface. Utilizing XML at the presentation layer allows multiple devices such as thick (laptops and workstations), thin (Web browsers and WAP-enabled devices), and bulgy (PDAs, car stereo systems, etc.) clients to interface with the CRM application natively.

- Standard schema entities and types. This would be a standardized format for items such as client records, product descriptions, prices, etc.

- All links between information and people on the Web. This would allow contact information to be updated automatically via LDAP-type services.

While it will take the majority of CRM vendors several years to obtain this level of architecture, make sure that your vendor shares their XML directions and development schedule with you.

Web Services

It is hard to imagine networked computing without the Web. The "Web services" movement leverages the advantages of the Web as a platform not only for information but also for services. Web services make up the service-oriented architecture that will give rise to the next generation of B2B, enterprise application integration, and business process management solutions. Web services will enable companies to:

- Dramatically cut application development time and costs.

- Simplify application integration across the enterprise.

- Safely expose both data and business processes to customers and business partners, enabling unprecedented e-business interactions and collaboration.

A more formal definition of a Web service may be adapted from an IBM tutorial on the topic.

Web services complete, independent Web applications that can be published, found, and used across the Web. Web services perform a variety of functions, which can be anything from simple requests to complicated business processes. Once a Web service is deployed, other applications (and other Web services) can find and use the deployed service.

The new Web services initiative is supported by the World Wide Web Consortium (W3C) whose goal is to lead the Web to its full potential as a forum for information, commerce, communication, and collective understanding.

The Web services basic platform is XML plus HTTP. Behind the facade of a Web server, the XML message gets converted to a middleware request and the results converted back to XML. The full-function Web services platform can be thought of as XML plus HTTP plus SOAP plus WSDL plus UDDI. At higher levels, one might also add technologies such as XAML, XLANG, XKMS, and XFS—services that are not universally accepted as mandatory. The emergent Web services platform is really a series of "in-development" technologies. Very few software companies have released software using this technology, although one that has is IONA, whose Total Business Integration package has just been adopted by Nordstrom, Inc. to power its online retail order fulfillment process. The IONA e-business platform provides nordstrom.com an application integration platform that facilitates business collaboration transactions and enhanced online order fulfillment for greater inventory visibility.

Another emerging technical standard that is likely to impact CRM is called document object model (DOM). W3C's DOM is a platform- and language-neutral interface that will allow programs and scripts to dynamically access and update the content, structure, and style of documents. The document can be further processed and the results of that processing can be incorporated back into the presented page.

A DOM implementation (also called a host implementation) is that piece of software which takes the parsed XML or HTML document and makes it available for processing via the DOM interfaces. Companies will take advantage of the DOM as the interpretation layer for XML in the exchange with PRM, B2B, and e-CRM applications. It is more effective to translate an order as a document rather than a data string. Make sure your CRM vendor is able to handle this back-end data exchange.

Enterprise Application Integration

Enterprise application integrations (EAIs) are tools that allow CRM vendors to connect their applications to other applications that may be in use within a company (e.g., EPR systems, legacy systems, e-business systems). EAI has been a mixed bag among CRM vendors. Some vendors have actually developed their own EAI offering; others have teamed with EAI vendors such as TIBCO, NEON, CrossWorlds, SAGA, Vitria, Microsoft, or Computer Associates, to name a few.

Other CRM vendors have chosen to provide native hooks to ERP and other systems. Nonetheless, this can create long-term maintenance issues especially if multiple native hooks have been created and each hook needs to be maintained. Other vendors have provided an XML integration toolset. Over the next few years, it is likely that we will see consolidation of the EAI vendor space and more CRM vendors will begin providing native interfaces to the leading EAI vendors.

Application Server/ Framework Architecture

Several vendors have begun to redevelop their architecture so that they are aligned with one vendor's application framework such as Microsoft's Biz-Talk, or .NET platforms, BEA Systems, IBM's WebSphere, webMethods, TIBCO, and others.

BizTalk was Microsoft's first offering of a single structure that brings together business process automation (BPA), business-to-business (B2B) applications, and enterprise application integration (EAI) services. BizTalk also contains tools for developers and administrators, which have hooks into Microsoft operating systems, server platforms, and networking infra-structures. During the later part of 2000, Microsoft announced an expanded product offering called .NET. .NET Enterprise Servers are designed to aggre-gate and deliver Web services. Many of these servers, including the Win-dows 2000 Server Family, Microsoft SQL Server 2000, and Microsoft Exchange 2000, are built in Extensible Markup Language (XML) at the core. XML ensures that structured data will be uniform and independent of appli-cations or vendors, which makes it ideal as a foundation for integrating Web services.

During the next few years, we will likely see several other CRM vendors align themselves with an application server/framework vendor. The devel-opment cost is getting too high for CRM vendors to develop all of the com-ponents in-house.

ASP-Enabled Applications

Chapter 23, "Application Service Providers (ASP): An Overview," provides a history to and current status of the ASP marketplace, particularly as con-cerns CRM. Despite past problems with low returns, customer dissatisfac-tion, inadequate training and support, and high integration costs, companies are turning a curious eye toward a new breed of ASPs. The new ASP model combines a focus on best practices in the CRM arena from a pro-cess perspective, as well as cutting-edge technologies that are integrated and deployed rapidly.

There are ASPs for field service, CRM, e-CRM, software solution provid-ers, contact center outsourcers, system integrators with multichannel man-agement and self-hosted independent software vendors (ISVs), not to mention ERP players hosting their own applications, as well as traditional outsourcers hosting ERP applications. ASP runs the spectrum from traditional outsourcers like EDS, CSC, and IBM Global to the pure online application provider, such as eBay, where a service is auctioned off to millions of people, with no off-line counterpart.

Statistically, there are more companies installing on-site than going to ASPs, however, IDC estimates dictate that ISPs, ASPs, and e-markets have the potential as IT distribution channels to account for almost 2.6 percent of total IT spending in 2004, which represents almost 30 percent of the overall online sales forecast for indirect channel partners. Most CRM applications are built upon best-of-breed processes. These are some of the major elements in today's SSPs (search service provider), which are emerging as one of the more popular varieties of ASPs.

SSPs offer a unique proposition and value; they take a variety of best-of-breed applications, like E.piphany, KANA, and other newer Web-based applications that are easily hosted. Then they augment them with a value-added integration layer. For example, they'll take an agent desktop and give it Cisco Webline chat functionality and CTI to create an application that is resold out to the customer. Some of these options are a lower cost alternative that provides seamless, frictionless, effective solutions for CRM implementations.

Enterprise/Satellite Server Architecture

Over the years, many CRM vendors have shied away from the enterprise/satellite server architecture. In most cases, the CRM vendors would say that they left the remote office synchronization to the database vendors. This created many problems because the database vendors do not concern themselves with the business logic and rules of the CRM application.

Recently, however, more CRM vendors seem to have realized that there are many organizations that do have global operations and cannot cost effectively or efficiently operate from a centralized server model. Therefore, we feel that over the next few years the CRM industry will continue to see more vendors provide this option.

CRM and CCC Modules

This area is a very big topic and several chapters could be written on the growth of the CCC (customer contact center) space (also see Chapter 19, "E-Service and CRM"). More CRM vendors are getting into this area and your organization might consider if your CRM needs include an interaction center which includes tightly integrated sales, service, e-business, call center, etc. Designing a CCC environment is not the same as rolling out a sales or field force component of a CRM system. Questions about telephony integration, IVR integration, skills-based routing, monitoring, chat, co-surfing, e-mail management, multimedia routing, and many other such issues must be addressed.

If a CCC is a requirement, make sure that the CRM vendors you consider have a full understanding of the CCC environment and significant product offerings.

Multilingual/Multicurrency

Many vendors have been struggling with the multinational customization problem. The reason is that multiple languages and multiple currencies were not part of the core architecture. Vendors who try to address this after-the-fact tend to have major integration problems with a resulting higher cost of localization. If you have a localization or currency conversion requirement, make sure that the vendors that you consider can demonstrate successful customization of multiple languages and multiple currencies. The successful vendors have placed language and currencies in a database table structure to facilitate maintenance and enhancements.

Graphical Workflow Mapping Tools

Graphical workflow tools allow you to quickly create a business process workflow, and instruct the CRM program to automate the workflow. Most CRM vendors have been very slow to develop graphical workflow, business rules, and scripting tools. It is not that the technology has not been there; in fact, some CRM vendors (e.g., Pivotal) and CTI vendors have been developing dynamic graphical tools for years. Over the last year, we have seen a movement towards more graphical tools and we expect that more CRM vendors will begin to release these tools over the next year. The better products will have the ability to work in both graphical and programming/scripting modes.

Business Intelligence

Anyone who has been following the stream of press releases issued by CRM and customer interaction companies this year knows that analytic applications vendors are quickly merging with customer intelligence and CRM providers. If companies are not privy to changes in their corporate landscape, they are likely to be blindsided. The convergence of BI (business intelligence) and the Internet—or e-solutions—is the critical next step to supplying company infrastructures with the decision-making capabilities and Web-enablement they need to move forward in e-business. From a BI standpoint, clients leverage their ERP investment by pulling information from that system into a separate, organized intelligent structure from which educated decisions can be made. This information helps them leverage their new Internet site with their existing data warehouse to create the overall infrastructure needed to support and supply BI information for CRM initiatives. Companies must continually gather information about their competitors to stay at the top of their game. Software is used to collect data daily and store it in a data warehouse.

This type of analytic application provides CRM and BI solutions with three key capabilities:

1. The ability to quantify the value of the customer interaction.
2. The ability to set thresholds to trigger rules and events, e.g., automate the delivery of specific content such as personalized offers and product recommendations.
3. The ability to help qualify customer information.

A data warehouse is a large analytical database that can serve as the foundation for BI activities. Data warehousing is a process supported by a number of underlying enabling technologies such as data extraction, transformation, and load tools. The underlying framework is the data store that is built on popular database engines like Microsoft SQL Server or Oracle both supporting OLAP (Online Analytical Processing) technology. The data extraction on the surface uses ETL (Extraction, Transformation, and Load) software. Some of the current ETL software include Cognos, Microsoft DTS, and Informatica.

Data mining can best be described as a BI technology that has various techniques to extract comprehensible, hidden, and useful information from a population of data. Data mining makes it possible to discover hidden trends and patterns in large amounts of data. The current technology for this is data analyzers; these can be integrated with your CRM suite, like Oracle's Performance Analyzer that generates data and makes it available to your CRM application, or others like Computer Associates' Intelligent CRM Suite is a comprehensive and intelligent e-business solution comprised of modules that include customer intelligence. Whichever you choose, being able to not only detect trends, but make future decisions based on competitive information will leverage your company into greater profits.

Summary

In summary, the last year has seen many changes in the technology that CRM vendors are using for development and application. We can expect to see more consolidation in technologies and companies. As you consider CRM solutions, make sure that you pay attention to how tightly integrated the CRM vendor's modules really are. Some CRM vendors have literally taken years to come out with integrated modules after purchasing a CRM-related technology vendor that had specific CRM technology or functionality. 2001 has also seen several CRM vendor mergers and acquisitions which should lead to more "best-of-breed" software choices. When evaluating CRM technology, focus on the CRM vendor as a whole rather than a specific aspect of the company's product/service offering. The technology may be "hot" but more importantly, the vendor must have the resources and experience to deliver that technology to you based on your CRM system requirements and schedule. Also remember that technology accounts for at most 20 percent of the overall success of a CRM initiative (with people accounting for at least 50 percent and processes accounting for at least 30 percent).

CRM: Benefits and Problems

8

There are three most often mentioned reasons why firms automate their sales, marketing, and customer service functions:

1. **High Costs of Direct Sales**—Today the average cost of a sales call is close to $211. Moreover, in most cases, direct selling costs continue to rise. CRM can help to increase sales force productivity and, in turn, contain or decrease the rising costs of sales.

2. **Increased Global Competition**—Conducting business is no longer restricted to local competition. Increasingly, companies work within a global marketplace. To beat the competition, whether local or foreign, effective market intelligence is often critical. CRM can assist firms to better monitor and track marketplace developments.

3. **Need for Information**—Sales, marketing, and customer service/support are information-intensive activities. Success in the marketplace is dependent on implementing an effective marketing mix strategy (product, place, price, and promotion), as well as on understanding and

addressing the marketing mix strategy of your competitors. CRM can assist in the collection, compilation, and dissemination of needed information about the marketplace, particularly your customers.

Benefits of CRM

The most frequently stated benefits resulting from CRM include:

- **Better Sales/Marketing Information**—For example, customer names, customer background, customer needs, competitive positioning, etc. are just some of the information collected as a result of inputting a CRM system.
- **Improved Productivity**—For example, effective target market identification, reduction in the number of cold leads, and the ability to provide accurate and on-the-spot quotations, look up inventory availability quickly, enter orders directly from the field, etc., all of which help shorten the sales cycle.
- **Enhanced Customer Care**—For example, more time to spend with customers due to a reduction in the sales administrative workload, an ability to monitor customer service levels, and ability to highlight existing or potential customer service problems and to react more quickly to customer needs, etc.

An increasingly important objective, and area that is related to each of the aforementioned benefits, is improved customer retention/loyalty. Corporations in the U.S. lose approximately half of their customers within five years. If the CRM system really focuses on the customer and the above benefits are realized, a company can expect to retain more customers over time. It has been shown that the longer a customer is retained, the greater the profitability will be for the retained customer.

For those who prefer hard numbers, studies by ISM and by Insight Technology Group concerning CRM systems confirm that the following level of benefit can be achieved:

1. A minimum 10 percent per annum increase in gross sales revenue per sales representative during the first three years of the system. This gain occurs because field personnel improve both their efficiency (e.g., more batting time to call on customers and implement strategy) and their effectiveness (e.g., improved quality of their sales call in that field because personnel are more knowledgeable about their customers).

2. A minimum 5 percent decrease in the general and administrative cost of sales during the first three years of the system. This takes place because field personnel (and the company) no longer need to send out costly literature and information in a shotgun approach to all existing and potential customers; rather, field personnel (and the company) can decrease their cost of sales by being selective in terms of which customers receive specific promotional materials.

3. A minimum 5 percent increase in win rates for forecasted sales during the first three years of the system. This gain results because field personnel select their opportunities more carefully, drop out of potentially bad opportunities earlier on, and concentrate on those opportunities with a high likelihood of closure.

4. A minimum 1 percent margin improvement in the value of a deal over the lifetime of the system. This gain occurs since field personnel are working closely with a carefully selected group of customers who place as much emphasis on value selling as they do on discounts, and field personnel thus tend to discount less often.

5. A minimum 5 percent improvement in the quality rating provided by customers. This gain results from happier customers who get the information that they need more quickly, who receive better service, and who enjoy building on the relationship marketing approach that field personnel are now able to offer.

Prior to deciding whether CRM is for you and your firm, ISM recommends that you review all potential benefits of CRM in detail. Our experience over the past 17 years in successfully helping companies to automate customer-facing functions is that senior management wants to see a list of detailed measurable benefits by which they can justify what may amount to a large capital investment, plus an investment of time, resources, and staff.

The good news is that there are a growing number of detailed tangible and intangible benefits associated with CRM, and there are ways to measure these benefits. For each of the following measurements, we have assumed that similar and valid measurement information is available today in some format within your company, or that similar and valid measurement information will be available by the start of any CRM project within your company.

Tangible Benefits

We define tangible benefits as those benefits that can be measured in hard numbers.

Increase in time spent by sales personnel with existing customers per day. To determine this benefit, consider measuring the number of service calls made per day by sales personnel or the number of hours spent by sales personnel in face-to-face contact with existing customers.

Increase in the number of new customer prospects pursued by sales representatives. Remember that most representatives prefer to call on their existing customers, with whom they have an ongoing relationship. But new customers spearhead future growth. To determine this benefit, consider measuring the number of new prospects versus existing customers contacted by the sales representative per day, per week, per month, or per quarter.

Increase in time spent by sales managers in contacting customers and working with sales representatives on customer issues. "Coaching" sales personnel is critical, and managers never seem to have enough time for this. To determine this benefit, consider measuring the number of hours per day which sales managers spend in contact with customers and prospects, and with sales representatives discussing customer issues.

Increase in customer service efficiency. Customer service may well be the key differentiator between those companies that lead and those companies that wonder what happened! To determine this benefit, consider measuring the turnaround time for customer service issues, as well as the number of customer service errors made as a result of misinformation.

Increase in timeliness of follow-up correspondence to customers/prospects. To determine this benefit, consider measuring the number of days between the date the customer/prospect was contacted and the date that the customer/prospect follow-up information is sent.

Increase in revenue per month per sales representative. This is an important benefit of CRM, though careful management is required to ensure that time saved as a result of automation is used productively to deliver more sales. To determine this benefit, consider measuring the increase in base revenue generated per month per sales representative.

Increase in overall business results. In one company that ISM worked with, the sales manager set up a competition between sales personnel based on their use of the CRM system. The results were overwhelming as healthy rivalry between the sales force led to a significant increase in overall business results (as well as a nice seven-day cruise for the winning salesperson and spouse). To determine this benefit, consider measuring the percent of dollar increase over budget for the entire sales team per month.

Increase in frequency that your company's name is in front of your customers and prospects. The "out-of-sight, out-of-mind" syndrome can be quite harmful to your sales efforts. To determine this benefit, consider measuring the number of pieces of correspondence sent to customers and prospects by sales and marketing personnel.

Increase in customer satisfaction. To determine this benefit, consider using a customer satisfaction survey rating and hanging these ratings in a location for all personnel to review.

Improved communications within your company. As more and more personnel spend time in the field with customers and prospects, there is a growing need to secure effective communications between personnel. To determine this benefit, consider measuring the time spent giving and getting information between the field and regional or headquarters offices.

Increase in "close" rates. In other words, an increase in the percentage of business orders closed.

Reduction in "close" time. In other words, a reduction in the speed of bringing new business orders to a close.

Intangible Benefits

We define intangible benefits as those benefits that can be measured by using "soft" criteria. Management may prefer the hard numbers but increasingly is learning to appreciate the soft criteria as well.

Overall smoother functioning within your company. To determine this benefit, consider measuring the time spent looking for needed information versus time spent utilizing information and getting on with your job. It can be shocking to learn how much time is spent by sales personnel on unnecessary administrative matters, or the amount of time a new salesperson spends getting up to speed in a new territory!

Increased employee motivation and satisfaction. While this may be difficult to measure, consider measuring feedback from those employees who use CRM. An alternative measurement is employee turnover rate for those personnel who use the CRM system.

Better trained and more skillful sales, marketing, and customer service personnel. CRM can provide an excellent training ground for personnel to quietly spend time learning facts and figures about your products and services. To determine this benefit, consider measuring the ability of sales personnel to quickly access needed facts and figures, including the implementation of required sales and marketing business procedures.

Improved use of mobile access devices. This benefit is important given that each of us has a different technological assimilation learning curve that impacts our future use of equipment and technology. To determine this benefit, consider measuring the comfort level over time of field personnel who use the mobile devices.

More up-to-date information and easy access to this information. Up-to-date information and easy access is a subjective measurement made by end-users. To determine this benefit, therefore, consider measuring the timeliness of needed information and ease of accessing this information based on end-user standards.

Improved responsiveness to customer and prospect requests. ISM worked with a domestic pipe manufacturer whose sales and marketing manager used the firm's automation system to "staple" himself to each customer request until the request got resolved. To determine this benefit, which may be tied in with customer service, consider measuring the time it takes to respond completely to a customer or a prospect request.

Improved image of your company. Automation can play a leading role in building your company's image in the eyes of your customers. To determine this benefit, consider measuring the reaction of existing and future buyers to your sales and marketing professionalism.

The ability to differentiate your company from the competition. It should be noted that many studies have tried or are trying to measure the competitive advantage resulting from CRM (one Danish company has tried to mathematically model this measurement). Consider measuring increased customer loyalty as well customer perception of your company versus the competition.

Support for organizational change(s) within your firm. ISM worked with an airline that significantly downsized its organization and needed increased support for the remaining sales and marketing personnel. To determine this benefit, consider measuring time lost training new sales and marketing personnel.

Improved understanding and eventual control over expenses. CRM can assist in this effort, assuming sales, marketing, and customer care expenses are tagged to individual sales personnel and/or accounts. To determine this benefit, consider measuring expenses per sales and marketing personnel and/or per account.

Based on this list of tangible and intangible benefits, it would not be inappropriate for one to conclude that the rewards of automation can indeed be great. For example, ISM conducted a sales and marketing audit for a copying machine manufacturer that measured both the impact and potential of automated systems on sales force productivity.

The audit determined that automating activities such as lead tracking, time scheduling, and account profiling would result in an average time savings of one hour per day per salesperson. This equated to an additional 26 days of work time a year per sales representative. Similar measurements for customer service representatives and top management showed savings of 30 minutes and 20 minutes per day, respectively.

But time saved isn't the only reward. Proposal generation, an arduous task for both sales and marketing departments, becomes far more user friendly, because many proposal components—such as standard proposal paragraphs, online pricing information, and customer information (names, addresses, discounts, etc.)—can be automatically incorporated through CRM system functionality.

This copier manufacturer also incorporated an external, third-party prospect database into their CRM system and supplemented this new database with a data entry function which permitted users to enter new prospects from a variety of sources including cold calls, telemarketing, trade shows, etc. The end result was more and better prospects that could then be sorted and assigned according to predefined criteria.

Most dramatic of all, however, was the ability, through automation, to deliver a 14 percent increase in sales force productivity by the end of the first year of operation, which as a result of careful management translated into a healthy contribution to the bottom-line.

By analyzing and identifying both the tangible and intangible benefits, you will be in a position to determine whether or not automation is for you, and to prepare your justification to senior management based on viable facts and figures.

While the list of benefits is impressive, those firms that have realized these benefits also have successfully overcome the problems typically associated with CRM.

Problems with CRM

There are several problems associated with CRM. The key problems include:

Lack of a sales, marketing, and customer service strategy. Firms lacking a sales, marketing, and customer service strategy often are unable to identify or prioritize areas which could benefit from automation. Successful CRM can be realized only when a strategy is in place.

Lack of corporate commitment. CRM requires a corporate commitment from the top. Often, this commitment is missing. Successful CRM requires the involvement of sales and marketing personnel, information systems personnel, external information sources, etc.

In-company politics. Information is power, and key individuals within the firms are often not prepared to share their own information with their colleagues. Successful CRM requires the sharing of information across the organization. There is little room for individuals who tend to create and protect their own information power.

Lack of proper training. The majority of today's managers have been exposed to computers, and today's computer software is increasingly simple to use. Nonetheless, proper training of sales and marketing personnel still remains an essential part of CRM success. Those firms that successfully automate sales and marketing functions claim that for each $1 spent on computer hardware and software, they spend between $3 and $15 on training over the life of the project. This requires a serious commitment within the firm.

Lack of know-how. Firms often feel that they do not have the required knowledge to automate the sales, marketing, and customer service functions. While this may be true for some firms, the use of outside expertise has proven to be a cost-effective way to transfer knowledge in CRM to the firm.

Resistance by system users. This is one of the most difficult problems associated with CRM. Those firms that have successfully applied CRM have learned the importance of creating a two-way flow of valuable information between corporate and field personnel.

Summary

To summarize, CRM comes with its benefits and its problems. Those firms that have successfully applied CRM have found that each and every problem can be overcome and that the benefits far outweigh the problems.

A Blueprint for Effective Customer Relationship Management

9

Despite the many benefits of CRM, recent polls have suggested that CRM remains a "mystery" to most corporate executives. Why? Because most executives do not understand the processes involved in CRM and are somewhat intimidated by the technological issues associated with automation.

Given the potentially large impact of CRM, it is well worth investing the necessary time and resources required to ensure that the automation process succeeds. ISM has developed a 10-step approach for the successful implementation of CRM systems.

Our experience over the past 17 years suggests that the implementation of the following 10 steps improves the chances of success for your CRM system, but does not guarantee it. Our experience also suggests that failure to implement any of these steps greatly increases the likelihood that the automation process will become bogged down, fail outright, or become a dinosaur soon after implementation.

Step 1: Organize Your Project Management Team _____

Initially, you should form a project team consisting of the following:

- **A project champion**, preferably a senior executive, responsible for ensuring appropriate managerial and financial backing throughout the project. The project champion will be involved, on average, six hours per month during the six- to twelve-month project life cycle.
- **A project leader**, who has business process and technical skills. This person will be responsible for implementing the project on a day-to-day basis. This will usually be a full-time position during the project's life cycle.
- **A project user group**, comprised of CRM end-users who are responsible for providing input to the project leader during the project's conceptualization phase, and who test the system during the design and implementation phases. The project user group will be involved, on average, eight hours per month during the six- to twelve-month project life cycle.

Step 2: Determine the Functions to Automate _____

Effective automation at a company starts with a CRM audit, which identifies the business functions that need to be automated and lists the technical features that are required in the CRM system. While there are several different audit methodologies available, we recommend one that contains questionnaires, face-to-face interviews with customer-facing personnel (e.g., anyone who has direct contact with a customer or serves a support role), face-to-face interviews with customers if possible, visits with sales representatives in the field as well as sales channel partners, a review of business processes, a technical assessment, and a final report.

You may choose to hire a CRM consultant to conduct the audit, or you may want to conduct the audit yourself. If you choose the latter, be sure to start by assigning a project team composed of internal and/or external personnel who are familiar with your sales and marketing operations. You may even wish to send one or more members of your project team to one of the many available CRM seminars (e.g., DCI's Customer Relationship Management Conference), at which audit implementation details are discussed.

Regardless of your approach, the audit step is critical. If the audit is not performed properly, you will most likely be unable to implement an effective CRM system. In ISM's experience, companies that took the time to audit properly have more easily and quickly realized the benefits of CRM than those companies that did not. The latter are now paying the price in terms of wasted time, effort, and money.

Automate what needs automating. Automating, for example, an inefficient business process, can be a costly mistake. During a visit with the CRM manager of one of Italy's leading car manufacturers, it was apparent that he wanted to use the CRM system to "once and for all, control his unstructured Italian sales force." This is not the correct basis for approaching CRM, and using CRM to control a sales force is a grave error. In this case, the CRM system never got off the ground.

To ensure that you automate what needs to be automated, your CRM audit should address a "wish list" of how salespeople, marketing personnel, customer support staff, and management would like to improve their work processes. At one company, while ISM was conducting an audit, the top salesman expressed the wish: "If only I could get updated information on both my potential client and my competitors prior to the sales call." Remember that the people doing the job know ways to do it better. Take the time to work with them and you will learn what needs to be automated.

Step 3: Gain Top Management Support and Commitment_____

Companies that successfully automate the customer-facing functions view the CRM systems more as a business tool than as a technological tool. Keep this in mind as you approach top management for support.

Top management commitment can be secured by demonstrating that automation does the following:

- Supports the business strategy—automation delivers the information required to make the key decisions which enable business strategy to be realized.
- Measurably impacts and improves results—this can be gauged according to both tangible and intangible benefits already described.
- Significantly reduces costs and thereby pays for itself over a specified time period.

Document your case for automation based on business impact.

Step 4: Employ Technology Smartly _____

Select information technology and systems that utilize open architecture, thereby making it easy to enhance and enlarge the system over time. Look for software applications that are modularized and can be easily integrated into or interconnected with your existing information databases. Ensure that the technology you select is portable. For example, it uses UNIX, NT, CORBA/COM/DCOM (Java/ActiveX) and other such standards. For firms conducting business between the field and headquarters, or across regions, select software applications that are network compatible and that permit easy Web connection and/or data synchronization between information held on field computers and information held on regional or headquarter computers. To accommodate future changes, be sure the technology you select can easily be customized as well as modified. In other words, let the technology help you to grow.

Although technology is only one step in the overall approach for successfully implementing CRM, it is vital to the functioning of CRM systems. Here is a list of the leading technologies users should be familiar with. The following technologies will continue to drive customer acceptance of CRM in the future:

- **Object-Oriented Programming (OOP)**—This new software technique is making software easier to program for the technical team and easier to use for CRM end-user. Recently introduced technology used in this category includes CORBA/COM/DCOM which are programmed with development environments such as Java, C++ and ActiveX.

  By using these object-oriented architectures, customer relationship management software vendors provide a framework into which new components can be plugged. As corporate cultures and business processes change, individual objects (applets and servlets) can be updated, rewritten, deleted, or added and quickly distributed and installed throughout the user environment, without having to rewrite the entire application, business logic, user interface, or back-office application.

- **Notebook computers**—These portable computers are the choice of sales and marketing executives who tend to spend much of their time in the field. Weight restrictions are quickly disappearing as new lightweight battery technology is introduced. From our experience, choose equipment of the lighter side, this tends to keep the mobile workers happier. In choosing the hardware be careful not to compromise on screen size, keyboard feel and ease of interfacing with options such as networks, CD-ROMs, etc.

- **Handhelds, Smart Phones, and PDAs**—Expect to see an increasing number of pen-based portable computers and PDAs (personal digital assistants) being used in niche CRM areas such as inventory management, route accounting, and additional or alternative sales force automation clients. 3Com and Handspring have been supporting the ISV (independent software vendor) community and this has resulted in several CRM thin-client packages running on the Palm platform. Microsoft has been growing their handheld offerings with new releases of Windows CE and their Pocket PC platform. Several ISVs are exploring the Microsoft platform as the seamless integration with Outlook, Word, and Excel showing lots of promise. Some vendors are introducing integrated Smart Phone platforms using one of the aforementioned handheld operating systems or lightweight browser features such as WAP, WML, J2ME, and other newly introduced wireless technology operating on the TDMA, CDMA, GSM wireless networks. Another wireless technology that we are seeing ISVs embrace is the BlackBerry platform by Research In Motion (RIM). While the beauty of the platform is its simplicity, a few vendors feel that this is what makes the platform so intriguing.

- **Voice recognition**—Despite the potential benefits of computers based on voice recognition, we are still several years away from the seamless integration of voice and computer. However, in recent years progress has been made in this direction. Over the past year, this market sector has seen business consolidation activities that have brought more strength to the segment. One key player, Dictaphone (the dictation pioneer), offers Naturally Speaking, Voice Express, and Kurzweil Voice Commands. Another leader in the market, IBM, has consistently been maturing its Voice Type product line.

  Once inside an application, such as a word processor or e-mail application, the user's continuous speech will be converted to text, with approximately 97 percent accuracy. The difficulty that speech recognition development companies have with voice command and control is that operating systems developed to date have been designed for the keyboard, the integrated pointing device and the primary interface. In order for voice navigation to be smooth and efficient, a new operating system paradigm will need to be designed. While companies like Microsoft and Apple are both developing these new operating system interfaces, they are still a few years off.

- **Modem support**—Most portable computers have the option to be configured with an internal modem, thereby permitting users to communicate to and from the field, including sending and receiving faxes as well as e-mail messages, and to connect to networks such as the Internet or virtual private networks.

- **Wireless technologies**—The new wave of data communication technologies is already available. Cellular and other mobile communications, which permit sales and marketing executives and field service personnel to send and receive data from virtually anywhere, will continue to improve their cost performance and will become, without a doubt, the technology of choice for busy, on-the-move sales and marketing executives.

  2001 to 2004 will bring about many new innovations in the wireless arena. The major problem that we still face is in the area of wireless standards adoptions, especially in the United States. Currently ISVs have too many wireless platforms that they need to support. The next one to two years should help to bring about more wireless technology consolidation.

- **Client/server architectures**—Client/server architectures permit the two-way transfer of selected new or modified data, thereby ensuring continually up-to-date data, decreased data communications costs, since only changed data is transferred between the clients and the server, and connectivity with existing databases regardless of their location, platform, or data format. This allows a company to maintain its current information technology investments. While several of the vendors still offer client/server architecture, we are in the midst of major rearchitectures. The main problem is that occasionally connected devices like laptop CRM applications that can operate with connectivity still require client/server architecture. Many vendors are trying to get away from this and go 100 percent Web-centric. The problem with this approach is that there are still major geographic areas where it is hard if not impossible to achieve network connectivity to the Internet. It is our opinion that we will see some form of client/server architecture for several years to come.

- **"N-tiered" CRM architecture**—This is a growth area. This new direction in system architecture accommodates multiple CRM clients— thick (laptops/desktops), thin (browser, WAP, BlackBerry), and bulgy (i.e., Palm, MS Windows CE, Pocket PC). This architecture allows CRM applications and database servers to reside in regional offices with synchronization of subsets of information on a regular or real-time basis. Multiple application servers and database servers can be integrated in order to provide information to the various CRM clients that are relevant for their particular task.

- **Graphics, video, and sound support**—This equipment, which is available today, will continue to improve because of better compression algorithms, larger storage devices in portable computers, and improved multimedia and streaming technology and improved network bandwidth. Graphics, video, and sound support enhances sales and marketing personnel's ability to easily display their goods and services in the field, e.g., showing color pictures of their products and services on the computer rather than having to carry around an out-of-date paper catalog. Other areas where graphics, video, and sound are increasingly important are CRM user community training (e.g., e-training), product demos and virtual sales meetings (e.g., evoke communications, Centra, WebEx, PlaceWare, etc.).

Step 5: Secure User Ownership

Get users involved early to make sure that your CRM system addresses their needs. One large information technology manufacturer automated their sales force in accordance with the results of the corporate headquarters CRM task force. The actual end-users were not sufficiently represented on this task force and ended up revolting against what they felt was yet another "big brother" system.

Generally, CRM users will respond to a 3X factor in accessing information from the CRM software package. For every one piece of information that the user requests, the CRM system should provide three pieces of information that the user personally values. The 3X factor will motivate users to use the CRM system.

Remember that a satisfied user will want to work with the system, and no one knows better what the users need and what they find annoying, than the users themselves. Do not be afraid to hand over "ownership" of the system to the users.

Step 6: Prototype the System

Prototyping your CRM system facilitates the phasing in of new technology, allows experimentation on a smaller and less costly scale, tests the system's functionality, highlights required changes in organizational procedures, and most importantly, demonstrates that automation objectives can be met. The availability of rapid prototyping software development tools reinforces the importance of "testing before you leap."

Step 7: Train Users

Training is a multistep process that should include: demonstrating to users how to access and utilize needed information, ensuring that users are provided with documentation which is understandable and frequently updated, offering online tutorials which can be customized for each user, providing a telephone help line to stand by your user, and training the "trainers" to ensure that new users can be up and running quickly on the system. In many cases, the use of Web-based training will help to increase training effectiveness while reducing cost.

At a leading air courier express company, several members of the salesforce requested that all electronic information on the CRM system be printed out in paper form. The reason for this request was that these users had not been properly trained and did not know how to properly navigate their way around the system to obtain needed information.

Over the life of your CRM system, training will end up costing 1–1.5 times the cost of the CRM system hardware/software. Budget for training accordingly, and remember that the best way to change work habits and to ensure systems success is via effective training.

Step 8: Motivate Personnel

CRM succeeds when users are motivated by the system's ability to help them obtain their objectives, and when users understand the strategic importance of CRM, there will be improved user productivity and a positive impact on the company's bottom line.

Trends come and go within an organization and it is critical that you determine ways to maintain individual motivation and commitment toward the CRM system. Show users their importance and their impact in terms of the CRM system.

Step 9: Administrate the System

One person/department must be held responsible for overseeing the welfare of the CRM system. This person/department must include an information "gate keeper," who is responsible for ensuring that the information is timely, relevant, easy to access, and is positively impacting users' decision-making needs.

It is a strong disincentive for system use, to be out in the field and using your CRM system only to find out-of-date or incorrect data. Be disciplined and pay careful attention to information and systems details.

Step 10: Keep Management Committed

Set up a committee that includes senior staff and users from the sales, marketing, and customer service departments as well as from the information systems department. This committee should brief senior management on a quarterly basis concerning the status of the CRM systems project, e.g., successes, failures, future needs, growth, etc. Measure the system's results and relay the impact of the system to management. Secure your "system's champion."

Summary

The benefits of CRM can be great, including improved productivity, enhanced customer service, and a strengthened ability to make sound business decisions. To realize the benefits of CRM it is necessary to audit properly, to successfully accomplish the 10 steps outlined above, and to address both technical as well as nontechnical issues. Let us therefore turn to the CRM audit, the centerpiece in implementing CRM in your organization.

Creating Your CRM Business Case

10

A successful CRM initiative is based on a solid CRM Business Case. The Business Case is a critical document that describes the company's current customer relationship management processes, the desired state, how the company intends to integrate people, process, and technology to get to the desired state, the costs and expected return of the CRM initiative, the risks and mitigating factors associated with the initiative, the organizational/operational impact of the initiative, and CRM program metrics against which success/failure can be measured. The CRM Business Case is as relevant to one-off CRM projects as it is to multiple CRM projects within a CRM program.

A company that embarks upon a CRM initiative but fails to create a comprehensive CRM Business Case risks being doomed from the start. The CRM Business Case should not be an option. Not only should it be done, but also it should include precise metrics that get measured throughout the life of the CRM initiative. Despite some analysts' unreasonable claims of CRM implementation failure rates, I can confidently state that those companies that have taken the time to create a comprehensive CRM Business Case containing metrics as described below greatly improve their likelihood of CRM program success. Remember the works of management guru, Peter Drucker, who reminded us some years ago "if you can't measure it, you can't manage it."

The following sections and their details comprise a successful, comprehensive CRM Business Case.

I. Executive Summary

CRM program background.   Provides the reasons for launching the initiative, current business issues that CRM is likely to address, and the impact that CRM is likely to have both internally as well as for customers.

CRM value proposition.   Describes which CRM value proposition components are applicable for the CRM program and offers measurable program impact. The CRM value proposition is based in large part on metrics identified and described below.

In addition to the CRM program background and the CRM value proposition, the Executive Summary section of the CRM Business Case will include:

Initial project scope and timetable.   Provides high-level goals, milestones, and dates associated with successful implementation of the CRM initiative.

Business sponsorship.   Describes the role of top management in approving the CRM Business Case and in actively participating in driving the success of resulting CRM projects (e.g., participation in the CRM Oversight Board which reviews the accomplishment of metrics every six months during a two-hour meeting).

Example of a Successful Value Proposition

Each CRM initiative will have its own value proposition. Here, nonetheless, is one example of a company's value proposition for a 150-person, multifunctional CRM effort:

At a high level, the CRM initiative promised to:

- Deliver more productive reps (freeing up 18.5 hours per week currently spent on unnecessary administrative work) leading to higher close ratios (going from 22 to 28 percent over an 18-month period).

- Reach new customers with more customer seminars (increase the number of seminars from 8 to 12 per year).
- Improve lead efficiency and speed (baseline of three days to get lead out to rep decreasing to one day over a 12-month period).
- Lower mailing costs (promotional mailing costs to decrease from $340,000 to $180,000 per annum).

At a more detailed level, the CRM initiative promised to deliver:

- Productivity impact (resulting from doing your job more efficiently because you no longer have to run around like a chicken with its head cut off to obtain needed information):

Each sales rep	18.5 hours per week (2+ days per week)
Each sales manager	5.8 hours per week
Tech services department	20.2 hours per week (2+ days per week)
Marketing department	36.8 hours per week (4+ days per week)
Each product manager	6.0 hours per week
Total for CRM user-base	1,182 hours per week (148 days per week)

- Revenue impact (resulting from doing your job more effectively resulting in higher close ratios):

Territory sales reps (total)	$ 3.55 million per annum
Sales managers (total)	$ 1.47 million per annum
Tech services department	$ 0.30 million per annum
Total	$ 5.32 million per annum

- Cost savings (resulting from no longer sending annual product catalogs to all customers, but rather specific catalogs and targeted mailings to specific customers based on known areas of interest):

  Marketing department savings $ 234,950 per annum

- A financial break-even point at month 16 (i.e., sufficient contribution has been generated from the CRM system through month 16 to pay back all CRM-related costs through month 16).

CRM Value Proposition Guidelines

For the past six years, ISM has conducted research into the CRM value proposition. As previously stated, while each CRM value proposition is unique, here are some generic guidelines for creating the CRM value proposition.

Companies that successfully implement their CRM initiative realize and benefit from one or more of the six CRM value proposition components:

1. **Enhanced productivity**: A 10–20 percent annual increase in the productivity of your customer-facing personnel, resulting from having needed customer information readily available. With proper discipline and incentives, this productivity improvement leads to a 5–10 percent increase in annual sales.

2. **Lower costs**: A 5–10 percent decrease in your sales, marketing, and customer service general and administrative costs. This benefit results from knowing your customers and servicing your customers better and more efficiently.

3. **Superior employee morale**: A 10 percent decrease in your turnover rate resulting from more satisfied customer-facing employees, along with a better pool of candidates applying for your customer-facing job openings.

4. **Better customer knowledge**: A complete, comprehensive "customer profile" as defined by your customer-facing personnel and customers within 18-months of the launch of your CRM initiative.

5. **Higher customer satisfaction**: A 10 percent increase per annum between 100 percent customer satisfaction and your current satisfaction rating. This results from customers who receive desired information promptly and completely.

6. **Improved customer loyalty/retention**: A 10 percent annual increase in customer wallet share, and a 10 percent annual improvement in customer retention rates. These result because customers like to do business with a company that really cares about their relationship.

II. Financials

Detailed financial information. Includes estimated costs for hardware, software, communication, consulting, training, internal costs, and other total-cost-of-ownership components needed to realize a successful CRM program. Also provides estimated revenues resulting from the CRM program, including identification of the break-even point and the resulting ROI.

III. Recommended Technical Solutions_____

Provides insight into key technical issues. CRM technical alternatives considered, description of the proposed CRM technical solution, interfaces with existing company systems (e.g., ERP systems), disaster recovery policy, hot spare policy, and support/help desk policies. This section tends to have heavy input from or be written by internal IT company personnel.

IV. Key Risks and Mitigating Factors _____

Key technology risks and mitigation. For example, lack of scalability, inappropriate security procedures, difficult data synchronization, and lack of data quality strategy.

Key user risks and mitigation. For example, bad or inappropriate training leading to an inability to properly utilize the system, or users don't perceive CRM value.

Key management risks and mitigation. For example, lack of management commitment to CRM, lack of management support for CRM, or management attention moves off CRM and onto a more attractive initiative.

V. Operational/Organizational Impact _____

Key processes affected. Describes the processes that have or will be impacted by the CRM program, including how processes will be enhanced.

Organizational issues. Provides the number of personnel affected by the CRM program, also identifies how the CRM program will impact job descriptions, individual performance requirements, and compensation.

Organizational buy-in. Details a CRM program communications plan along with appropriate change management issues that need to be addressed to ensure success of the CRM initiative.

VI. Appendices _____

For each CRM business functional area (e.g., time management, sales, sales management, telemarketing/telesales, customer contact center, marketing, business intelligence, e-business, and so on), there is a high-level description of potential areas of improvement. This includes, for example, key current activities, the current state of these activities including time spent per activity, and the likely benefits and results of the CRM system quantified in terms of time saved, monetary gain, and/or cost savings achieved.

The appendices point out common CRM business functionality such as a common customer profile or a limited number of common management reports that are needed across all customer-facing functional areas. Identifying common CRM functionality is very important for the overall success of a CRM project and/or program since common business functionality allows multiple functions/departments to share common information on an as-needed basis. The appendices also point out unique CRM system customer-facing functionality needs. Unique needs may be important due to, for example, cultural differences within a global company; but unique needs should be kept to a minimum if at all possible since there are costs, often times significant, associated with creating unique needs. Moreover, unique needs often lead to incompatibility of business processes and ultimately to an inability to share or report against common customer information.

Summary _____

Each CRM Business Case is unique, and therefore it is difficult to provide a sample or generic CRM Business Case here. If you feel that you would benefit from seeing a sanitized version of a CRM Business Case, please contact ISM.

The CRM Business Case is not an optional item. Not only is it mandatory, but also it must be measured quarterly to ensure that the CRM initiative stays on track. Effective use of the CRM Business Case is how a company proactively achieves CRM project or program success.

CRM Software Selection and Implementation Roadmap

A company's decision to pursue a customer relationship management (CRM) system for automation of the sales, marketing, and customer service processes, may be prompted by the sales force, sales management, marketing, customer service, or other members of the executive staff. It is not so important who initiates the procedure. What is important is that sales, marketing, customer service, and other executives work together to ensure that the CRM process integrates differing needs across these functions, and that sufficient time is allocated to this integration process. While this may seem apparent, this is not always the case.

Avoid the Quick Fix—Do Your Homework

In helping industry giants and small-scale companies to automate their sales, marketing, and customer service functions, we often come across a dangerous situation in CRM that we call the *quick fix*. The quick fix is defined as a desire, on behalf of existing and potential CRM users, to realize the full benefits of CRM but to short cut those steps required to ensure that these benefits materialize.

ISM has found that when the quick fix is employed, not only do benefits often not materialize, the likelihood for a CRM disaster increases substantially.

Case Studies of CRM Disasters

To describe the quick fix, let us turn to two case studies.

Case Study 1.   Company A is a global computer manufacturer based in the United States. For a number of months, sales management complained to their sales force that new customer prospects were not being followed up properly. The sales force in turn complained that the customer/prospect follow-up procedures being used by this company were both outdated and unproductive, and that sales force automation would help to address this situation. To address this situation, the company implemented a sales force automation system, which required that users use laptops to access needed customer prospect data. This sales force automation software package included lead management, telemarketing, and direct mail business functions.

Unfortunately, the strategic impact of this application never materialized. Why? Because this sales force automation application had been quickly thrown together by management without identifying and incorporating the needs of the sales force. Moreover, the application proved to be neither intuitive nor easy to use, resulting in the sales force abandoning the system after a mere three months.

Result: a multimillion dollar write-off.

Case Study 2.   Company B is a large consumer goods wholesaler/retailer located in a European country. The sales force complained that it spent too much time counting stock at the many stores located throughout this country, which led to low sales force productivity. To address this situation, the company implemented a sales and marketing automation system, which employed large electronic scanners to read and record stock figures. These stock figures were then uploaded from the scanners to a centralized mainframe computer at corporate headquarters, using a very well defined but rigid database structure.

Unfortunately, the strategic impact of this application never materialized. Why? Given the need to get this automation system up and running quickly, the company selected available electronic scanners that were large and heavy and employed out-of-date technology. Moreover, the application was selected without sales force input, and proved to be inflexible both for the sales force as well as for management. After a six-month trial period, the system was dismantled.

Result: a $500,000 write-off.

The previous two case studies clearly indicate how the quick fix approach to CRM can lead to disastrous and costly results. They are not anomalies in an otherwise successful field of CRM. The quick fix exists today for a very intoxicating reason, namely sales and marketing executives have been falsely lured by the potentially large benefits of CRM. Impatient by nature, sales and marketing executives have often overlooked the need to do their homework to ensure successful automation.

The quick fix promises of software vendors have further complicated this situation, as sales and marketing executives have become a receptive target for unrealistic quick fix solutions. The following are two examples of this phenomenon.

In the first situation, a sales executive from a large California-based corporation requested that we recommend the most appropriate CRM software package for his firm. This executive was proud to inform us that his corporation had spent one full day deciding on CRM needs, and that we easily could base our software recommendation on the results of this needs analysis.

Yet when we challenged this executive concerning his needs for an integrated and modular sales and marketing solution (e.g., sales assistance, customer service, marketing intelligence, and/or executive information modules), this executive was quick to admit that these important issues had not been addressed during their automation needs analysis meeting. Moreover, as we continued to question this executive concerning required business functions, technical features, and user friendliness criteria, it became increasingly clear to this executive that his firm had not properly done its homework, and that it was necessary to return to the drawing board.

In the second situation, the sales and marketing vice president of a Maryland-based multinational company decided to drive the implementation of a sales and marketing automation project within her corporation. This meant traveling from one sales and marketing automation trade show to the next, each time reviewing one or more new vendor software packages that often promised to "do it all."

After viewing each new vendor software package, this executive requested that an information package be sent to her, including a proposal outlining the vendor's charges to automate this executive's sales force. After reviewing most of these information packages herself, this executive made her sales and marketing automation software selection. A few weeks later, however, she learned from her Information Systems department that the software package she had specified was incompatible with the order entry system being used by the corporation. Given the need to work with this firm's order entry system, she received no further corporate funding and little IT support for the package she had selected. Needless to say, the potentially large benefits of this CRM system never materialized for this firm.

Case Studies of CRM Successes

On a more positive note, with proper planning and careful attention to implementation details, many companies reap the benefits of CRM. Following are two examples of international companies that have been successful in their sales and marketing CRM projects.

Case Study 1.   Company C is one of the world's leading clothing manufacturers. Management complained that it needed to more easily monitor the day-to-day results of its 5,000 stores worldwide and to improve its responsiveness to changing market conditions. To address this situation, the company implemented a sales and marketing information system which (1) read barcode labels attached to each garment sold in each store each day, (2) sent the corresponding sales figures from each store to corporate headquarters on a daily basis, and (3) used a colorful graphical user interface to display these sales figures to senior management.

Result: The strategic impact of this application has been tremendous as management is now able to obtain a quick, efficient view of their business; management decision-making has been enhanced and overall business results have improved.

Case Study 2.   Company D is a European corporation and one of the world's leading manufacturers of plastic drainage systems. To stay competitive, the company needed to: (1) consolidate its operations across Europe, (2) undertake new manufacturing and distribution business strategies, and (3) integrate the sales and marketing functions into these new business strategies. To address this situation, the company implemented a sales and marketing information system that included online inventory verification, and online ordering and bidding from any country in Europe, tied together via a global data communications network.

Result: The strategic impact of this application allowed this company to effectively realize its new manufacturing and distribution business strategies, improve its pan-European customer service, and enable sales and marketing personnel to spend more time in the marketplace securing additional business with its client base.

Lessons Learned

We have reviewed four examples of companies that have gone through the sales and marketing automation process. Companies A and B fall into the quick fix trap and have failed outright in their CRM automation efforts. Companies C and D avoided the lure of the quick fix and have been successful in their sales and marketing automation efforts.

What lessons can we learn from these case studies?

Lesson 1. From the two companies that failed in their CRM automation efforts, we can learn that the complexity of automation must never be underestimated and that jumping into the deep end of automation, without careful planning, is a costly mistake. In addition, the needs of sales, marketing, and customer service automation users cannot be bypassed and automation cannot be thrown at the users in the belief that this will deliver measurable business benefits.

Lesson 2. From the two companies that succeeded in their sales and marketing automation efforts, we can learn that to ensure the successful implementation of sales and marketing automation, one must do the necessary homework. The successful implementation of sales and marketing automation begins with an effective CRM audit.

Components of an Effective CRM Software Selection Process

Several excellent CRM software selection methodologies currently exist. Here is a ten-step methodology that ISM has developed and has implemented with reasonable success at more than 300 companies worldwide.

Step 1: Technical Baseline Review

Your technical staff should define your current technical platform and capabilities, including issues of data synchronization, links to ERP systems, and potential system expansion (i.e., the Internet/Web for e-business).

Step 2: Customer Visits with the Customer-Facing Personnel

A CRM project team member will visit with a cross-section of customer facing representatives (e.g., sales, marketing, customer service, partners) for one-half to a full day per representative. Observations gleaned from the visits serve as input for the brainstorming session and the needs analysis questionnaires.

Step 3: Brainstorming Session

Your CRM project team should conduct a structured three-hour session with between 10 and 18 personnel (e.g., sales representatives, marketing and sales managers, executives, customer service managers, IT specialists) to reveal their perceived CRM business functional needs. These participants are typically chosen as a *superuser* group that will participate in further CRM audit steps and be ambassadors for the eventual CRM system.

Step 4: Needs Analysis Questionnaires

A customized needs analysis questionnaire should be administered to between 30 and 60 potential users of the CRM system (including brainstorming session participants). There are typically three different questionnaire types sent to three different decision-making groups, namely customer-facing personnel, managers, and executives. While the three questionnaires may ask several of the same questions, these questionnaires should also ask separate questions that take into account the different decision-making responsibilities of these three groups. The questionnaires serve to confirm and consolidate findings revealed during the field visits and the brainstorming session, as well as force the respondents to do a preliminary prioritization of the business functional needs, technical features, and user friendliness issues.

Step 5: Business Process Review

Your business processes need to be reviewed and highlighted to address existing business process issues as well as business process requirements. Recommendations for a step-by-step approach for implementing best-in-class business processes applicable to the CRM system should be defined in order to properly plan for short-term as well as long-term business needs that can be addressed by your CRM system.

Step 6: Business Functional Prioritization

Based on the results of the field visits, the brainstorming session, the needs analysis questionnaires, and the business process review, the identification of your prioritized business functions can be made for presentation to your management team.

Step 7: Technical Platform Recommendations

In view of your prioritized business functions, and the results of your technical platform review, recommendations for appropriate technical platform alternatives can be made for CRM software, hardware, and communications.

Step 8: CRM Report

The report, which is presented to your management team for approval, contains information needed to formulate your system specifications, including business and technical requirements.

Step 9: Software Selection

If you opt for external software, it is recommended that you consider between three and five software packages appropriate to the CRM functions identified. It may be of considerable value to bring in an experienced CRM consultant to assist you in writing your Request For Proposal (RFP) and reviewing, selecting, and negotiating with your CRM vendor of choice.

Step 10: Software Implementation Assistance

Once you have made your software selection, a CRM consultant can assist you in implementing your CRM project, primarily in the areas of project management and systems assurance. This includes:

- Helping to select your systems integrator.
- Helping to choose your training partner and approach.
- Evaluating project plans.
- Participating in weekly operations review meetings.
- Assisting in the implementation of specific tasks/project management (e.g., training manuals, pilot rules, performance measurement criteria, etc.).
- Assisting in system assurance/customer satisfaction (e.g., on-going process improvements).

The CRM software selection process should in most cases be accomplished within eight to twelve weeks (assuming the prospective company has committed to an aggressive CRM timeframe).

Summary

In summary, we have reviewed case studies of CRM successes and failures, and looked into ISM's ten-step methodology for selecting CRM software. Regardless of the methodology you use, be sure to use a structured approach.

In the following section, we intend to review in greater detail how to prioritize your CRM system.

CRM System: Requirements Analysis

12

One of the key results of your CRM software selection and implementation roadmap process will be a list of requirements, which typically includes business functional, technical, and user friendliness/support items. These requirements come directly from your brainstorming session, your field/corporate visits, your questionnaires, as well as any business matrices that you may have employed (e.g., technical infrastructure review).

You should not be surprised if your requirements list is long; in fact, this may well signal the results of a successful software selection and implementation roadmap. Nevertheless, in ISM's experience we find it unfeasible and even unwise to try to deliver all defined business functionality during your first system release. Here are the key reasons why:

- While all business functions may seem important, experience suggests that once a CRM system is implemented, users employ considerably less that 100 percent of the functionality available from the system.

- Too many business functions may overwhelm even the best technical staff's capabilities, and may lead to confusion between business functions that are needed versus business functions that are nice to have, thereby delaying delivery of high priority functions.
- Automation changes the way customer-facing personnel work, and this in itself can be quite a shock to the user. To overwhelm the user with too much functionality too quickly can actually bring about lower productivity and a longer technological assimilation period.

For these reasons, our suggestion is to start small and build your system functionality in phases. This in turn requires that your business functionality list be prioritized to ensure that there is a clear understanding of which business functions will be implemented first, second, and so forth.

Business Functional Requirements for Your CRM System

Prioritizing your business functional requirements can be a difficult exercise. Assuming you are implementing a multifunctional, integrated system, it is likely that your business functional requirements list will contain requirements elicited from job functions which include sales, sales management, marketing, customer service, and top management. It is also likely that each of these job functions will feel that its own requirements are the most important requirements for the system. Moreover, unless there are clear rules for prioritizing your business functional requirements, internal politics can lead to inappropriate prioritization, which may have long-term unfavorable system results.

Here are our suggestions to avoid these potential problems, and to prioritize your business functional list in a way that will ensure maximum results:

- Conduct a prioritization meeting. Bring together senior managers responsible for sales, marketing, and customer service for a prioritization session that should last no more than three hours. To this group of senior managers, add potential system users, e.g., one or two sales representatives, a marketing representative, and a customer service representative, preferably individuals who have participated in the brainstorming session, field/corporate visits, and questionnaire exercise.

- During this prioritization meeting, the potential system users should brief senior management on how the business functional requirements list came about, and what each desired functionality means. In turn, the senior managers should brief the potential systems users as to the key priorities of the company, based on business strategy and direction.

- Participants in the prioritization meeting should next discuss how each of the proposed business functional requirements supports both the company's key priorities as well as the needs of potential systems users. Compromises will need to be made during this part of the meeting.

- Participants of the prioritization meeting should next prioritize the business functional requirements list (No. 1 being the most important function to automate, No. 2 the second most important function to automate, etc.). Responses to this prioritization exercise should then be tabulated.

- Finally, participants of the prioritization meeting should review the prioritization exercise results, iron out any remaining disagreements or difficulties, and agree to the final prioritization list, which will be used either for your internal specification or for your Request For Information/Proposal to external vendors. During this final session of the prioritization meeting, remaining disagreements or difficulties should be worked out by referring to the company's business strategy and direction. The value of your prioritization meeting includes (1) a final list of prioritized business functions, and (2) buy-in from both senior management as well as the users concerning the direction forward for your CRM system.

On one occasion, ISM ran a prioritization meeting for a large consumer goods company. It became apparent 30 minutes into the meeting, following the user and senior management briefings, that the marketing director felt he owned the system, and that the sales manager really wasn't very interested in it. Acknowledging the long-term dangers of this situation, a few pertinent business questions were asked (e.g., how could the sharing of marketing and sales information benefit each party) that forced these two directors to address the need for an integrated CRM system.

This type of situation is not abnormal and reminds us that while the prioritization meeting should be structured, sufficient flexibility needs to be built into the timetable for issues that may arise.

Technical Features Requirements for Your CRM System

A second key result of your CRM software selection and implementation roadmap will be an initial list of technical features requirements. These features come directly from discussions with key placeholders in the development of the CRM system.

There may be confusion between technical features for your CRM system, which facilitate usage of the system, and technical platform issues, which deal more with what technical architecture will be used to support your CRM system.

Decisions concerning technical platform issues most often rest in the hands of the company's IT department. Here are some examples of technical platform issues:

- Will your CRM system have a Web-centric architecture or is a Web-enabled client/server architecture adequate?
- What operating system environments will be compatible with your CRM system (e.g., MS Windows 95/98/ME/NT/2000/XP, Novell, UNIX)?
- How will your CRM system be accessed (e.g., Internet/Web, virtual private networks, handheld devices, wireless technology)?
- How will data be synchronized between CRM system components and users (e.g., servers, databases, locations)?
- Which database(s) will be used for your CRM system, including the number and location of database servers (e.g., Oracle, MS-SQL Server, Sybase, IBM DB2)?
- How will back-office or legacy systems be integrated into the CRM system?
- What groupware platforms (e.g., Lotus Notes, MS Exchange) will your CRM systems need to interface with?
- What e-business platforms will (e.g., BEA, IBM WebSphere, Vignette, BroadVision) your CRM systems need to interface with?
- What security features are available to protect CRM system data?
- Will your existing computer hardware support the CRM system, and if not, which new hardware will be necessary?

While CRM users should be aware of these issues and provide input where needed (for very good reasons such as technical integrity across multiple company systems), decisions on technical platform issues remain largely out of the hands of the CRM users.

To define which technical features should be in your CRM system, here are a few guidelines:

1. Work with your IT department and/or an external consultant to help define possible technical features that could be included in your CRM software.

2. Remember that technical features are required in your CRM system to facilitate the eventual implementation of your prioritized business functional requirements. For example, if placing your company price lists online is a prioritized business function, you will want to make sure that the software you use has appropriate technical features that allow for easy updating of price lists.

3. Learn possible technical features by reviewing existing CRM software. Whether you end up building or buying your CRM software, review some of the vast quantity of packaged and hosted CRM software solutions to gain insight into the latest thinking vis-à-vis technical features.

In one CRM assignment that ISM worked on with a publishing company, the project leader had a technical background. During specification of the system, he showed us the latest available technical features for CRM. While many of his proposed technical features would be of some value to his company's system, others were little more than technical toys. To bring some reality to the playing field, we asked the project leader what were the top 10 business functional requirements for the proposed system. After getting four out of 10 correct, he finally began to listen more carefully to his users needs.

Ensure that technical features will directly assist your CRM system users to successfully implement prioritized business functions. While they can be dazzling, technical features should not be judged on technical wizardry, but on business value. Based on our observations of CRM users in the field, the greatest value of technical features is their ability to help users feel comfortable with the system, to help users access and navigate the system, and to help make the system intuitive to the user.

User Friendliness/Support Requirements for Your CRM System

A third result of your CRM software selection and implementation roadmap will be an initial list of user friendliness/support requirements. These requirements come directly from your brainstorming session, your field/corporate visits, your questionnaires, as well as any business matrices that you may have employed.

User support requirements are critical since many potential users of your CRM system may not be familiar with the CRM software you select, with using CRM software in general, or even with using other computer systems. To complicate the process of determining user support requirements, CRM software is being developed for hardware platforms other than desktop or laptop computers, such as handheld devices (e.g., Palm) and wireless devices (e.g., WAP phones). Nonetheless, too many good CRM systems have failed because user support requirements were overlooked; so pay attention to these requirements.

Who decides on the user support criteria? In actuality, it is a collaborative process, but the users should have a large voice. This decision must not be left up to technical or managerial personnel. Moreover, only via trial and error will your company learn what is the correct level of user support, as this level differs from company to company and from system to system.

With these thoughts in mind, here are some of the key user support requirements that you should take into consideration when specifying and designing your CRM system:

Graphical User Interface (GUI).   For thick and thin client CRM interfaces, MS Windows GUIs and browser GUIs predominate. Some vendors have developed GUIs that mimic those of MS Outlook. Most recently, vendors have been taking cues from the Web world and designing interfaces that in many ways mimic the interface of a Web browser. This makes sense, because most new CRM software is being developed based on Internet/Web platforms and technologies. Handheld devices such as PDAs use a different GUI due to the smaller screen size. Regardless of the interface, there are key questions that you should consider. Does the screen layout appear to be cluttered, or does the screen layout appear to be nicely designed in terms of ergonomics and flow? Have the screen fields been laid out in a logical manner? Is it easy to get to a secondary or a support screen from the main screen?

System Navigation.   This is the ease with which users can move from field to field within a screen, from screen to screen, as well as from function to function within the system. Several studies confirm that system navigation is a key success factor for user acceptance of the system. While system navigation may be a subjective issue, let the users inform you whether system navigation is sufficiently easy to implement. Navigation schemes for CRM software primarily use MS Windows or Web browser metaphors, which should have familiarity to the majority of computer users. Increasingly, different functions of the software are being ported down to handheld and wireless devices, which have their own navigation schemes.

Intuitiveness of the System.   This is a hard requirement to define since each user will have a perspective on what constitutes intuitiveness. Moreover, intuitiveness of the system is impacted by screen design, graphical user interface, as well as system navigation. Based on ISM's findings, users feel that an intuitive system reflects the developer's knowledge of the customer-facing processes behind the interface. In a nonintuitive system, users feel as if the system has been designed by technical personnel who are out-of-touch with the way customer-facing functions (e.g., sales, marketing, and customer service) work within organizations.

Effectiveness of the System.   Increased competition between software vendors has led to divergent philosophies within the industry as to what constitutes effective functionality. The business principle driving this split is defined on the basis of how a company can best take advantage of its information resources to increase sales. Some software vendors have answered this question by incorporating a sales methodology, which requires the user to input a substantial amount of data to provide a more extensive profile of the contact, account, or opportunity. Other vendors have chosen to simplify the user's responsibilities by requiring less data input and offering a more appealing screen design, with colors, shading, and easy-to-read text, to increase user support and the use of the program. This is where the software buyer must decide whether acquiring more information or offering a simpler data entry environment defines effectiveness.

Customer Self-Service via the Web.   The influence of the Internet/Web is affecting automation efforts in countless ways. The vendors that are more advanced in Web interaction technology are offering online Web pages that provide customers with a "window" into some customer service portions of the corporate knowledgebase (subject to security restrictions). Using the customer service Web pages, a user can perform operations without the assistance of a customer service representative. Users might input service request information, check on the status of a problem resolution, request technical documentation, search FAQs, or request follow-up from a customer service representative. What Web self-service support capabilities are provided by your short-list of vendors?

The Help Function. Most users prefer a field-sensitive Help Function rather than a screen-sensitive Help Function, since less work is required by the user to find specific answers to questions that the user may have. Another important Help Function requirement is the ability for the systems administrator, either internal or external to your company, to modify (add, enhance, delete) or to customize the verbiage within the Help Function. The ability to customize the Help Function is particularly important if your system contains specific business processes which are unique to your company and which your users may need to refer to regularly. Lastly, does the Help Function contain the User Documentation online so that users can leave their often heavy User Documentation books at home?

Online Chat. What interaction channels are available to customers as an alternative to making a phone call, sending an e-mail, or searching a knowledgebase of information to get answers to support questions? Increasingly, vendors are offering an online chat feature that allows customers to interact with customer service representatives via a company Web page. Typically, this interaction entails typing in questions and receiving feedback via a dialog box, which shows the questions and answers. This capability augments the other customer self-service features that a vendor may provide.

Online Training. Does the vendor offer modes of training in addition to the standard training options for classroom training provided on-site or at a company location? With the increase in Web-based CRM applications, there has been an increase in availability of Web-based, online training. So, users can participate in training exercises via the Internet/Web without the limitation of geographic location (e.g., travel). Trainees log into a scheduled session, which is held using Web-based collaboration services such as Centra or WebEx. Some CRM vendors offer Web-based CRM applications training via OEM agreements with companies like Knowledge Impact. Online training is particularly suited to periodic training, because there is typically less material to present. This online training capability allows users to increase their skills and not consume additional time away from work, while the vendor can provide the same quality of learning as the on-site training at a lower cost of delivery.

User Documentation.   Is the documentation comprehensive and up-to-date? Are there plenty of practical examples shown in the documentation, including screenshots of software functionality? How do system users receive documentation updates? Can updates be delivered electronically? Can the User Documentation be accessed online while the user is on the system?

Internationalization.   Does the vendor offer multilanguage and multicurrency versions of the software? What types of translation capabilities are provided for local versions of the CRM solution? What international support office locations are available to customers that have global CRM system implementations?

Data Synchronization.   Is the process of sending and receiving data to/from the field with headquarters a "one-button" operation, or do you need extensive training to perform this critical function? Also, how simple is it for the user to determine what went wrong and what to do to correct the problem if in the middle of data synchronization the telephone line or wireless modem disconnects?

System Support.   Given the importance of this topic (e.g., training, help desk, system administration), and the impact that system support can have not only on user support but also on the overall success of the system, ISM has devoted a separate chapter to this topic (see Chapter 17, "The Necessity of Training, a Good Help Desk, and Effective Systems Administration").

Here is an example of how one company addressed the user support issue. A large international pharmaceutical company implemented a comprehensive CRM system for its sales and marketing personnel a few years ago. To ensure that the system was user friendly, this company invited sales and marketing personnel participation from the inception of the project. Specifically, as this in-company system was built module by module, the sales and marketing personnel were given the right to veto any screen as well as to reject the navigation, the Help Function, etc., as "unfriendly."

While this approach led to a longer than expected development period, and a few battles between users and developers, the users ultimately owned the system which they had created based on their own needs and their own user support criteria. We can confirm that to this day, sales and marketing personnel belonging to this company connect to this system on a daily basis.

This example shows that by letting the users define and approve user support, you will greatly enhance the likelihood of overall system success.

Summary

In summary, the requirements analysis portion of your CRM software selection process is of great importance to the success of the CRM initiative. You will want to carefully consider and prioritize the business functional, technical features, and user friendliness/support requirements for your CRM system.

How to Write Your Systems Specifications Document

13

Once you have completed your CRM system needs analysis, prioritized your business functional requirements, and defined both your technical features and user friendliness/support requirements, you are now in a position to write your systems specifications document for sending to a qualified short-list of external vendors in the form of a Request For Proposal (RFP) or for use by internal IT personnel.

ISM has devoted an entire chapter to this topic since we feel it is imperative for you to remain in charge of the external vendor process, yet provide sufficient information so that external vendors as well as internal IT personnel are able to customize and deliver to you a system which fulfills your unique set of CRM needs. Additional information about selecting a vendor is provided in the next chapter.

Writing an RFP

It is not our intention here to suggest a "best" way to write your systems specifications document. We respect the fact that each company has its own set of rules and regulations concerning the writing of a technical specifications document. Nevertheless, here are ISM's recommendations to assist in structuring your CRM systems specifications document to send to a qualified short-list of external vendors in the form of an RFP:

1. **General Conditions Section**—This is where you list general conditions of significance to your company such as right to reject, performance conditions, response verification and conditions, and so forth.

2. **Vendor Instructions**—This is where you provide a clear description to the CRM vendor concerning the purpose of the specifications document, communications regarding the proposal, timetable for the proposal, selection and award process, vendor response deadlines, vendor presentation rules, contract negotiations, and so forth.

3. **Proposal Guidelines/Formats**—This is where you specify the format of the proposal (e.g., in electronic format), of how to present exceptions to the RFP, what is needed concerning vendor contact information, and evaluation criteria (e.g., product features and operational capability consistent with specified requirements, specialized relevant experience of the firm, completeness in addressing all aspects of the RFP, financial stability of the vendor, and so forth).

4. **Vendor Profile**—This is where you ask the vendor to provide the following types of background information:
   - Size of the company and whether it is local, national, or international.
   - Location of the office which will handle your account.
   - An affirmation that the vendor does not have a history of providing substandard work.
   - A profile of the vendor's product lines along with the industries they serve.
   - A list of those elements that differentiate the vendor from other organizations.
   - A list of at least three clients, and so forth.

5. **Business Functional Requirements**—Here we recommend that you use the following type of approach (the functions have been selected for exemplary purposes):

After most of the business functions listed, you will be asked to fill in the ranking space according to five categories:

F+ *Functionality fully provided.*

F *Functionality partially provided, and can be enhanced to full functionality.*

D *Functionality does not exist, but can be provided at no additional cost.*

DB *Functionality does not exist, but can be provided at additional cost.*

X *Functionality does not exist, and vendor has no plans for development.*

For F and D, indicate if Company X can develop or if vendor support is needed. For F, D, and DB, provide time estimate for development.

After each business function that you have checked F+, F, DB, or D, please provide a comprehensive description of the business function as it is presently offered in your software package (use additional sheets as needed).

You would then list your business functional requirement, as well as your technical features and user friendliness/support criteria and have the vendors assess how well their software meets your needs. The enclosed list provides an example of the types of business functions, technical features, and user friendliness/support criteria one would expect to find in an RFP. Remember, your RFP will probably only contain a subset of these criteria, based upon your prioritized list of required functions and features.

Business Functions	Description
Contact Management	
Contact profile	
Organization Chart	
Contact history	
Account Management	
Account information	
Business relationships	
Account planning tool	
Activity management	
Order entry	
Order history	

Sales contract generation	
Quote/proposal generation	
Sales Management	
Opportunity management	
Sales cycle analysis	
Sales metrics	
Territory alignment/assignment	
Activity reporting	
Mapping tools	
Sales coaching	
Expense reporting	
Literature/samples management	
Equipment loan management	
Time Management Tools	
Calendar (i.e., native or third-party)	
Single user scheduling	
Group (multiuser) scheduling	
Task lists	
Tickler/alarm	
Electronic mail	
Fax	
Notes	
Transaction log/audit trail	
Customer Contact Center	
Customer self-service	
Automated e-mail response	
Customer profile screen-pop	
Interactive support	
Multimedia portal management	
Workforce management	
Customer Service	
Incident assignment	
Incident escalation	
Incident lifecycle management	
Incident reporting	

Interactive calendar	
Order management	
Return authorization management and analysis	
Service level agreement management	
Warranty management	
Field Service	
Call handling/dispatching/scheduling	
Workforce management	
Inventory management	
Problem resolution management	
Time and expense reporting	
Telemarketing/Telesales	
Call list assembly	
Call planning	
Scripting	
Call recording	
Call statistics/reporting	
Auto-dialing	
Marketing	
Campaign management	
Marketing (media) encyclopedia	
Special events management	
Predictive modeling tools	
Product/price configurator	
Integration with geographical information systems	
Customer lifetime value	
Customer engagement tools	
Literature fulfillment	
Letter writing capabilities	
Mail merge	
Label creation	

Lead Management	
Enhancement	
Incubation	
Qualification	
Prioritization	
Routing	
Tracking	
Partner Relationship Management	
Channel program management	
Opportunity management	
Reporting capabilities	
Sales management	
Marketing	
Lead management	
Product/price configurator	
E-service	
Partnership agreements	
Knowledge Management	
Information feeds	
Information attachment	
Inference engines	
Document management	
Business Intelligence	
Predefined reports	
User-defined reporting	
Predefined queries	
Ad hoc query generator	
Automatic roll-up/drill-down capabilities	
Forecasting/planning tools	
Graphical or statistical modeling tools	
Dashboard/portal interface for key indicators	
Notification of Web site updates/changes	
Alert/alarm capabilities	

E-Business	
Personalization	
Portal capabilities	
Content management	
Storefront	
Order/transaction processing	
Cross-selling	
Online customer behavior analysis and reporting	
Supply Chain Management	
E-procurement	
Interfaces to B2B exchanges/software packages	
Logistics management	

Technical Features	Description
Workflow	
Process configurability	
Alerts/notifications	
Task reassignment	
Workflow personalization	
Architectural Consistency	
Are all your software modules on the same architecture?	
Are all your software modules seamlessly integrated together?	
Technical Specifications	
Desktop/laptop operating systems supported	
Handheld operating systems supported	
Application server operating systems supported	
Wireless technologies supported	
Scalability	
Users per application server	
ERP integration	
Point solution integration	

Telephony switch and/or PBX integration	
Software programming language(s) used for development	
Software architecture(s)	
Current architecture release date	
First software release date and platform(s)	
Last software release date and platform(s)	
Security features	
LDAP compliant	
Minimum hardware requirements for desktop/laptop client	
Minimum hardware requirements for application server	
Minimum hardware requirements for handhelds	
Toolkits used in software development and customization	
Database servers natively supported	
COM and/or CORBA compliant	
Laptop databases supplied with package	
Handheld databases supplied with package	
ODBC compliant	
Connection mode	
Client-to-server synchronization	
Server-to-server database synchronization supported	
Portal technology tools supported	
Speech recognition supported	
Thin-client supported	
Source code available/included	
Office productivity package integration	
Bi-directional integration with Groupware platforms	
EAI vendor(s) supported	

User Friendliness	Description
Help Function	
Help menu	
Context-sensitive help	
Detailed error messages	
Internationalization	
Multicurrency	
Multilingual module support	
Translation capabilities/integration	
Foreign office locations	
International support	
Training	
Range of available options	
Training charges	
Support	
On-site support	
Phone support	
Toll-free number	
Technical and user documentation	
Web, bulletin-board, online forums	
Maintenance/support charges	
Software warranty period	
List your company's top tier integration firms	

Once RFP responses are back from your short-list of vendors, the next step is to review their responses and to invite between one and three vendors to make a presentation at your facilities. These presentations take on average of four to eight hours each. To help focus the presentation on your company's specific needs, it is useful to request that the selected vendors demonstrate those functions and features which the vendor has responded to positively in their RFP response. Moreover, to help ensure a realistic assessment of the software, it is preferable to have selected vendors set up their software at your site on equipment and within a technical environment similar to the one that you will be using for the eventual system (e.g., with 80,000 user records loaded onto the system).

If your CRM system is to be built internally by your IT department, obviously your system specifications document would concentrate on specifying, in great detail, needed business functional requirements, technical feature requirements, and user support requirements.

Summary

In conclusion, we recommend that you take the time to carefully write your systems specifications document for sending to a qualified short-list of external vendors in the form of an RFP or for use by internal IT personnel. In this way, you will improve the likelihood that the CRM system you receive closely mirrors that CRM system that you have specified.

Sizing Up Your CRM Software Vendor

14

The 12-Question Software Vendor Evaluation Test

Selecting the best software vendor for your customer relationship management automation project is no easy task. Software vendors come and go, many are backed by venture capitalists who can opt to pull the plug if financial returns are not met, technological changes often shake the very base on which vendors build their application, and so forth. With these potential difficulties in mind, ISM recommends that you ask each vendor that ends up on your vendor "short-list" the 12 questions that are detailed in this chapter.

Here are a couple of observations prior to the 12 questions. First, if you find that a short-listed vendor is evasive in responding to any of these 12 questions, continue to demand answers now rather than later. Second, do not rely on the answer to any one question as the basis for your vendor selection decision. Rather, get answers to all 12 questions, and then apply business judgement as to how well the vendor's 12 responses hold together in view of your specific needs.

Question #1:   How long has the vendor been in business, and what is the history of their business?

The Customer Relationship Management automation industry celebrated its 22nd birthday in 2001. To the best of our knowledge, there are no CRM software vendors older than 18 years and most CRM software vendors are between 5–10 years old. Perhaps this makes the number of years in business less relevant, though we think not.

A software vendor like Firstwave, which began in 1984 as Brock Control Systems, has been through the good times and the bad times, through an initial public offering, as well as a number of organizational acquisitions and structural reorganizations. Over the years, Firstwave has proven itself a resilient CRM player, whose products consistently score high in independent user reviews such as ISM's *The Guide To Customer Relationship Management (CRM) Automation*. While we do not want to infer that being around for a long time is an essential characteristic of a solid CRM vendor, we do want to make the point that longevity has a value.

There are, nonetheless, dozens of outstanding CRM vendors, several of which are today's market leaders, who have been around 5–10 years, and whose CRM software offerings are excellent today and are likely to remain excellent in the future. For example, McGraw-Hill may have been seen as taking a risk when it became the first customer of YOUcentric (recently purchased by J.D. Edwards), a CRM vendor that was reasonably new to the CRM industry. McGraw-Hill was willing to take that risk with YOUcentric's Java-based Web CRM offering, and has not looked backwards ever since. So, despite some vendors having venture capital behind them or despite some vendors being brand new to the CRM industry (e.g., the emerging Web-based CRM vendors), there are no hard and fast rules concerning their long-term viability.

In fact CRM software vendors come and go whether they are established players (e.g., Sales Technologies decided to pull out of the CRM marketplace in the early 1990s) or new players (e.g., Corepoint, a CRM vendor backed by IBM in the late 1990s, never really got off the ground). Our conclusion is that years in business, while important, are not sufficient to determine whether the CRM vendor in question is appropriate for you.

Question #2:   Do they have experience and customers in your particular industry?

Experience in your particular industry can be quite important. A software vendor who demonstrates to you their understanding of how your industry works, including, for example, your industry's best demonstrated practices within their software offering, may be a real plus. You should not, however, be overly swayed by a vendor's demonstration of industry-specific software, since creating impressive demonstrations using today's software tools is reasonably easy. More importantly, therefore, you will want to ask questions about their active customers in your industry, and whether they are willing to provide you with the names/contacts of these customers. Answers to these types of questions will allow you to conduct your own due diligence concerning how well the CRM vendor in question has met the needs of a live, industry-specific customer.

You may find yourself in a dilemma in that new CRM software vendors may not have specific industry experience, yet have software whose technology and flexibility seem ideal based on your specific needs (e.g., Talisma for customer contact center). Increasingly the industry is seeing vertical focus from CRM software vendors (e.g., Siebel in the pharmaceutical industry) and thus the need for experience and customers within your specific industry may soon become a moot point.

Question #3:   What is their technological direction (e.g., Web strategy, CRM module expansion intentions)?

It is imperative that your CRM vendor's technological direction is known, and that this direction "fits" within your own company's technological direction. The best way to determine this is to hold a half-day technology session with the vendor's chief technical officer. The objective of this session is to determine where the vendor is headed (i.e., new business modules, new development tools, and the likely timeframes in question), to reveal as best as possible what your specific business functional and technical feature needs are, both today and in the future, and to come to an understanding as to whether you and the vendor see eye-to-eye. Don't be surprised if you are asked to sign a nondisclosure agreement, which is standard for these types of meetings.

Question #4:   Who are the members of their management team, and what are their backgrounds?

The cumulative background and experience of a vendor's management team can provide some insight into the stability and credibility of the vendor within the CRM market. Ideally, you would want to see a mix of business discipline backgrounds (e.g., accounting, finance, information systems, operations) as well as industry background (e.g., healthcare, CPG, etc.) that is representative of the vendor's product focus and offerings. Also, educate yourself about the companies where the management team members were previously employed. Are those companies thriving? Are those companies no longer in existence?

Question #5:   How are they financed?

It is very important to know the financial backing of a prospective CRM vendor. Venture capital groups finance many new companies in the high-tech area, particularly software companies. In many cases, the payback periods for the venture capital funds are very aggressive. In other words, the venture capitalists want to be paid back in a short period of time. Therefore, there is additional pressure on the software vendor to sell as many seats or licenses as it can, in as short a period of time as possible. In addition, if the venture capital organization has dictated an exit strategy by acquisition, there is increased pressure on the software vendor to do whatever it deems necessary to make the financials look attractive. In other words, in the process of reviewing the financial stability of the vendor, go beyond the financial statements.

Question #6:   Is source code included with the product?

Increasingly, vendors are providing toolkits that allow the customer to make changes to the software without using third party implementation consultants. Much of the underlying code is programmed into reusable objects. Nevertheless, the ability to customize the CRM system without the help of vendor technicians or third-party consultants may be limited by the lack of provided source code. If the vendor does not provide the source code, you need to know why this is so. What happens if the vendor goes out of business? Do you get source code to ensure the continued functioning of your system? Pay close attention to the fine print about what is and what is not provided.

Question #7:   What training do they offer (e.g., end-user, train-the-trainer, systems administrator training)?

Remember that over the life of the CRM system, the cost of training will probably exceed by 1 to 5 times the cost of the software itself. Does the vendor provide any training? Is the training provided in-house, on-site or online? Does the vendor pass the training responsibility on to the resellers or implementation partners? Regardless of whether the vendor offers some or all training programs, it is extremely important to ask how the vendor measures the performance of their own trainers and how they will measure the effectiveness of their own training methods, for resellers or the final end-users. Do they have structured plans for ongoing training, refresher training, and training for new hires? Is the vendor using the latest technologies to provide training services (i.e., Web-based training)?

Question #8:   How do they support their software (e.g., do they have a guaranteed response time)?

Many vendors provide support services as part of some type of maintenance agreement. It is imperative that you ask what types of support are offered with a maintenance agreement (e.g., phone support, Web-based self service, on-site support). Some vendors are offering à-la-carte support programs like pay-per-incident or per-support interaction. Are the support services passed on from the vendor to the third-party implementation partner? If the support services are "outsourced" to a third-party company, what certification programs does the vendor have to teach, train, and certify third-party partner personnel?

Question #9:   What is included in their maintenance agreement (e.g., fixed number of upgrades per year)?

The maintenance programs provided by CRM vendors vary greatly in cost and complexity. Be prepared to get specifics on what exactly is provided by the agreement, the timeframe of the agreement, and who will provide the service and support (the vendor and/or the vendor's implementation/service partner.) Ask the vendor how upgrades and updates will be made available (i.e., via download from a Web site, via a reseller). Will you have access to a dedicated technician or group of technicians, whether it is by phone, e-mail or Web site? Can the vendor guarantee a particular turn-around time for problem resolution? What kind of resources has the vendor devoted to the particular support/service options? These are all questions that should be asked.

Question #10: What is their warranty period, and what is their bug-fix policy during this period?

It is important to know what type of warranty policy a CRM vendor has for its product(s). Many vendors offer a standard 90-day warranty period. Be careful to ask the vendor what is included in this warranty and if it is exclusive of an annual maintenance agreement. It is absolutely appropriate to question the vendor as to how, when, and where any software "fixes," updates and upgrades will be made available. In addition, you should question the vendor about the extension of the warranty and any costs associated with the extension.

Question #11: How do they implement their software (e.g., themselves, via a third-party implementer)?

Most of the CRM vendors that provide comprehensive suites of products employ the services of third party CRM implementation companies. If the vendor does the implementation using their own technical staff, how many consultants are dedicated to implementation efforts? You might want to know if the vendor provides any type of "rapid implementation" option and if so, is this really appropriate to your own business situation. Ask questions about the qualifications of the vendor's implementation staff and in the case of third-party implementation partners, the type of certification, and length of training required in becoming a vendor implementation partner. In the event that the vendor uses third-party implementation companies, ask how the vendor ensures the quality of the implementation company. Also, make sure that the vendor and/or the implementation partners are actually using the CRM software for their own front-office operations.

Question #12: How important to them is your piece of business?

Will you be an important customer to the vendor? Will the vendor commit the necessary resources to ensure the successful implementation of your CRM system? To ensure that the software vendor provides appropriate attention, some customers insist that they sit on the software vendor's management board of advisors! Regardless of how you do it, secure guarantees from the software vendor that it is prepared to commit the necessary resources to ensure the successful realization of your CRM project.

Summary

Once you have received answers to these 12 questions, you will then need to apply business judgement as to which of these questions are most applicable to the success of your CRM automation project prior to deciding which software vendor best meets your needs. There are few "good" or "bad" vendors. What you need to determine, when sizing up a CRM software vendor, is the fit between your CRM project direction and that of the vendor. When you have determined this, put your stakes in the ground, and get on with the implementation of your CRM project.

The Importance of CRM Project Communications

15

CRM brings with it a myriad of questions from the users that require careful thought and analysis. It is paramount that you create communication and feedback mechanisms to deliver information about the vision, objectives, planning, and development of the CRM system.

Users of the CRM system as well as nonusers will have questions and concerns regarding the aforementioned areas, so you need to be proactive in planning for the needs of the various placeholders in the organization that will be impacted by the CRM initiative. Our recommendation is that you should plan on preparing your CRM project communications efforts well, thereby improving the likelihood of long-term success for your CRM efforts. By internal marketing, we mean your ability to build and maintain interest within your company for your CRM project over its entire life cycle. Effective internal marketing consists of the following five initiatives.

Announce Your CRM Efforts Internally _____

The launching of your CRM initiative should be done with great pride and with great care. There are many people within your company who will be curious to know what your initiative is all about. You should not be surprised if people start to ask questions like: Will the initiative include me? Who has been selected to participate in the initiative and what were the selection criteria? How many people have been included in the initiative? How long will the initiative last? How quickly will the initiative spread to members outside the initial user group? What will persons participating in the user group need to do? Will persons participating in the initiative get PCs or other access devices from the company? Will there be additional people brought on to support the initiative, or will the initiative lead to a decrease in the number of jobs within the company? Will my job change as a result of the initiative?

Carefully prepare your responses to each of these types of questions, as you will want to make sure that initially the appropriate messages are passed within your company, thereby ensuring that your initiative gets off to a healthy start.

To highlight the importance of internal communications, let's examine an ISM software selection roadmap completed for a U.S. manufacturer of industrial pipes. In this particular situation, the CRM project leader was overly secretive about the project, and this created considerable initial and unnecessary misunderstanding among personnel who were to be associated with the project. The result was that several of these personnel asked that they not be considered for further participation in the project.

Carefully Select Your Superuser Group _____

You should ensure that your initiative is supported from the beginning by a project leader who coordinates all aspects of project design and implementation. In addition to the project leader, your initiative should be supported by a group of "superusers": members from sales, sales management, marketing, customer service, and top management whose role is to represent the voice of the user. Your superuser group should consist of representative individuals who are among the best in their respective job functions (i.e., leaders) and who are not afraid of computers. While it is not essential that these individuals be computer literate, it does help.

Responsibilities for the superusers consist of participation in meetings (including the brainstorming session, the questionnaire process, and perhaps field/corporate visits), in your business matrices work, and throughout the specification/design/implementation stages of your CRM initiative. The number of days that superusers need to devote to the CRM initiative will depend on several factors, though three to five man days per month during the first three months of the project is not unreasonable, with the level of participation usually decreasing after month three of the project.

Your project leader may be one of the members of the superuser team, or you may wish to appoint another individual who is not a part of the superuser team. In addition to your project leader and the above mentioned superusers, you also may want to include in the overall project team one or more members from your company's IT department, as well as from other departments who may play a significant role in designing and/or influencing the final outcome of the project (e.g., finance, production, etc.). If your organization sells products through distribution channels, you may want to consider adding a channel representative to the superuser group.

In one success story, ISM worked with a leading U.S. publisher who was in the process of automating their 500+ sales force throughout the world. The project leader hand selected his superuser team, and this team was carefully looked after during the project initiation, design, and implementation. The value of this successful superuser group paid for itself many times over as project disputes and disagreements, normal within every CRM project, were quickly resolved, thereby enabling the project to move forward with minimum interruption.

Manage Your Communications to All CRM Initiative Participants

Once you have announced your CRM efforts internally, and have carefully selected your project leader and superuser team, your next internal marketing effort should be focused on maintaining ongoing and effective communications with all members of the automation project. It is particularly important at this stage to ensure that there is an open and constructive channel of communications between your project champion (your project champion will be the highest possible executive who is willing to promote your system throughout the organization and ensure that bureaucracy does not get in the way of your success), your project leader, your superusers, your IT department, and any external consultants or vendors that you may be working with. You may want to include key customers in the communication channel as well.

Remember that people within your company will talk about your CRM project, and therefore you want to send a continuous stream of factual and relevant statements so that you build ongoing internal support and excitement for your project and keep all parties up to date on progress. What you will want to prevent is an internal rumor-mill filled with irrelevant or untrue facts concerning the project, as this can negatively impact participation in the project as well as the long-term success of the project. We suggest that you consider the following forums for your CRM project communications:

- Web page or section on your Intranet dedicated to the CRM project
- Company newsletters or periodicals (primarily internal)
- Articles in specific departmental communications
- Presentations at company special events
- CRM project status presentations at departmental management meetings
- E–mail updates, which occur on a regular basis
- Letters from executive sponsors

Managing your communications well can be particularly important if the project is to be implemented in more than one region or country. It may be useful for you to keep potential superusers within regions or countries abreast of the trials and tribulations of your current CRM efforts, thereby preparing for a more smooth transition as you enlarge the system from one set of users to the next.

In one overseas project that ISM worked on, managing communications translated into holding quarterly review meetings with designated personnel from 12 different European countries. The benefit of these meetings was quite evident when the project was rolled out across Europe with minimum difficulty and maximum country participation.

Keep Your Project Champion Involved

Initial support from senior management for your CRM project tends to be quite high. The key, therefore, is to secure your project champion early. Once you have secured your project champion, you should keep this individual briefed on a monthly basis during the first six or so months of the project, and then quarterly thereafter. Your briefings should be a one-page list of bulleted points (be sure to inform your champion of both good as well as bad news!), and be followed up by a face-to-face meeting.

Senior management can quickly become busy with other issues and priorities, and thus you must insist on holding your briefings on a regular basis. Otherwise you risk losing your champion to another more aggressive initiative within the company. Lack of senior management support is a sure way to bring a project to a premature end. In ISM's experience, a situation occurred in one company where the project champion lost interest in the CRM initiative and failed to provide bureaucratic support when required; the initiative died within three months.

If possible, show your project champion the emerging CRM system as it evolves. Of course, be careful that the system works (i.e., does not crash) prior to any senior management preview. Senior managers talk with other senior managers on a regular basis and good news can travel quickly at this level, which in turn can add potential support to your CRM efforts.

Maintain a Long-Term Systems View _____

Lastly, it is valuable for you to maintain a long-term systems view, i.e., there will be successes and failures during your CRM project, and you should prepare to survive both the good and the bad times. A failure or two that is overcome during your project often strengthens your resolve and demonstrates to senior management that the project indeed has needed user commitment.

We have been in many situations in which a CRM project hits a snag, and the first reaction from management is to get overly excited rather than to quietly take the time to properly address and resolve the situation. We have found that maintaining a long-term systems view will help in these situations.

Also remember that your current initiative in CRM is likely to form a part of a larger, more comprehensive corporate information systems offering in the future. Thus your ability to maintain this long-term system view and to deliver a system that is flexible and adaptable is key to the long-term success of your CRM initiative.

Summary

Let us reiterate the importance of preparing your CRM project communications well. Assuming you take the time to address the above five key CRM project communication issues, your chances for overall project success will improve significantly. It is people who create CRM systems and it is people who use these systems. Therefore, you need to remain highly sensitive to the strengths and weaknesses of your users and to work diplomatically within the boundaries set by these individuals.

Eight Key Implementation Issues for Effective CRM Systems

At this stage in the development of the CRM industry, the weakest link remains the less than optimal implementation of CRM systems. In the past, some distinguished CRM analysts published research that indicated very high CRM system failure rates. ISM has never concurred with these high figures. Too often, success in the form of metrics is not specified at the outset of the CRM project, leading to one division of the company calling the CRM project a failure while another division calls it a success. Nonetheless, ISM does concur that the CRM industry needs to improve the level of implementation professionalism, and that there are few, if any, implementation shortcuts.

With this in mind, let us turn to the eight key CRM system implementation issues. Please note that the following eight issues refer to post-CRM software selection implementation (i.e., assume that the company involved in the CRM initiative has specified the software vendor of choice, or has agreed upon internal specifications for building the system).

Step 1: Prepare for Your CRM Implementation _____

Preparation means that you and/or your systems implementers need to create the following:

- A financial plan that demonstrates commitment to the required financial resources for personnel, equipment, and integration activities.

- A clear project methodology to ensure that the project stays on track and within budget. There is no one best project methodology, but use of one is non-negotiable.

- An implementation plan for your project that lays out each To-do step, assigns responsibility as well as a date for each To-do item, and provides milestone checks for each To-do item.

- A communications plan that describes the types of internal marketing communications that you intend to realize during the implementation of your CRM project. This includes, for example, weekly communications to all potential users in the form of e-mails, a CRM "notice board" on your Intranet, printed material from your executive sponsor, discussion at quarterly sales meetings, etc. While the exact content of the communications will differ per project, typical communications will include weekly project implementation accomplishments, training/ support schedules, user issues and success stories, pilot outcomes, etc.

- A training plan that describes in minute detail who will be trained, when the training will occur, where the training will be held, how many participants per training session, number of trainers, training materials to be used, etc.

- A support plan that describes first-, second-, and third-tier support, and that outlines help desk/support intentions (e.g., support hours).

Step 2: Set Up an Effective CRM Project Management Team _____

Successful CRM implementation requires an effective project management team that consists of the following types of personnel: the CRM project leader; the executive sponsor; one or more representatives from sales; representative from marketing; a representative from customer service; the CRM software vendor; a representative from the system implementer; and an external CRM advisor.

Typically, the project management team meets every week, say Monday from 8:00 a.m. to noon, during which time the project implementation plan is reviewed. The previous week's implementation deliverables need to be reviewed and categorized into green (fully accomplished), yellow (minor action items that remain To-do), and red (not accomplished with a problem getting to green). In addition to reviewing the previous week's To-do items, the project management team also needs to discuss each and every one of the coming week's To-do items and identify any issues that are likely to impact the full accomplishment of each To-do item.

From time to time, the project management team may also want to call upon heads of the subproject management teams to provide the full project management team with a status report on the subproject team's deliverables.

Subproject management teams often include the following entities: a business process subproject management team (responsible for modifying and/or creating new business processes that will be supported by the CRM system); a help desk subproject management team (responsible for creating the help desk/support plan, which includes help desk scripts, help desk hours of operation, etc.); a training subproject management team (responsible for creating the pilot training plan, the rollout training plan, and post-rollout training); and a quality control subproject management team (responsible for ensuring that project implementation is realized at the highest standards of quality standards).

Step 3: Integrate Legacy and Third-Party Information Systems

Integration is an issue that, if not carefully planned, can delay the on-time implementation of a CRM system. Integration concerns which type and what quantity of data your company intends to bring into your CRM system, and may include information from legacy systems as well as from third-party sources. You will need to determine what data conversions need to be performed to get the data into your CRM system in a usable format, and what data needs to be populated into your CRM system. Since not all data formats are compatible, integration can be a tricky issue. All too often, companies attempt to integrate too much information from too many systems into the CRM system.

One piece of advice concerning integration: don't bite off more than you can chew! It is better to integrate less and bring your CRM project in on time than to integrate more and bring the project in late.

Step 4: Customize Your CRM System _____

Customization is a necessary part of all CRM systems. For example, the graphical user interfaces (GUIs) can be customized to reflect the specific needs of each user or each user group. So, for example, the sales reps may want the opening screen to show all opportunities, whereas the customer service reps may want the opening screen to show all outstanding customer service incidents. In addition to user GUIs, business functionality within the system can be customized. For example, if your company manufactures textbooks for university students, you will likely need to customize your CRM system to accommodate the need to send samples or "comps" to professors, since a comp function is not standard in most off-the-shelf CRM systems.

If not carefully monitored, customization can become another activity that delays the CRM implementation. All too often, users want to customize too much, too quickly. To avoid this tendency, be sure to have a customization plan that clearly describes the phases in your customization efforts, prior to commencing your customization work. And remember the 80-20 rule: if you can get 80 percent of your customizations completed on time and within budget, forget the remaining 20 percent.

Step 5: Pilot Your CRM System _____

The objective of piloting your CRM system is to test the system before you "leap." A good CRM implementation should include one or more pilots, during which very important feedback is gathered from system users as to likes/dislikes of the emerging system. In preparation for the pilot(s), you should develop a Pilot Plan that describes what the pilot is trying to accomplish (e.g., proof of concept, increased productivity, etc.), and describes the metrics against which the pilot is going to be measured. One or two pilots should be run simultaneously, as one pilot alone may not include a mix of users that are representative of the larger group of users that will be using your CRM system. Each pilot should consist of 10–12 users (e.g., eight sales reps, and two to four managers). The pilot should last no less than three weeks and no more than six weeks. You should have a clear understanding of what constitutes a successful pilot, since a failed pilot may signify a need to halt your CRM rollout.

The proper training of pilot users will be critical to your pilot. Remember that, in effect, pilot users are your live systems testers. They will know little if anything about the system, and it is unlikely that you will have well thought-out user training materials or documentation for pilot users. As a result, it becomes your responsibility to ensure that pilot users have been properly trained. Poor training of pilot users may lead to poor pilot results, an avoidable outcome if training is managed properly.

Pilot measurements also are important. How will you judge the success or failure of a pilot? For the IT division, success may mean simply getting the new CRM system to exchange data with existing legacy systems. Yet for the sales division, success may mean proving that it takes less time to create and send a customer a proposal, and thus productivity has increased. Unless all parties agree on metrics prior to the pilot, the pilot's success or failure becomes a subjective measurement, which can be dangerous. ISM recommends three measurements for a pilot: ease-of-use of the system, as measured by the users; proof-of-concept, as measured by the IT department; and business impact, as measured by business management. ISM establishes a baseline, as well as a measurement scale, for each of these three measurements prior to the pilot, and then measures results during and directly after completion of the pilot.

Step 6: Roll Out Your CRM System

The rollout of your CRM system will mean bringing together many small, yet significant pieces that the sub-project management teams have been working on through completion of the pilot. Therefore, there should be a Rollout Plan that describes in great detail each of the pieces associated with the rollout, including who will be trained, where the training will occur, and for how long. Training is not restricted to rollout training, and should include pre-rollout training, such as computer literacy training. You do not want noncomputer literate users to participate in your CRM rollout training classes. Your rollout plan will also describe the exact content and timetable for each rollout training session, as well as the test that all users must pass prior to "graduating" from rollout training class.

When planning a rollout, you should employ pragmatic timing, given that people do take vacations, children do get sick, emergencies do occur, etc. Thus, your rollout plan needs to have contingency plans in case there are glitches (and there always are!). Your rollout plan should also describe how you intend to update the system for field or remote users, and demonstrate exactly how system updates will work once users return to their respective day-to-day jobs. Do not underestimate the complexity of a CRM system rollout. Also, the rollout gets considerably more complex if the implementation is global.

Step 7: Support Your CRM System

Support for your CRM system is the next area that you need to be concerned with. Do not underestimate the impact of excellent support. This can greatly impact the success of your CRM system. You should have a support plan that describes the levels of support your company offers to system users, the hours of operations of the support function, and the procedures to escalate a support issue that may not be easily resolved. Thus, for example, your support plan needs to define who is your company's first-tier support (e.g., an internal help desk, an 800 number, your boss, etc.), who is your company's second-tier support (e.g., your systems administrator or IT department), and who is your company's third-tier support (e.g., the CRM software vendor). Your support plan needs to clearly describe the international hours of operation for your support or help desk—is it seven days per week and 24 hours per day, or is it five days per week and eight hours per day? Your plan also needs to describe the role of your systems administrator.

Increasingly, companies that are implementing CRM are turning to third-party CRM support companies to provide support for the system. Companies like C^3i in New York specialize in this area and offer a full line of training and support services, including a "hot spare" program that guarantees delivery of a ready-to-use replacement PC computer in the event that your PC breaks or is stolen. Whether you create your own support function, default to support by your CRM software vendor, or use a third-party support company, take the time to lay out a clear, comprehensive support plan. There is nothing worse than being in the field, logging on to the CRM application, and getting stuck because of a support issue.

Step 8: Grow Your CRM System

One of the most important CRM implementation issues concerns growing your system. This means growing system functionality, beyond the initial rollout and the initial business functionality. A key factor for growing your system will be your ability to maintain enthusiasm for the system among its users, and to help users manage the changes that inevitably take place when applying technology to day-to-day business circumstances. From a management perspective, you will need to measure and demonstrate the system ROI and business impact if you are to receive continued system funding. Our experience with several hundred CRM-related system implementations worldwide over the past 17 years suggests that successful companies grow their CRM system using a phased, pragmatic approach.

Summary

There are eight key implementation issues associated with the successful implementation of your CRM system:

1. Prepare for your CRM implementation.
2. Set up an effective CRM project management team.
3. Integrate legacy and third-party information systems.
4. Customize your CRM system.
5. Pilot your CRM system.
6. Roll out your CRM system.
7. Support your CRM system.
8. Grow your CRM system.

It is very important that you pay careful attention to each of these key implementation issues, and that you get them right. As stated at the beginning of this chapter, systems implementation is the weak link in today's booming CRM industry. Continued strong growth within the CRM industry will require that this weak link be strengthened considerably, and soon. Needless to say, this presents an excellent opportunity for CRM systems implementation entrepreneurs.

In the interim, however, CRM software vendors are providing professional service organizations to implement their own systems at customer sites (e.g., Firstwave), or more carefully managing the implementation of their system by third-party systems implementers. It also explains why some companies choose to take on CRM systems implementation efforts themselves.

The Necessity of Training, a Good Help Desk, and Effective Systems Administration

Training, an effective Help Desk, and comprehensive systems administration play key roles in ensuring happy CRM system users as well as long-term systems success. Let us look into each of these areas in greater detail.

Training

ISM has previously published that for every $1 you spend on CRM automation technology (e.g., hardware, software, communications equipment), you should budget $1.50 for training over the life of the project (which is typically about five years). The training costs are spread over the life of the project. In other words, if the technology costs are $1 million, your training costs would be $1.5 million, but that amount is spread over five years (or whatever project duration), with a greater percentage funding allocation to the first year of the project. Other well-known consulting firms have used a ratio as high as $15 of training for every $1 of equipment. While we consider the latter ratio excessively high, the message is the same, namely, you should never underestimate the importance of training in your overall project success.

Training can take many different formats. Among the most common are:

Initial User Training.   Assuming you end up purchasing off-the-shelf software, initial user training is often included or can be negotiated into the overall price of the software. Initial user training may consist of training sessions held at your facilities, at the vendor's facilities, or at a third-party site. A small number of vendors, especially those that provide Web-based software applications, are beginning to offer online training using collaboration tools and services. If your company has developed the software in-house, you will need to plan for this training separately.

Initial user training sessions tend to last one to two days, though some carry on into a third and even fourth day depending on the complexity of the system. Typically, the number of user participants at these sessions range from three to 15 participants, but should not exceed 15. Ideally, there should be one instructor for every three or four participants.

It is essential that these training sessions include hands-on training, i.e., participants should have equipment for system access (e.g., PCs, handheld devices) assigned to them, with printers, Internet access, etc. so that as the instructor explains a function or feature, participants can immediately perform the same function or feature on their PCs. In this regard, it may be useful to have a teaching script prepared to ensure that the training realistically supports your company's way of conducting business.

The objective of the initial user training is to provide users with an overview of the system, then to go into individual system functions and features. After each section of the training, be sure that participants are required to complete a hands-on test to show that they have understood how to use that section of the system effectively. This may be accomplished via the use of a computer-aided training program, whereby the user takes a test and the program automatically scores the user's test results. Each participant also should be provided with a set of User Documentation during this training session.

Train the Trainer.   This type of training is used when your company prefers to do its own training or when there are so many system users that it becomes unrealistic to train them all at once. The objective of this session is to bring together internal trainers so that they may learn how to use the system as well as how to teach others to use the system.

This session should follow the format for initial user training, but in addition, each trainer should be provided with a training manual from which to implement required user training.

There are advantages and disadvantages to training the trainer. The key advantage is that you have an internally controllable, cost-effective means to train a large number of company personnel. The key disadvantage is that you are dependent on your in-company trainers and should these individuals get busy on other assignments, as often may be the case, this may delay the training of users on your CRM system.

Systems Administrator Training.   If the software has been purchased from an external vendor, this training takes place between the vendor and your assigned systems administrator(s), that is, the individual(s) who will be performing day-to-day maintenance on the system such as assigning passwords, customizing screens, updating databases, etc. If the software has been built in-house, it is still critical that your systems administrator receives proper training.

Typically, this training takes three to five days to complete (though up to two weeks is not unheard of). Again, the training should be hands-on training, and there should be one instructor for every two to three participants. In addition to hands-on examples, each systems administrator should receive comprehensive system documentation during this session.

Periodic Training.   Individuals trained on the system and who use the system shortly thereafter are likely to retain much of their training. Nonetheless, the most seasoned learner benefits from periodic training, particularly if there are new systems releases that include new functions and features. Therefore, we recommend a periodic training session no more than six months after the system has been implemented, and at least annually thereafter. As was mentioned before, supplemental training can be accomplished via e-learning and Internet/Web-based online training. Ask your vendor what capabilities are available in this area.

Regardless of the training format(s) you choose to implement, your company should take training very seriously. On more than one occasion, ISM has seen a CRM automation system fail because of insufficient training. One company, where we had been asked to assist in the training, did not have PCs set up, the software had not been loaded, there were no printers available and there were no modems installed to properly conduct training. It should come as no surprise that this company's CRM system was in trouble from the start.

Help Desk

As previously discussed, every system user should have a comprehensive Help Function included within CRM software, which may or may not include system User Documentation online. In addition to the Help Function, there also should be a Help Desk set up in support of your CRM system. Most often users call the Help Desk using a telephone, though some companies have implemented a Help Desk that offers multimodal access (e.g., e-mail system or Intranet system).

The Help Desk fulfills several important needs, including one phone number to dial when the user encounters a problem that seems unfixable. This in turn implies that the Help Desk should be staffed with properly trained personnel and supported by a system that allows for proper logging and tracking of callers' questions. In smaller companies, the Help Desk may be integrated with the systems administrator function. In larger companies, the Help Desk may contain staff specifically trained to support CRM applications only or individuals trained to support more than one application within the company.

For a Help Desk to be successful, strict business procedures need to be in place to handle incoming questions. For example, each question received needs to be logged in so that there is a record of the types of questions received. When a caller's question cannot be answered on the spot (often called first-line or first-tier assistance), the Help Desk should then route the question to the appropriate individual within your company (second-line or second-tier assistance), such as the systems administrator, and track the question until it has been successfully resolved. In the worst case scenario, the question may require changes to the software code (third-line or third-tier assistance), which may mean that the Help Desk routes the question to the systems administrator, to the IT department, or even to outside software vendors (especially if third-party software packages are being used).

Regardless of the type of question received and its subsequent routing, once the caller's question has been resolved, a summary of how long it took to resolve the question as well as the solution to the question needs to be logged into the Help Desk's system. Reports generated from this information, are used to improve the functioning of the Help Desk as well as to prioritize training needs or system alterations and enhancements.

Systems Administration _____

In most companies, a Systems Administrator is required to manage the CRM system. The responsibilities of the Systems Administrator include:

- Making sure that the systems data is kept up-to-date (timely and relevant).
- Backing up the system files and data on a regular basis.
- Providing new users with an ID and initial password.
- Making changes to screens and pull-down menus.
- Delivering new software releases and updates to the users.
- Creating and/or reporting on system usage statistic (e.g., how many uploads/downloads/synchronizations are being made, how often, and with what success ratio).
- Reporting on any problems that may be occurring with the system.
- Writing new systems reports and implementing other technically related systems tasks (e.g., workflow routines).

A good Systems Administrator works closely with the Help Desk, with the external software vendor(s) or internal IT department, and maintains a close working relationship with system users. As a rule of thumb, once the initial systems integration and training are completed, most CRM systems require a half-time Systems Administrator for up to 100 users. In excess of 100 users, one or more Systems Administrators may be needed, though this will depend in large part on the capabilities of the Help Desk, the number of users, and the complexity of the system.

Be sure to staff your systems administration function with qualified individuals. There is nothing worse to a customer-facing (e.g., sales, field service) representative or executive than to be out in the field and use the system only to realize that the system isn't working correctly or system information is out-of-date or factually incorrect. This is a sure way to lose the support of your users.

Summary _____

Finally, be sure that in your CRM project planning, you address the need for comprehensive training, an effective Help Desk, and systems administration functions up front. Case after case has shown that these items can make the difference between systems success or failure.

E-Business
and CRM

18

Electronic business, or e-business, is not a new concept in the business world. The electronic commerce portion of e-business has been available since the late 1960s. Nonetheless, the advent of the Web has led to an explosion in technologies that facilitate the processes involved in building individualized relationships with customers before, during and after the purchase of goods and services. In this chapter, we will discuss what e-business and e-commerce are, observations on the status of e-business, the key applications of e-business, the benefits and challenges, e-business infrastructure, a sample of software that is available and what the future looks like for e-business.

What Is E-Business?

Possibly, because of the rapid development of technologies, processes, and models underlying e-business, there are myriad definitions of e-business.

We will use the following definitions, adapted from TechWeb's online *Tech-Encyclopedia*[1]:

E-business: Having a *total* presence on the Web in order to do business online. The business conducted from the company's Web site might feature the selling of products and services, *as well as* the ability to, for example, track shipments, have discussions, or provide feedback.

There is sometimes confusion as to the difference between e-business and e-commerce.

E-commerce: Implies that products and services can be purchased online through electronic data interchange (EDI) features in which purchase orders are transmitted from computer to computer via the Web.

E-commerce is essentially the exchange process (i.e., buying, selling, and collaborating) between internal and external business partners as well as end customers across electronic platforms such as Intranets, extranets and the Internet/Web. It is a component of an overall e-business strategy.

Many companies that have made business and financial investments into e-business have proven that online business is not only possible but also very profitable. E-business is more than allowing customers the ability to view a few Web pages of company information, it's the ability to extend the enterprise out to customers. To do this in the past would have required major efforts in custom software on the customers' computers—oftentimes a very difficult proposition.

Keep in mind though that e-business is only one piece of the puzzle, as discussed in Chapter 2, "CRM: A Working Definition"; it is a component of the overall Customer Relationship Management (CRM) framework. Other CRM components like sales and marketing, call centers, etc. are required to provide the full customer experience depending upon the type of organization that implements e-business.

Unlike brick-and-mortar operations, e-business need not be constrained by space, time, or type of currency. Today, goods can be purchased, paid for, and shipped globally (subject to physical constraints like weather conditions) at any time. E-business is inherently shifting more power to customers, producers, and distributors because there can be direct connections between entities involved in the exchange process, in some cases eliminating the need for intermediaries (see Figure 18.1). E-business is reflective of the changing roles in the producer-customer relationship, where the consumer has increased participa-

1. TechWeb's *Tech Encyclopedia* can be found at *www.techweb.com/encyclopedia*.

tion in the way the producer is doing business. An example would be the feedback mechanisms that are provided to consumers via e-business, which allow for more feedback and more immediate response and measurement/ analysis of that feedback. In this way, e-business is bringing the customer closer to the actual producer of products and services.

E-business and CRM is more than just purchasing and installing software, it means that organizations have to do business and leverage technology in a different way. In order to maintain a competitive industry position, management must realize that the business rules are being rewritten. The vast majority of the Global 2000 have significant e-business components to their overall business.

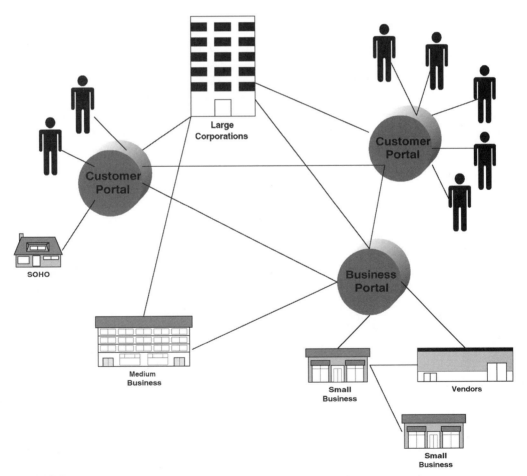

FIGURE 18.1
The connections between those involved in the e-business exchange process.

Supply chain management is another area of e-business. Electronic linkages between suppliers, distributors, resellers, retailers, etc. are increasingly incorporated into the e-business framework. These various entities, using Web-related technologies and architecture, are taking advantage of opportunities to exchange information, products, and payments to expedite the transaction process. For example, suppliers that use CRM software applications to automate sales, marketing, and customer service functions are also using e-business via the Web to share information on customers, competitors, shipping/delivery, inventory, financials, etc. with members of the supply chain. In other words, e-business facilitates communication and cooperation with members of the supply chain, which can increase the business effectiveness of the channels. This also fosters interdependencies, which force supply chain members to mutually consider strategies, knowledge base and business structures/processes.

E-business technology is evolving. Electronic data interchange (EDI) had been the leading platform for conducting e-business before the rapid expansion in Web technology. EDI was generally used by large companies with substantial financial resources that were able to buy their own proprietary infrastructure for interchange of information about payments, deliveries, inventory, etc. EDI provides for secure data communications between organizations, with the translation of data between disparate computing systems. EDI nonetheless requires significant investments in computers (e.g., hardware, software), third-party service providers and telecommunications (e.g., dedicated data lines and Value Added Networks [VANs]), regular maintenance, and training. Web technologies such as the emerging industry standard XML (Extensible Markup Language) provide EDI functionality at a lower overall associated cost. Also, Web technologies provide reach and accessibility of e-business to small businesses and consumers that do not have the resources available to implement EDI. XML, EDI, and Web technology are being integrated together and used concurrently. This integration is in turn fueling the expansion of e-business.

Business-to-business e-commerce far outpaces that of business-to-consumer in terms of volume of revenue generated. Sales, technical support, customer service, and public relations are the main reasons cited by 70 percent of Fortune 500 companies that have or are building e-business structures.

What Are the Key Applications of E-Business?

E-business is being used to augment or replace existing models of transaction and interaction with customers. For example, in business-to-consumer e-commerce, Barnes & Noble bookstores is using e-business to evolve from brick-and-mortar retail outlets to click-and-mortar (i.e., customers can order via an online store as well as in retail outlets). The focus of most e-business efforts has been related to the following business functions:

- Sales of products and services (e.g., including payments).
- Product development (e.g., gathering customer feedback).
- Customer self-service (e.g., Frequently Asked Questions, online tutorials, chat/discussion groups, automated e-mail response).
- Post-sales support (e.g., order status, billing, technical support).

Here is an example of a company that uses e-business processes and systems:

Company:	Works™
Type of e-commerce:	Business-to-business

Works is another Web-based business that changes the online purchasing paradigm much like Amazon.com has done. By forming a Web-centric company, Works is able to transcend the traditional geographic constraints of brick-and-mortar operations.

Works has developed a supply-chain, workflow-enabled software suite that allows companies to order business products online and manage both online and offline expenditures from indirect goods and services.

What Are the Benefits of E-Business?

The benefits that can be derived from application of e-business include:

- Enhanced customer service
- Market expansion
- Cost reduction
- Customer retention/loyalty
- Streamlining of the sales cycle

What Are the Challenges to the Growth of E-Business?

E-business provides many opportunities for companies to grow their business. Nonetheless, given the short history of e-business using Web technologies, there remain several issues associated with the implementation and use of e-business. These include:

- Resistance to organizational change
- Business process redesign and systems integration hurdles

- Lack of e-business expertise
- Difficulties in matching technology to business needs
- Security concerns

Setting Up the E-Business Infrastructure

Since e-business opens up the corporate information technology infrastructure to potentially millions of users, there are several important points that must be considered when designing and implementing an e-business system:

- The information technologies infrastructure must be designed from the ground up to handle this environment. In other words, the infrastructure must be designed to be massively scaleable.
- It must be able to provide consistent service quality with low administrative overhead allowing companies the ability to take advantage of new business opportunities.
- Must be able to offer 24×7×365 availability while providing security and transaction integrity.
- The system must be able to tightly integrate and leverage existing business systems.
- The system must be able to handle hundreds of applications and new services that can be transformed in "Web-time" (4 months = 1 Web-year).
- The systems must be able to support the complexity of integrating both business-to-business and business-to-consumer trading.

Where Is E-Business Going? _____

All business functions from the front office (e.g., sales, marketing, customer service) to the back office (e.g., accounting, manufacturing, logistics/distribution/delivery) will continue to be automated, primarily via software that is built on or takes advantage of Web technologies. Closing of sales, payment, and delivery of product will occur electronically, especially for products that are created in digital media (e.g., music, books, videos, reports, financials, etc.). Potential customers will to a greater extent be able to participate in their own "lead qualification" process by filling out an online form or survey, the results of which are analyzed by e-business software and fed back to the potential customer in real-time (where applicable).

E-business will be augmented by customer self-service and e-service applications that allow customers to find information about products/services without or with the assistance of live human customer service agents. Customer expectations regarding the availability of information about their respective purchases via e-commerce, will definitely increase. If a product or service is not being offered through e-business, customers will question why this is not so, because they expect the e-business environment of rapid results. This applies for business-to-business as well as business-to-consumer transactions. In addition, customers will expect that any organization that the customer does business with will have CRM systems, which will capture all transaction-based, permission-based, and observation-based knowledge and make this information available to any "customer touch-points" so that a company presents a unified voice to the customer.

E-business is blurring the lines that divide business departments and functions such as manufacturing, marketing, sales, and distribution. Advances in the development of XML and other Web-centric languages, architectures, and systems will further facilitate movement of data across the Web. Nonetheless, the integration of people, process, and technology between remains the key to success for e-business and CRM.

Summary

In summary, we have defined e-business and e-commerce, provided observations on the status of e-business, examined the key applications of e-business, looked into the benefits and challenges, described e-business infrastructure, offered a sample of software that is available, and provided a vision concerning the future of e-business. Keep in mind that e-business is only one piece of the CRM puzzle. In the next chapter, we'll take a look at another important element—e-service.

E-Service and CRM

19

One-to-one marketing, launched in the late 1980s, emphasizes individualized marketing relationships with customers. One-to-one customer service, launched in the late 1990s, emphasizes individualized servicing of a customer. While the two initiatives increasingly work hand-in-hand, as a result of new and powerful Web-based tools, one-to-one customer service has taken on increased significance. Let's examine why.

Why Is E-Service Important?

It is undisputed that customer service and support is an important piece of the CRM picture. The rapid growth of e-business has verified the need to provide customer access to presales or postsales information across multiple interaction points (channels). Driven by advances in Web technology and customer demand for unassisted and assisted customer support, CRM vendors are offering various Web-based customer service options, across multiple contact channels, to supplement the telephone support that has in many cases been offered via a call center. The customer interaction center (CIC), a component of the overall e-service area, integrates customer self-service, interactive support, and multimedia portal management to provide that access to customer data.

E-service products, which attempt to integrate all customer interactions into one coherent "string" of communications, can include:

- Self-service via frequently asked questions (FAQs)
- Self-service via a knowledgebase, which can be searched using different query methods, including natural language query
- E-mail management and response
- Interactive Web text "chat" with a live agent, including "Call Me Now" option
- Real-time voice chat via the Web connection (e.g., voice over IP or VoIP)
- Virtual agent, artificial intelligence "bot," or assistant that processes natural language queries and presents responses from a knowledgebase

It was estimated that greater than 25 percent of all customer contacts and inquiries will be conducted through the Internet (Gartner Group, 2001). Dynamic self-help customer service solutions will rise from 7 percent in 2000 to approximately 40 percent in 2001. It is clear that the e-service component of CRM is growing rapidly.

Companies that have a Web presence and/or are planning to sell or interact with customer online would be well advised to consider e-service options. Vendors that have e-service solutions typically provide Web-based customer self-service with assisted service to create a consistent customer service capability as a substitute for the standard call center staffed by live agents. This approach can increase customer satisfaction and build customer switching costs. Many organizations experience 20–25 percent increases in Web-based conversion rates (actual closed sales) by simply adding real-time interaction capabilities (e.g., chat, callback) at the appropriate places on their Web sites (META Group, August 2000).

Cost reduction is one potential benefit of implementing e-service. Based on a Forrester study of 46 companies offering CRM, 54 percent of customers who call a toll-free call center choose to speak with an operator, which costs a company an average of $33 per inquiry. This compares with $9.99 per inquiry for the 9 percent who use e-mail correspondence, and $1.17 per inquiry for those customers who desire to perform self-service on a Web site.[1] For example, Dell's call center in Texas saves between $10 and $80 per transaction due to the e-service capabilities that it promotes to customers as an alternative to calls to the 800 number.

Who Provides E-Service Solutions? _____

Now that you understand why e-service is becoming more important, it is necessary to understand more about who provides e-service solutions. e-service products primarily come from two main areas:

CRM Vendors. CRM (sometimes referred to as eCRM, e-business, or IM [interaction management]) vendors offer specific CRM functionality centered around the e-service capabilities described above. Many vendors that provided just interactive text chat, e-mail management, or FAQ, have rounded out their respective offerings to include multiple interaction channels. Some vendors focus on e-service as a point solution; point solutions are typically easier to install than large frameworks, which have higher rates of failure in the implementation process. Companies such as KANA, eGain, Synchrony Communications, Chordiant, LivePerson, NativeMinds, and Primus offer e-service solutions.

Call Center Vendors. This group is trying to reposition themselves as e-service vendors. This means that these vendors must have full call center functionality including IVR and CTI. In addition, they must have connectivity to PBX/switches, VoIP (voice over IP), e-mail management, self-service, media blending, skills-based routing, interactive text chat, assisted browsing, and preferably workforce management. Call center vendors that have moved into the e-service space include Apropos, Genesys, and the more traditional call center hardware providers such as Lucent (Avaya) and Cisco. Nortel Networks (Clarify) has been associated with the CRM space for some time.

---

1. Zimmerman, Christine, "E-Commerce Searches Get Smarter: Engines That Understand Can Drive Down CRM Costs," *Internet Week*, October 24, 2001. Found at: *http://www.internetweek.com/lead/lead102400.htm.*

It is increasingly common to see companies using e-service solutions as or along with a CRM application to capture customer information and use that information to forge better relationships. For example, a travel services company in Florida implemented CosmoCom technology for customer interaction via the Web which was then integrated with a leading CRM application, utilizing a standard SQL database. Since the e-service capability was implemented, there has been a drastic reduction in calls placed to a toll-free number for customer service.

When evaluating e-service applications, you should consider if the solution can:

- Provide the option for a personalized self-service experience.
- Provide the end-user with the ability to escalate to assisted service and seamlessly transfer information across all communication channels (i.e. VoIP, Web chat, e-mail, Web forms, CTI (voice integration).
- Accommodate more than one account or tenant on a system server.
- Queue all forms of customer/agent interaction—voice, Call Me Now, e-mail, Web chat, and provide media blending with integrated skills based and load balancing capabilities.
- Consolidate the knowledgebase and intellectual capital throughout the organization and make it available throughout the extended enterprise. This could be accomplished by providing both COM and CORBA objects that can be called from CRM and e-business frameworks like IONA, BEA, WebSphere, etc.
- Learn through cumulative customer feedback and rapidly develop solutions to allow the enterprise to provide proactive service to end-users. The ability to transfer customer history from your platform to other systems provides a good competitive advantage.
- Enable enterprises to rapidly deploy e-service technology without large integration/implementation efforts. Companies are spending their time on implementing CRM, ERP, MRP, e-business and they do not have large amounts of time to integrate point solutions.
- Scale cost effectively as an organization's service needs grow.
- Provide seamless integration between all technologies using architectures like COM/COM+ wrappers, C++, EJB wrappers, XML, ODBC and native tools.
- Handle multiple sessions concurrently, regardless of contact method used to reach the contact center (e.g., phone, interactive text, e-mail).
- Provide strong workflow functionality.

- Provide dynamic self-service and custom Web page presentation through inference technology.
- Be purchased on a pay-per-usage basis or a licensed, per-seat basis.

Customer Self-Service

As was mentioned earlier, customer self-service has become such an important part of the overall customer service and support options for CRM systems, and we feel that there are particular items that should be considered when evaluating customer self-service. Let's investigate further.

Traits of the E-Customer

Web-based CRM architecture allows for more and more customers to have access to your company's products and services. Needless to say, all customers and particularly e-customers have become savvy buyers. E-customers know how to quickly get to the competition. They expect that you will offer them either enhanced speed to purchase needed products or services, lower prices, improved quality, or some combination. They anticipate quick and comprehensive answers to all of their questions. They want to be able to contact you at one moment via telephone and the next moment via the Web, and they expect you to have one holistic profile of them regardless of the contact mode they choose to use. Increasingly e-customers are requesting personalized entry and services, all within a secure environment. Moreover, they look to you to provide them with "communities of interest" that allow them to meet other buyers sharing similar traits.

Given the increasing demands of the e-customer, it should come as no surprise that Web-based customer self-service is on the rise and has already become critical in attracting and retaining your customers' loyalty.

Cisco: A Case Study

A good example of a company effectively using Web-based customer self-service is Cisco, which integrates complete customer service and support functions through Web-based applications across the following areas: customer service call centers, Web self-service tools, field service management systems, and problem resolution technologies.

A host of Web-based Service and Learning tools provide the customer with complete support, service, and training. When the customer is unable to answer their own Service questions online, integrated click-to-talk tools provide immediate access to live agents who see what steps the customer has taken and leverage all existing customer information to help resolve the issue. The agent can take direct control of the customer's browser and show where the information can be found online.

This initiative, which Cisco calls "New World Customer Care," has delivered some mighty impressive results:

- By implementing New World Customer Care Solutions, Cisco has realized over $300 million in savings.
- Cisco has improved customer satisfaction (from 3.4 to 4.3 out of 5).
- 82 percent of Cisco orders are placed online.
- 83 percent of support questions are answered through Web self-service tools.
- Cisco has been able to redeploy more than 1,000 engineers and 600 customer service representatives to its higher value-add core businesses.
- More than 12,000 customers worldwide have access to Cisco online support tools.
- A 20 percent increase in customer purchasing efficiency has been realized through Cisco online ordering.
- Cisco has realized savings of over $330 million by avoiding headcount growth and limiting the infrastructure required to support that growth.
- Delivery times have been reduced by 3 to 5 days domestically, and over 7 days internationally.
- Order error rates are now less than one percent.
- Cisco customer service and technical support call centers have more than doubled in size since 1995, but have avoided headcount growth of over 1,600 people.

Customer Self-Service Has Enormous Potential

When implemented successfully, Web-based customer self-service gives customers the capability to access needed information and perform service functions their way. This includes:

- Incident assignment, escalation, tracking, and reporting
- Problem management and resolution
- Order management
- Warranty and contract management

Knowledge management engines, which help your company to learn from each customer service incident, further enhances the ability for customers to conduct their own self-servicing.

How to Assess Web-Based Customer Self-Service Options

If you are considering Web-based customer self-service for your firm, consider the following recommendations:

1. Learn about the leading e-service vendors that offer Web-based customer self-service options. Some companies that provide customer self-service solutions are outsourcers. Companies that provide customer self-service solutions include eSupportNow, Servicesoft, PeopleSupport, Support.com, and Primus. There are many other providers; this is just a sampling.

2. Understand the key risks:
   - Potential customer dissatisfaction, even loss, resulting from frustration of having to using your inefficient self-service offering.
   - Customers feel that you have dehumanized the customer service function.
   - Failure to provide customers with proper responses to their questions.
   - Overlooking the need to tightly integrate your customer self-service system with other components of your CRM system (e.g., sales, marketing) to ensure closed loop servicing.
   - Customer displeasure of being up-sold or cross-sold during a customer service experience.
   - Failure to properly train customer service personnel that field questions online.
   - Failure to provide alternative servicing options to customers when your self-service system is down.

3. Understand the key rewards:
   - Lets customers do business with you the way they want to, (i.e., "their way").
   - Provides the ability for customers to track and configure products 24 hours a day online.
   - Increases your ability to cross-sell and up-sell your customers during a customer service experience.

- Increases customer satisfaction/loyalty rating resulting from customers getting what they need faster, at a lower price and/or with better quality.
- Places emphasis on maximizing customer satisfaction rather than the effectiveness of your customer service staff.
- Lower service costs resulting from the reduction of customer support and IT staff expenses (20 percent per year savings are being achieved by best-in-class companies today).
- Allows you to redeploy customer support representatives and IT staff to revenue generating activities.

Summary

In the 21st century, ISM believes that outstanding customer service will be the key differentiator that distinguishes leading companies from all the rest. Of the various components of CRM, e-service and customer self-service are particularly exciting, because the solutions available today can really help organizations to achieve outstanding customer service. You will probably want to expand your research beyond this brief overview of e-service and customer self-service. As you investigate e-service solutions, don't lose focus on the people and process issues that will be integral to the success of the system, no matter which technology you ultimately decide upon.

Ensuring Consistent Customer Service Across Channels

20

"Focus on your customers, figure out what they need and want.
Make it easy for your customers to do business with you!"

Excerpted from Customers.com, *Patricia Seybold (1998)*

A knowledgeable friend recently asked me whether customer relationship management (CRM) was truly a new business approach or simply a repackaging of old concepts. Needless to say, having been in the CRM industry for 17 years, this question got me thinking. I conclude "yes," CRM really is a new business approach resulting from two complementary factors. First, CRM allows customers to conduct business with a company the way the customer so desires; this is new and quite important to many customers. Second, CRM offers new technology tools to make this happen. For this new approach to work, you have the need for consistent customer service across multiple channels.

When properly implemented, consistent customer service across channels allows customers to reach your company any way they so desire. Increasingly, customers opt to use multiple contact channels that include voice, leaving a message on voice mail, fax, regular mail, e-mail, Web chat, collaboration, assisted browsing, and customer self-service (e.g., FAQs or knowledge-based queries). Equally important, once customers have reached your company, they expect your front-line agents/reps to be knowledgeable about them regardless of how the customer may have contacted you in the past.

So when the customer informs you, "I am phoning you today about the e-mail that I sent to you earlier this week, which was in response to last week's Web chat session that resulted from the letter that I sent you via regular mail last month," they expect your company's agents/reps to know about all of the contacts that they have had with your company and they expect your agents/reps to be ready to assist them accurately in real time. How you realize consistent customer service is your concern, not theirs. Moreover, achieving consistent customer service is indeed a concern for most companies in that it may be technically complex and costly, is likely to require a rethink of existing customer-facing processes and may require extensive retraining of your agents/reps who initially may be resistant to change. Nonetheless, those companies that successfully realize consistent customer service will be the winners in today's increasingly competitive marketplace where competition is but one mouse click away.

Current State of the Art

Technology tools that help companies to realize consistent customer service were first offered in 1998 (e.g., Quintus's eContact offering). Moreover, while there is no shortage today of technology-driven options to ensure consistent customer service across channels, there are few if any standards driving this area of CRM. *Result:* consistent customer service technology is still finding its way.

Consistent customer service has, to a large extent, been delegated to customer service centers (now more commonly referred to as customer contact or customer interaction centers). Most often, an existing call center desires to become Web-enabled to expand contact channels for Web chat, e-mail, and possibly other Web-based interactions in addition to voice calls. Alternatively, an e-business department that has installed Web and e-mail functionality (i.e., some portion of available eCRM offerings) now wants to link to a call or customer service center.

CRM software that is aimed at delivering consistent customer service across channels works as follows. Assume that there are three customers seeking assistance. Customer A comes in via a voice call on a toll-free 800 number. Customer B comes in via an e-mail. Customer C comes in via Web chat. Today's technology allows the requests from each of these customers to be lined up in a common queue. Assuming the customer service agent is trained to handle multichannel requests, the agent then begins to interact with Customer A, B, and C in whatever order the requests are listed in the queue (some companies opt to send all e-mails to one agent, all Web chat requests to another agent, and so forth). Automated e-mail and Web chat responses allow the agent to respond to more than one customer at a time. All customer interactions are recorded and placed into the customer's contact file. Reporting tools consistently monitor customer service efficiencies and highlight needed areas of improvement.

The majority of companies that now offer consistent customer service face a dilemma discussed below: do I continue to build my offering using my existing telephony infrastructure or do I move over to the emerging IP network alternative.

Benefits of Consistent Customer Service Across Channels

Customers who take the time to contact a company expect to be serviced quickly and efficiently. Customers visiting your Web site may need help right now. If they send you an e-mail, they expect a rapid response. If they register a complaint, they want confirmation that you are on top of resolving that complaint. Also of concern is that the majority of customers feel that their complaint will not be heard or resolved properly, and thus do not even bother to contact the company; they simply move over to the competition. This in part explains why U.S. corporations now lose half their customers in five years. Moreover, the impact of losing customers can be significant: if you lose one customer per day who spends $100 per week, you lose $1,900,000 a year in sales.[1]

As companies increasingly supplement their service capability with electronic capabilities (e.g., e-mail, Web offerings), the situation remains equally grave; Jupiter Media Metrix for example found that 65 percent of all companies offering e-mail service do not respond to a customer's e-mail within 24 hours.

---

1. Taken from F. Reichheld, *The Loyalty Effect: The Hidden Force Behind Growth, Profits, and Lasting Value*. Harvard Business School Press, 1996.

On the flip side of these rather depressing statistics, consistent customer service across channels does appear to deliver real benefits. Our research shows that customers, who are engaged quickly and efficiently regardless of the channel they use tend to be more loyal to a company, which drives customer retention and profitability in the long term. Moreover, from the company perspective, there is increased opportunity to cross-sell and up-sell. By training an agent to handle multiple channels, companies are finding a reduction in agent frustrations and turnover (a serious problem in most companies who face up to a 50 percent annual turnover rate). Companies also reduce their costs; a Forrester Research study concluded that Internet-based customer self-service slashes call-center costs by 43 percent. Also, as stated in *iQ Magazine*, "...54 percent of the customers who used a toll-free telephone-based call center choose to speak with an operator. These types of calls cost a company an average of $33 per inquiry, compared to $10 per e-mail inquiry (9 percent of customer) and $1.17 per inquiry for customers who use Web-site self-service (37 percent)."[2] For those interested in customer service benchmarking information, I encourage you to peruse the work of John Anton, a professor at Perdue University.

In short, there seems to be sufficient existing and potential benefits resulting from consistent customer service across channels.

Leading Vendors That Offer
Consistent Customer Service Products _____

Leading software solutions for some or all aspects of consistent customer service include:

- PCC by Cisco (a part of their emerging customer contact software platform), *www.cisco.com*
- Quintus by Avaya, *www.avaya.com*
- Apropos, *www.apropos.com*
- Aspect, *www.aspect.com*
- Genesys by Alcatel, *www.genesyslab.com*
- Clarify by Nortel, *www.nortelnetworks.com* (acquired by Amdocs Ltd. in 2001)

---

2. Goldenberg, Barton, "Knowledge Management for Customer Care," *iQ Magazine*, Cisco Systems, Inc., March/April 2001. Found at: *http://resources.cisco.com/app/tree.taf?asset_id=49581*

- Vantive by PeopleSoft, *www.peoplesoft.com*
- KANA, *www.kana.com*
- eGain, *www.egain.com*
- E.piphany, *www.epiphany.com*
- Firepond, *www.firepond.com*
- Trilogy, *www.trilogy.com*
- Telephony@Work, *www.telephonyatwork.com*
- CELLIT, *www.cellit.com*

Key Issues Related to Consistent Customer Service Across Channels

If your company is to benefit from consistent customer service across channels, here are the questions you will want to answer:

- Has your company taken the time to understand the customer service methods most preferred by your customers? Whereas there is a value in reviewing current customer service statistics, it also is necessary to provide incentives for target market customers to participate in focus groups. These focus groups aim to obtain additional, valuable information concerning consistent customer service requirements.

- Has your company formulated a clear vision that articulates a consistent customer service strategy?

- Has this vision and strategy been communicated effectively to internal customer-facing personnel as well as to external customers?

- Do the current customer-facing processes support consistent customer service across channels or do your processes need to be adjusted or even reinvented?

- How will your company effectively train customer service agents to think outside of silos (e.g., I am responsible for handling telephone inquiries whereas you are responsible for handling e-mail inquiries), and to be desirous of participating in your multichannel support efforts?

- Will your current telephone network (PSTN) allow for consistent customer service across channels, or should you be implementing emerging IP network technology that is capable of effectively integrating both voice and data information?

This last question is important, as well as complex. Today's customer service technology is in a transition phase, and the IP network initiative has the potential to transform the way customer service centers will be set up in the future. Most of today's customer service centers currently have two networks, an IT network on which their computer and their data runs, and a telephone network that Lucent, Siemens, Nortel, or others provide, which has all of their call routing functionality on it and which tends to be proprietary. Many middleware vendors currently offer CTI integration between these two separate networks but the middleware solutions are not cheap and may take considerable time.

Here is where Cisco's emerging IP network product offering comes into play. Cisco is suggesting that two networks are unnecessary and that the hardware switch-oriented nature of a PSTN bucks the trend of the emerging switchless data world. Cisco wants to provide a solution that supports a company's telephone as well as data network needs within the customer service environment. In February 2001, Cisco launched its IPCC (Internet Protocol Contact Center) offering, aimed at allowing customers to seamlessly transition from traditional PSTN applications to new world integrated IP applications (e.g., unified messaging, integrated Web collaboration, instant messaging, chat). Cisco openly admits that it is in the process of testing its IPCC offering within a high-volume environment, and that IPCC's current strength is more in its integration capabilities rather than the richness of its feature set. Cisco can expect stiff competition from Avaya, Nortel, Siemens, and 3Com, all of which are committed to offering their own IP network solutions.

There are several issues that should be considered related to the IP network alternative:

- There is a large installed base of customer service centers that currently run their customer services over a PSTN. Despite technical shortcomings of PSTN telephone switching equipment (e.g., the inability to support multimedia customer interactions such as voice, chat, e-mail, browser-sharing, call-me-now, etc.), the large installed base of customer service centers may be, for financial reasons, reluctant to dispose of their telephone switching equipment (never mind their reluctance to get rid of their green screen applications) and to replace it with an IP network. To be sure, vendors that currently sell PSTN products are not necessarily promoting this transition.

- Using current PSTN technology, a customer service supervisor can monitor customer voice calls but cannot monitor integrated voice and e-mails in real time. Using an IP network, simultaneous monitoring is feasible.

- By moving to an IP network, a company incurs at most a one- or two-minute network carrier charge (two cents per minute) while the call is passed over to the IP network. Compare this to a PSTN call whereby the company incurs this two cents per minute carrier charge during the entire voice call until the calling party hangs up. Net result: potentially significant cost savings per customer call.

- In the IP world, there really is no such thing as queuing, so when a packet gets sent in an IP network it goes across the wire and it looks for an IP address. When it finds the address, it expects to be consumed. But what if that IP packet is voice; how do you queue voice?

Up to now, there has not been a way to queue voice packets on an IP network, which is what most customer service centers need in order to provide consistent customer service across multiple channels. Here again is where Cisco comes into the picture. By purchasing Geotel, Cisco now offers a new IVR and queuing functionality within the IP network.

Summary

There have been and will continue to be new and exciting technologies that aim to provide consistent customer service across channels. While impressive, companies must not underestimate the importance of implementing processes that support consistent customer service. Moreover, companies must not downplay the significance of ensuring that in-company personnel and external customers feel comfortable and agreeable with the changes that consistent customer service inevitably brings.

In the beginning of this chapter, I stated that CRM really is a new business approach that allows customers to conduct business with a company the way the customer so desires, that CRM offers new technology tools to make this happen, and that consistent customer service across channels has arisen as a result of these two factors.

If I were to step back for a moment and look at the emerging trend of consistent customer service across channels, my biggest concern would be that this initiative is being too heavily driven by customer service, customer contact, or customer interaction center personnel. Line management, whether sales reps, sales managers, marketing personnel, or top management have as much a need for a complete customer picture as do customer service personnel. While customer service is a key component of CRM, the time seems ripe to ensure that consistent customer service across channels is based on the inputs related to the remaining four components of CRM, namely sales, marketing, business intelligence, and e-business as well as customer input. For example, sales personnel may want to view a comprehensive customer profile that includes list and summary details of personal visits to that customer, or letters ("snail mail") sent from that customer, as much as voice or Web transactions with that customer. My research suggests that to date, few if any customer service systems support this type of integration. In this regard, the CRM industry still has a way to go.

E-Marketing and CRM

21

The Emergence of E-Marketing

As recently as 25 years ago, some marketing professors at the Wharton School were stating that the marketing profession was half science and half art. The scientific part consisted of gathering valuable marketplace information about customer needs, customer satisfaction, and competitors. The artistic part consisted of applying this information to create marketing mixes to ensure that the right product/service was delivered to the right segments, and that the product/service was distributed, priced, and promoted in such a way so as to entice the segment buyers. It was suggested that there is no one right way to segment a market and that the two greatest tools that a marketing person could be born with are a nose to smell and a belly to feel shifts in the marketplace.

Has technology changed this way of thinking? Absolutely. Starting in the mid-1990s, several CRM software companies began to offer basic marketing automation functionality. This included helping companies to create marketing encyclopedias as repositories for valuable marketing information, to manage key events such as a trade show, and to manage basic marketing campaigns. Customer profiling, assisted by predictive modeling tools, also began to emerge.

In the late 1990s e-marketing vendors, taking advantage of the booming Internet and building on the work of marketing automation vendors, extended marketing functional capabilities. In fact, today's e-marketing can be defined as an expanding set of automation tools to help companies identify their most valuable prospects and customers, to convert and grow them, and to keep their loyalty for life. The expanding set of tools includes:

- Targeted Web marketing (e.g., Web banner advertising)
- Permission-based e-mail direct marketing (e.g., special promotions)
- Online customer behavior analysis (e.g., click-stream monitoring)
- Lead acquisition, distribution, and management for sales reps as well as for distribution channel partners
- Customer profiling and segmentation
- Integrated campaign management and measurements
- Customer engagement tools (e.g., reward-based surveys)
- Customer personalization tools
- Customer-driven services (e.g., collateral fulfillment, event management and execution, inquiry processing, direct mail requests, placement of orders)

Today's leading e-marketing vendors and their key strengths include:

- E.piphany—customer analytics
- Unica—customer analytics and campaign management
- Deuxo—lead incubation
- Annuncio—marketing process and marketing interaction automation
- Aprimo—campaign management and analytics
- Engage—customer profiling
- KANA—customer interaction platform and many of the above functions

Many of these players have been or currently are in an aggressive acquisition mode (e.g., KANA buys Broadbase, e.phiphany buys Octane). ISM sees these acquisitions as a way to compete within the more established CRM space by offering comprehensive e-CRM offerings rather than one or more "best-in-class" e-marketing "point" solutions. ISM recognizes that today's e-marketing vendors are focusing attention on the integration of data from operational CRM systems (e.g., sales, marketing, customer service, executives) as well as back-office ERP software packages such as Oracle, SAP, PeopleSoft, and others in order to create more universal customer profiles and increase the effectiveness of marketing efforts.

At the core of an e-marketing system is an effective knowledge base that continuously learns from it users. The knowledge base serves as a repository for the structured and unstructured data, drawn from various systems, and is critical to the execution of e-marketing functions. Some e-marketing vendors have written their own knowledge base whereas other e-marketing vendors opt to integrate a third-party "best-in-class" knowledge base solution.

E-marketing systems are red-hot for some very good reasons. For example, a recent Forrester Research finding stated that e-marketing, when properly implemented, can reduce costs for the production and delivery of promotional materials from $.50 to $1 (per unit) for a single catalog mailing to $.10 for a highly personalized e-mail campaign. E-marketing can also speed up marketing campaigns (e.g., e-mail direct marketing), allow you to test a marketing campaign before incurring large costs, and provide higher campaign response rates. Moreover, e-marketing can eliminate waste by focusing on the most profitable customer segments, helping to generate more revenues from the existing customer base, helping understand the behavior of your customer base, and helping to generate customer loyalty via personalization of services. Many companies are turning to e-marketing as a way to help them manage leads via distribution channels, as well as to provide headway into other CRM software modules (e.g., customer [self] service, cross- and up-selling).

While the future of e-marketing remains vibrant, there are challenges that users will likely confront and need to resolve. These challenges include traditional Web challenges such as:

- What to offer once the customer gets to your site.
- How to create an environment which makes the visitor want to stay on the site (i.e., site stickiness).
- How to maintain customer loyalty given that competition is a mouse click away.
- How to create a meaningful "Internet community" for e-customers to relate to.
- How to use interactivity as a replacement for the loss of persuasive human interaction.

- How to understand a customer's needs beyond inferential click-stream monitoring.

- How to build trust. Customers may wonder whether the information they provide about themselves will be kept secret or used inappropriately.

There is an additional set of e-marketing challenges that revolve around the integration issue, e.g., the integration of new e-marketing tools with existing marketing automation tools (e.g., process management tools for campaign workflow, response management, lead management and routing, event coordination), the integration of e-marketing with other CRM core functions (e.g., sales, sales management, customer service, business intelligence, e-business), the integration of e-marketing with regular marketing activities (e.g., the integration between "click" marketing and "mortar" marketing), and the integration of e-marketing with classical marketing activities (e.g., decisions concerning which products for which segments at what prices).

While these challenges can be daunting, those companies that have successfully implemented e-marketing systems rave about the results. Here is a case in point. Recently, ISM worked with a leading DSL provider in North America. Prior to implementing their e-marketing project, the VP of Marketing explained that his company was being overwhelmed by the number of hot customer leads they were receiving from a variety of sources. Yet there was no system in place to efficiently send leads to the sales force nor was there a system in place to track these leads. Of greater concern, this DSL provider had no way to monitor the work of a key member of their distribution channel, namely the local telephone company who was responsible for provisioning the customer's DSL line. This DSL provider was often in the dark as to when provisioning had or would take place. Meanwhile, the hot customer leads were inundating the DSL provider with calls and complaints concerning the availability of their DSL and when it would be installed and unfortunately the DSL company had no way to accurately respond.

After installing their e-marketing system, which was eventually linked to the local telephone companies, the DSL provider was able to effectively capture, distribute and track their hot customer leads. Moreover, they could quickly provide hot customer leads with an exact status of their order over the phone or via their Web site using self-service.

As lead and order fulfillment problems began to ease, the DSL provider turned to other functions of their e-marketing system to obtain new customers (e.g., permission-based e-mail direct marketing) and to service these customers (e.g., direct ordering by customers and use of customer self-service built on a knowledge base to correct DSL line problems). Approximately six months after installing the e-marketing system, the VP of Marketing provided this good piece of news: the customer satisfaction rating had risen from below 60 percent to above 85 percent during the six-month period.

Summary

In summary, the future of e-marketing is bright and may well prove to be the engine growth to both CRM and e-CRM, particularly as digital marketplaces (many sellers to many buyers) develop. ISM sees an increasingly important role for e-marketing as a set of tools that will help to segment, attract, and keep customers satisfied (the artistic side), while simultaneously offering a way for sellers to monitor customer behavior and satisfy customer needs (the scientific side). While technology has dramatically altered the way we conduct business today, the basic ideas and premises for marketing remain unaltered.

Knowledge Management and CRM

What Is Knowledge Management?

What is knowledge management and why is important for CRM? There are many definitions, but essentially knowledge management technology helps companies to capture, organize, manipulate, and share explicit and implicit data.

In CRM systems, knowledge management adds the ability to learn from each customer interaction. In CRM, information can be turned into actionable knowledge which can be made available to employees for customer profiling and personalization, or to the actual customer for self-servicing. Over the past few years, knowledge management technology developments have propelled the use of customer self-service, which enhances customer retention rates while driving down customer service costs.

Driving the impressive growth of customer self-service is the boom in knowledge management software, which is exploding in its own rights. IDC predicts the two market segments that make up knowledge management software—knowledge management access and knowledge management infrastructure—will carry the worldwide market from $1.4 billion in 1999 to $5.4 billion in 2004. According to IDC, the knowledge management access software segment will lead the way in terms of revenues and growth and will overtake the infrastructure software segment in 2002.[1] This prediction is significant in that new and enhanced knowledge management software will further drive the self-service functionality within customer contact centers.

Knowledge management technology focuses primarily on the following areas: expressing knowledge, storing knowledge, sharing knowledge, refining knowledge, and retaining knowledge. Moreover, knowledge management technologies allow for multiple data access and retrieval methodologies including keyword search, natural language queries, case-based reasoning, decision-tree reasoning, and expert-based reasoning. Knowledge management technology progressively narrows a user's search down to an answer that is currently held within a knowledge base. For example, a knowledge base can be used to respond to online user queries. If the user querying the knowledge base determines that the response is inappropriate, this knowledge goes into the knowledge base and the knowledge base then searches for a more appropriate response. This process continues until a response to the user query has been found. In some cases, the process may even involve human interaction if an appropriate response cannot be found within the knowledge base. In turn, this solution then gets added to the knowledge base (subject to verification).

Customers appreciate getting answers to their inquiries quickly and correctly. This helps to build customer satisfaction and ultimately increase customer loyalty over the long term. These same customers will increasingly gravitate towards those companies that offer a customer contact center (CCC), particularly a CCC that incorporates enhanced knowledge management tools that facilitate self-service.

The Table 22.1 illustrates some of the pros and cons associated with knowledge management systems.

Vendors that provide knowledge management solutions or a knowledgebase as part of a CRM-related offering include: KANA (purchased Broadbase), Ask Jeeves, RightNow, ServiceWare, and Primus.

---

1. IDC Research, October 2, 2000.
   Found at: *http://www.idcresearch.com/software/press/PR/SW100200pr.stm*.

TABLE 22.1
Pros and cons of knowledge management systems.

Pros	Cons
Available 24 hour, 7 days/week, 365 days/year	Possible inaccuracies/errors in response(s) to customer queries
Fast response to customer queries	An organization may have a limited number of customer contacts
Flexible based on sophistication of user	Tends to require serious process reengineering
Very scalable	

Companies that are implementing e-service aspects of CRM realize that the knowledge base should be accessible via multiple communication channels (e.g., Web chat, e-mail, phone, fax, mail). One of the key benefits of a centralized knowledge base is the ability to hold a single, integrated dialog with a customer regardless of their preferred communication channel. If implemented correctly, a knowledge base enables every CCC agent (or customer) to be as up-to-date and informed as the best agent because the knowledge is automatically available to any agent that uses the system.

There are a growing number of companies that are utilizing knowledge management tools. For example, Nike has a search engine that allows customers to easily search for comprehensive product/service information, while helping Nike to cut internal costs associated with live agents responding to basic phone and e-mail inquiries. In another example, Eddie Bauer has integrated a knowledge base into its CCC that provides users with self-service options including a library search of frequently asked questions (including natural language query) and interactive chat.

Cisco Systems uses Servicesoft technology for its Cisco Connection Online service (CCO), a global support organization that integrates with Cisco's global call center. A very large percentage of Cisco customers' self-service inquiries are resolved using the CCO.

Developing a Knowledge-Based CCC _____

There are two important developments that should be followed as concerns knowledge-based CCCs: the emergence of CCC knowledge management analytical tools that will provide powerful customer reports (e.g., which customers are contacting you when, and about what) as well as internal efficiency reports (e.g., how effective is your knowledge base and which areas need to be enhanced), and the emergence of truly multilingual CCCs.

Things to look for in a knowledge management solution include:

- Speed
- Flexibility of usage
- Open data model
- Accuracy
- Multiple hardware platforms and operating system environments

To get started on the development of knowledge-based CCC:

1. Analyze the quality and quantity of interactions with your customers across different access methods.
2. Compare the interaction costs across the different access methods.
3. Analyze the available resources and infrastructure to support a knowledge-based CCC.

Summary

As you investigate knowledge management as a component of your CRM system, do not forget to refer to your requirements analysis to determine what the real needs are and how knowledge management might be applied to filling those needs. Remember also that now, more than ever, is the time to extend your enterprise out to your customers and to let your customers conduct business with you in the ways they so desire.

Application Service Providers (ASP): An Overview

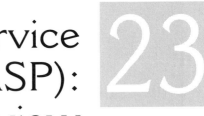

What is an Application Service Provider (ASP), and why is ASP a relevant acronym in the world of CRM? In this chapter, we explore the history and growth of ASPs, the applicability of the ASP to your organization's CRM efforts, as well as provide information on some ASP vendors.

Today's chief information officers (CIOs) are being asked to roll out electronic commerce initiatives such as CRM and e-procurement in weeks, not months, and to be ready to adapt or draw up entirely new strategies at a moment's notice. In addition to these dynamic business pressures, CIOs are wrestling with labor issues, speed of technological change, and the emergence of broadband networks. All of these forces support the ASP value proposition.

While analyst predictions for the growth of the ASP market have been slow to materialize, researchers such as IDC are predicting sales (from ASPs) of $24 billion by 2005. And although, Gartner Group has predicted that 60 percent of existing ASPs will go out of business within the next year, funding for existing and new ASP players continues. The message is that while the ASP model may be ideal for your organization's CRM needs, it is prudent to research the financial stability and long-term viability of the ASP you may be considering.

ASPs: A Brief History

The term ASP is a renaming of an old practice sometimes called "outsourcing." Businesses in the 1960s through the 1980s sold time-shares on mainframe computers and hosted subscribers' applications. Model 3270 terminals functioned as thin clients. Mainframe tools and networking protocols provided control over, and insight into usage, reliability, availability, performance, and service levels.

These time-shares or outsourcing companies even owned or leased the communications network. Mutual trust between provider and customer was possible because the provider controlled the quality of deliverables and the customer could validate that quality.

With the advent of client/server computing, the technical industry's progress toward distributed and open technology caused an unintended side effect. Somewhere in the evolution from old to new, precise control and measurement of service levels were lost. Not surprisingly, there were fewer and fewer providers of application services.

Today within the CRM industry, we are witnessing a full 360-degree circle. ASPs are now integrating new technology with meaningful, measurable service-level agreements and have the ability to efficiently deliver. Moreover, ASPs are winning corporate customers back with messages of security, reliability, and cost containment.

There are many examples of best-in-class companies that have moved their data and applications onto the site of an ASP. This has been complemented by communications infrastructures that have moved from private networks to Frame Relay connections, the Internet, or private VPNs (Virtual Private Networks).

In the simplest terms, an ASP uses the Internet or private Extranet to host, manage, and support software applications for companies. ASPs make it possible for enterprises to access enterprise-class software solutions without deep investments in the software, hardware, and personnel to support those solutions. The basis of the relationship between customer and ASP is a contractual Service Level Agreement (SLA); ASPs provide predictable monthly subscription fees for software, infrastructure, and operations support as well as application services.

Why are so many companies suddenly feeling comfortable with something that was treated as questionable-at-best only a few years ago? One of the primary points is the scarcity of raw intellectual talent, created by the World Wide Web itself. Demand for information technology specialists is so high that companies are at times unable to find or to afford the talent they need to run their critical applications. Even when they do find the talent, they are under constant threat of losing those specialists to headhunters. Information technology employees are holding jobs for months, not years or decades. Intellectual capital is going out the door just as fast as it is coming in.

There is an old proverb that says "there is nothing new under the sun." For those of you who have been around the SFA market long enough to have gray hairs, you will remember a company in Atlanta, Georgia called Sales Technologies. Back in the 1980s, Sales Technologies had large mainframe-based SFA systems that remote sales personnel synchronized to. During the time that they were in business, Sales Technologies primarily served the pharmaceutical and petroleum industries. Sales Technologies was truly the pioneer in being an SFA ASP.

Several pessimists have suggested that ASPs might only be able to thrive in small to mid-sized businesses. Sales Technologies proved this wrong; their well designed business model attracts larger corporations that are willing to sign up for these types of service offerings. Nonetheless, some CRM vendors (e.g., Neteos) that had originally offered their solution only via an ASP offering found that going exclusively down the ASP route can be dangerous since some companies do not want to place all their eggs in one ASP basket (Neteos went out of business). Increasingly, CRM software vendors are offering ASP services and providing software on a licensed basis as well.

Application developers and independent software vendors view the ASP arena as a new channel for delivery of their applications. There are, of course, some big questions about how the application developers will react since this movement represents a major shift in the revenue model, from higher up-front revenue for each customer to longer ongoing revenue in much smaller increments, from potentially many more customers. The pay as you go model of renting applications makes the revenue a three- or four-year equivalent to traditional license fees. Needless to say, not all application developers are buying into this model.

To help drive the ASP model faster, 25 companies formed the ASP Industry Consortium in mid-1999. The ASP Industry Consortium has grown from 200 members a year ago to approximately 700 at the time this book went to press. The consortium is composed of service aggregators, including value-added resellers, systems integrators, professional services groups, outsource providers, infrastructure/network services vendors, ISPs, Web-hosting providers, TSPs (Telephony Service Providers or Total Service Providers), VSPs (Voice Service Providers or Total Service Providers), FSPs (Full Service Providers), and companies such as Cisco, Sprint, and Qwest.

Despite the presence and promotion by the ASP Industry Consortium, during the last year several CRM vendors have been forced to make significant changes to their ASP model or to their ASP teaming partnerships, or to stop offering an ASP option altogether (e.g., Siebel closed down their sales.com offering). Many ASP vendors also have gone out of business (e.g., AristaSoft, marchFIRST, FutureLink, Agillon).

With this mixed track record in mind, I caution you to look very carefully at a vendor's long-term commitment to the ASP model. In fact, should you opt for the ASP model, I strongly recommend that your ASP contact provide mitigation for these types of risks.

In researching the ASPs, I was able to identify several vendors that can address CRM needs. Some ASPs listed below in Table 23.1 are very sales focused whereas others have greater enterprise capabilities. The list provided is a representative list and is not comprehensive.

TABLE 23.1
Partial list of CRM vendors.

Broad-Based ASPs	
Agilera	*www.agilera.com*
Corio	*www.corio.com*
Jamcracker	*www.jamcracker.com*
Oracle.com Online Services	*www.oracle.com/online_services*
Outtask	*www.outtask.com*
Qwest Cyber.Solutions	*www.qwestcybersolutions.com*
USinternetworking	*www.usinternetworking.com*

TABLE 23.1
Partial list of CRM vendors. (Continued)

Small and Mid-Sized Business ASPs

Breakaway Solutions	*www.breakaway.com*
Foreshock	*www.foreshock.com*
ManagedOps.com	*www.managedops.com*
NDUR	*www.ndur.com*
Surebridge	*www.surebridge.com*
TeleComputing	*www.telecomputing.net*

Specialized CRM ASPs

CrystalWare	*www.crystal-ware.com*
eLoyalty	*www.eloyalty.com*
Onyx	*www.onyx.com*
Pivotal	*www.pivotal.com*
Salesforce.com	*www.salesforce.com*
Salesnet	*www.salesnet.com*
UpShot	*www.upshot.com*
Xchange	*www.xchange.com*

Vendors are approaching the emerging ASP market segment from all angles. Some ASPs are providing only point solutions such as Sales Force Automation. Other vendors are providing an integrated suite of CRM, ERP (Enterprise Resource Planning), employee portals, and data warehousing. Several vendors have formed new corporations or business units to address specific market segments such as Sales Force Automation. Much of the new funding for ASPs is directed at ASPs that specialize in specific vertical industries.

Broad-Based ASPs

Agilera

Agilera has introduced a new total-solution outsourcing model. In their offering, they will install, configure, operate, and support top-tier applications such as SAP and Siebel. Other second-tier offerings will also be available on the Agilera ASP network. Customers connect to the Agilera Business Applications Network™ over secure, high-speed private or Internet connections.

Corio

Corio has been in stiff competition with USinternetworking for the number one ASP rating. The difference between the two organizations primarily is the amount of customization that they are willing to do for the hosted application.

The following applications are offered: Siebel CRM, BroadVision e-Business software, E.piphany eMarketing, and PeopleSoft or SAP for ERP. All of the offerings are integrated together and presented through a unified presentation layer.

Jamcracker

Jamcracker is the first pure-play application service aggregator. It is assembling a portfolio of pretested offerings from several ASPs and Internet-based software vendors, which it will offer to enterprises through their own customized application portal. The environment provides secure, single sign-on, 24×7 global support, and full accountability for service levels. As well as a choice of applications covering finance, human resources, customer relationship management, and other business operations, Jamcracker offers IT services such as remote access, desktop management, and infrastructure monitoring.

Oracle.com Online Services

In September 1998, Oracle became the first major applications vendor to offer application service provider (ASP) services based on its own applications and database technology. While many of the software vendors have been trying to negotiate deals with as many ASPs as they can, Oracle has decided that if you want an Oracle solution, you will have to come to Oracle.com Online Services for the hosting.

Oracle does not rent the applications. They require that the software be purchased, an annual maintenance contract be executed, and then Oracle.com Online Services will host it for you. This, of course, is after customization and implementation fees.

Outtask

Outtask provides ASP applications in the areas of CRM, financial management, executive productivity, human resources management, travel, and expense reporting. The company targets Fortune 1000 companies in the retail, publishing, manufacturing, professional services, high-tech, and healthcare fields. Outtask supports Siebel for CRM, Primus for customer service, and Microsoft Great Plains for financial management.

Qwest Cyber. Solutions

Known for its build-out of one of the largest fiber backbones, Qwest has recently begun to build large data hosting centers. Qwest is hosting several ASPs in these centers and has recently announced they now have a full ASP offering.

They have announced that SAP is their ERP offering hosted on Oracle databases. For their CRM offering, they have chosen Siebel.

USinternetworking

USi is currently the largest ASP. USi has their own data centers and touts this as a strategic business advantage unlike other ASPs who say that they focus on their core competencies, application hosting. In addition to being an ASP, USi has a program that application developers and other ASPs can use to become an instant ASP.

USi has one of the most comprehensive enterprise application offerings. They recently announced that they were the first to offer Storage Area Networks (SANs). This capability offers companies high reliability, performance, security, and fail-over capability using external storage for mission-critical systems. For the enterprise groupware environment, they recently began offering MS Exchange.

For their CRM offerings, they have teamed with Siebel Systems. As one of the first ASPs to offer PRM, they have teamed with Partnerware.

USi has two different ERP offerings, Lawson and PeopleSoft. They have also teamed with BroadVision and Calico for their e-commerce offerings, and Ariba and Clarus for e-procurement offerings. With these offerings, they provide a full end-to-end solution.

For publishing high-value B2B business data on the Web, USi has teamed with Actuate and for internal data mining and business intelligence, they offer Sagent software. USi fuses the Sagent OLAP Data Mart software modules for data extraction, transformation, and loading.

Small and Mid-Sized Business ASPs

Breakaway Solutions

Breakaway merged with Eggrock Partners to form a larger systems integration and ASP provider. The company refers to themselves as Full-Service Providers (FSP). They claim that they offer a fully integrated strategy, e-business implementation, and application hosting solutions for growing enterprises. Their Web-enabled offerings include integrated CRM (Onyx), e-CRM (KANA Communications/Silknet, MarketSoft Corporation, and Tara Software), e-back-office (Microsoft Great Plains), and an e-productivity (Microsoft) offering.

Foreshock

Foreshock provides multiple ASP services to mid-market companies. The offering of Internet solutions, front-office (Onyx), back-office (Microsoft Great Plains), and creative services gives Foreshock a different approach to a market segment that is getting harder to segment. Foreshock will provide services and applications in three different ways: monthly rental, rent to own, and outright purchase. All offerings have three pricing phases: customization and implementation charges, monthly enterprise hosting fees (per user), and application rental of one-time license fees.

ManagedOps.com

ManagedOps.com is a full-service application service provider with a complete Managed Operations service for Siebel Systems, Microsoft Great Plains, and Microsoft e-business solutions.

Managed Operations is the outsourcing of a managed data center using thin client technologies to deploy mission critical Microsoft-based applications to one or more locations. ManagedOps.com is targeted to small and mid-sized companies.

The company offers a secure 24×7 data center environment for both client/server and Web-based business applications. The Managed Operations service extends beyond traditional hardware hosting by providing a single point of support and system administration for business applications and the underlying technologies.

NDUR

NDUR Corporation is an Information Technology Service Provider. NDUR provides managed application services on a Microsoft-based platform. NDUR offers an ASP-hosted model of the SalesLogix.net CRM package to customers.

Surebridge

Surebridge provides outsourced enterprise application solutions for CRM, ERP, e-business, and productivity applications. The company's service offerings include application deployment, upgrade services, secure hosting, and application management. Surebridge deploys and hosts applications for mid-market companies. Surebridge's customers include manufacturing, professional services, financial services, healthcare, distribution, and trade services firms. The company provides a PeopleSoft v.8 upgrade program to implement PeopleSoft v.8 products and also supports Siebel 7.

TeleComputing

TeleComputing offers applications for the mid-market and has also begun to design service offerings for larger companies that have multiple offices. In addition to the CRM and ERP offerings, this organization is also one of the first to offer the full complement of Microsoft products via the Web.

The representative list of applications they currently offer include: MS Office 2000, MS Outlook 2000, MS Exchange Server, MS Access, MS Project 98, SalesLogix2000 CRM, and Microsoft Great Plains ERP.

Specialized CRM ASPs

Here I would like to make a distinction between ASPs that host "traditional" packaged CRM solutions (e.g., Pivotal, Onyx) and "next-generation" Web services vendors that have developed their CRM solutions specifically for the hosting model (e.g., UpShot, Salesforce.com, Salesnet).

CrystalWare

CrystalWare was formed as a software development and professional services provider. The company expanded into providing ASP offerings and today provides a suite of CRM applications for small to mid-sized enterprises via the Internet.

CrystalWare has developed CRM applications like several of the other specialized CRM ASPs.

eLoyalty

eLoyalty is a systems integration company and ASP that has 900 employees working from offices in North America, Canada, the United Kingdom, Germany, France, and Australia.

Their CRM ASP offering provides browser-based access to eLoyalty's customer contact technologies, Loyalty Foundation. The company allows companies to rent or lease access to applications that automate marketing, sales, and customer service.

Onyx

Onyx is a "traditional" packaged CRM solution that offers functionality in CRM such as contact, account, sales, time, marketing, and lead management. The Onyx CRM application is Web-based and sold on a license to customers.

Pivotal

Pivotal is another "traditional" packaged CRM solution with tight integration to Microsoft products to the front and back office. The Pivotal CRM application provides comprehensive CRM functionality to its users. Although the software is generally sold on a licensed model to customers, Pivotal does offer its CRM application on the ASP model via a third-party ASP provider, Interpath. Interpath can host the Pivotal CRM application and offer the ASP option to Pivotal customers who desire use of the ASP model.

Salesforce.com

The Salesforce.com business model is to provide a comprehensive CRM application that can be used to get a sales organization running in days at a monthly rate of $50 per salesperson per month.

The online application provides forecasts by employee, contact, account management, and reporting.

Founded in March 1999 by a former Oracle executive, Marc Benioff, Salesforce.com has put together a well-known management team and board of directors with Larry Ellison (Oracle CEO) as one of the board members.

Salesnet

Salesnet is a Web-based CRM ASP that offers salesforce automation tools, including account and contact management, forecasting, and reporting, primarily to small companies. The company has also entered into agreements with business content and service providers, including Dow Jones & Co. and Hoover's Inc. The site provides support for personal digital assistants and scheduling tools such as MS Outlook. Import tools for ACT! and Gold-Mine are also integrated into the site. Pricing for these services is $49.95 per month per user.

UpShot

This is one more site that is in competition for the sales professional. UpShot has teamed with WebEx to provide Web conferencing, and focuses more on the individual user.

Xchange

Xchange's software provides market analytics for effective customer/market segment targeting. The Xchange 8 package enables users to analyze the profitability of each customer and identify profitable opportunities. The Xchange 8 package is designed to complement the analytical capabilities of traditional CRM software packages such as Siebel, PeopleSoft, Onyx, Pivotal, etc. Xchange 8 includes ASP components such as the e-messaging ASP component, which provides plug-ins to e-messaging applications that facilitate personalized outbound online communications from the sales staff to customers for marketing purposes.

ASP Conferences

To get more information on trends and directions, conferences tend to be a good source. One of the leading ASP conferences is the ASP Summit. This conference series is directed towards the emerging application service provider industry, however it is a good conference to attend for companies looking to choose an ASP.

The ASP Summit, developed in conjunction with the ASP Industry Consortium, provides forums where the leading players in the emerging ASP marketplace come together to assess market opportunities, evaluate technology infrastructure requirements, and define new business models and best practices.

Pricing Model

As outlined above, ASPs have several different pricing models. Application vendors like Oracle have a business model where you buy the software license, pay the maintenance fee, and then pay them to host your application.

Corio, USi, and others allow you rent the application and hosting services for a monthly fee. Remember that in almost all cases, you pay for setup and implementation costs. With certain ASP providers, these costs can be almost as expensive as if you hired your own systems integrator. Be careful to evaluate the details carefully before you sign any ASP contracts.

The next-generation Web services vendors such as Salesforce.com, UpShot, and Salesnet provide subscription-based pricing that is typically much less costly than ASPs that host traditional CRM packages.

Things to Consider

Key challenges to the success of ASPs revolve around the network bandwidth to let the applications perform at a necessary level for consistent, acceptable service-level agreements and 24×7 availability. While most companies are still undecided on the future, the companies that are providing robust integrated application suites seem to be gaining the momentum.

Will ASPs become the way of the future? This is still the subject of many debates. Voicemail supplied by the telephone company is the equivalent of outsourcing your answering machine service, for a monthly fee. Many consumers feel very comfortable with an outside organization managing this mission-critical service. Nonetheless, there are still questions about control and security of CRM data. Many businesses do not feel comfortable housing mission-critical data at some ASP site somewhere, and prefer instead to have that data located at the company site.

Overall, the ASP market is still forming. Vendors are still working on service definitions and priorities, network availability, and bandwidth issues as well as partnership strategies.

According to a recent ASP Industry Consortium survey, 56 percent of companies currently renting business applications from an ASP have less than 500 employees. The survey indicates that small to mid-sized companies still form the largest market for the ASP model.

Renting applications seems like a logical solution for many businesses. However, time will tell. The promise of computing as a utility has been touted for several years now.

Companies deploying CRM might consider ASP as a potential software delivery method. But, be forward-thinking in terms of your business model. To date, ASPs have not really addressed requirements like call centers or customer interaction centers. Does this mean that your organization should outsource only half of your CRM application, if you need call center functionality as part of the CRM system?

Another issue is that there are varying levels of willingness among ASPs to integrate their applications with your existing legacy applications, ranging from import/export integration to more complex integration capabilities. Do not be surprised if an ASP informs you that you have to manage your own legacy systems. Again, does this provide a good business case if you still have to have an IT department just to manage your legacy? If you do interface your legacy applications to the ASP, third-party ASPs' mixed-bag approach to application hosting makes it unclear where accountability lies. So, pay attention to what integration services the ASP will provide.

Whereas some ASPs use co-location facilities and buy bandwidth from network carriers, other ASPs opt to control every aspect of their service. This impacts the important issue of the ability and willingness of ASPs to offer varying levels of SLAs. The SLAs offered by the ASP generally cover only the services over which the ASP has direct control. In general, the SLAs cover availability, functionality, and performance, from the applications to the network.

The SLA should include, but not be limited to:

- Purpose of the SLA
- Description of service
- General payment terms
- Duration of service
- Termination conditions
- Legal issues such as warranties, software ownership, etc.
- Start date of service indemnities, limitation of liability, etc.
- Installation timetable

ASPs also are struggling with the customization issue and this does not appear to be going away anytime soon. Shared services always means more generic offerings. However, remember that many companies unnecessarily customize applications. To help address the customization issue, ASPs also are turning to more configurable solutions that customers can tailor to their needs without doing expensive source code customization.

Summary

In the final analysis, there are indeed benefits for the ASP model, e.g., specific CRM software can be deployed quickly to key personnel, and CRM offered via ASP requires little IT infrastructure. Nonetheless, be careful in your due diligence, be realistic with your expectations and, most importantly, make sure the ASP can meet the prioritized business requirements that you have determined for your CRM system.

Addressing CRM
System Security Risks

Nothing in this world is gained without risk. When you are about to launch a new application that is months in the making or are about to sell your wares over the Web or are allowing your field service reps to get to their data over the net, you realize there will be risks. The growth of CRM and e-business is exposing our organizations to more access than ever before. There are too many variables in terms of hardware, firmware, operating systems, middleware, applications, and networking for anyone to account adequately for all the possibilities. In fact the only truly secure system is one that is switched off and good to no one.

Patrice Rapalus, director of the Computer Security Institute (CSI), notes that companies that want to survive in the future need to develop a comprehensive approach to information security, that embraces both the human and technical dimensions. They also need to properly fund, train, staff, and empower those involved with enterprisewide information security. In the Computer Security Institute's 2001 annual report, the following range of attacks and abuses were noted:

- Forty percent of respondents detected system penetration from the outside. Only 25 percent reported system penetration in 2000.

- Thirty-eight percent of respondents detected denial of service attacks Only 27 percent reported denial of service in 2000.

- Ninety-one percent detected employee abuse of Internet access privileges (for example, downloading pornography or pirated software, or inappropriate use of e-mail systems). Only 79 percent detected net abuse in 2000.

- Ninety-four percent detected computer viruses. Only 85 percent detected them in 2000.

Addressing Security Weaknesses

Addressing the security of our company infrastructures addresses the various threats that put our CRM and e-business networks at risk. Information systems security policies primarily address threats. In the absence of threats, policies would be unnecessary—one could do as one chooses with information. Unfortunately, threats do exist and information systems security policies are necessary to provide a framework for selecting and implementing countermeasures against them. A well-designed information security policy defines the objectives of the information system of an organization and outlines a strategy to achieve these stated objectives. An enforceable written policy helps ensure that everyone within the organization behaves coherently in an acceptable manner with respect to information security. *A security policy establishes what must be done to protect information stored on computers. A well-written policy contains sufficient definition of "what" to do so that the "how" can be identified and measured or evaluated.* Policies must be implementable and enforceable, concise and easy to understand, and balance protection with productivity. But more importantly they must define responsibilities and how violations will be handled in order to be effective. No matter how diligently a company is in maintaining a security policy, it is impossible to remove all security risks. One of the reasons is that there are so many areas where a security breach is possible in the enterprise CRM and e-business environments. These areas include:

- **Remote Access**
  - Laptop: virus, password protection for applications and operating systems, encryption, personal firewalls, encryption devices, token management, enterprise firewalls and data backup.

- PDA/Web Phone: password protection, virus protection, enterprise firewalls, encryption and potentially wireless encryption.
- Virtual private network (VPN): enterprise firewalls and network provider password management.
- Remote Access Service (RAS): RAS server passwords and enterprise firewalls.
- CRM application level security: workgroup, user, field level.

- **Partner Relationship Management (PRM)**
  - PRM/CRM application security: workgroup, user, field level.
  - Demilitarized zones (DMZ): Extranet passwords, log-on passwords.
  - Partner versus competitor data and information security issues.
  - Public key infrastructure (PKI).

- **E-Business/E-Commerce**
  - CRM, Portal, Web self-service and e-business application security: user, field level.
  - Public key infrastructure (PKI).
  - VPNs and Web services.

- **Call Center E-Mail**
  - Virus protection.
  - HelpDesk access.

- **Enterprise E-Mail**
  - User list management.
  - Lightweight Directory Access Protocol (LDAP): used for e-mail user management.
  - Password management.
  - Server e-mail attachment virus protection.
  - Web access management.

- **Enterprise Security**
  - Intrusion detection.
  - Lightweight Directory Access Protocol (LDAP): used in firewalls, segmentation, authentication, firewall and e-mail user management authorization.
  - Password management.
  - Network operating system password management.
  - Virus protection.
  - Demilitarized zones.

- Firewalls (external and office-to-office) network, proxy, packet filter gateways.
- Internet access: surf-control.

Becoming Aware of the Risks

While companies must accept that not all security holes can be plugged, they should nonetheless strive to define an acceptable level of risk at a reasonable cost. Identifying the threats or risks that your enterprise may face will help in identifying the vulnerabilities and will assist in selecting the appropriate security measures for protection. Management today must learn the new industry terminology and become proactively aware of the security issues out of necessity. Prior to setting the security policy, the following are critical trends and areas in which to be educated:

The Human Factor

People are the weakest link in your organization. Everyone in your organization, from the customer service representative at the call center to the sales executives equipped with wireless-enabled laptops, has the ability to inadvertently—or intentionally—create a security breach. One aspect of human behavior is that if you try hard enough, you can find someone who will believe nearly anything. Hackers know this and many create plausible stories to entice information from your employees. Unwittingly, your employees open the door to these attacks, most times innocently, such as by passing e-mail. The malicious employee is the individual who intentionally inflicts damage to the network. This type of damage can consist of anything from releasing a virus, stealing information and poisoning data, to bypassing security controls to play games on the company's dime. All statistics show that millions of dollars are lost each year due to employee security breaches.

Of course, people outside your organization who inflict chaos are commonly known as hackers. The Internet provides them with potential access from anywhere in the world. Some of these people are seeking some sort of intellectual high, while others are fueled by more treacherous motives such as revenge or stealing for profit. In any event, no intrusion is innocent and no intrusion is benign.

The other people issue is difficulty in attracting and keeping skilled staff. Lack of skilled staff leads to another common threat to an organization's network from the inside, which can be as simple as misconfiguration of servers and firewalls—sometimes from the manufacturer but also from the system administrators themselves. Out of this you can see one common theme emerges—education. The people involved with setting the policy and making the system secure need to make intelligent decisions. The threats to your CRM network come in many forms—disgruntled employees, corporate espionage, lax system administrators, faulty products, and poorly educated users.

The Systems and Software

Other risks to our CRM enterprises reside on our own PCs. Malicious code (sometimes called "malware") can take different forms. It may be in the form of a computer virus, a Trojan horse (a program that purports to do one thing, but creates a security vulnerability), or active content like Java and ActiveX programs. The latest harmful agents are the worms, like Nimda and Code Red, that can distribute themselves without people actively distributing them. E-business is especially vulnerable as the Internet is the lifeline of these viruses. The good news is that some very good virus protection tools exist, but they must be coupled with prudent end-user behavior to be effective. Anti-virus software has also been developed for PDAs, but there are also threats because of access to networks by Web cell phones (e.g. WAP, WML). The immediate need is to secure the network where these devices communicate. Companies must look at company firewalls and even personal firewalls for employees with home based PCs who connect via cable modems and DSLs.

Software vendors make installing software easy for us. Even if you know nothing about software, you can take the system defaults. From a security standpoint you only open a potential security door by allowing all options. Any capabilities and services that you don't plan to use should be turned off until needed in order to reduce the number of attack points. Firewalls are only as good as they are configured to be. Eliminating risk through this method is known as hardening, and offers fewer entry points into your network. Because our networks are in a constant state of change due to upgrades and add-ons, constant adjustments are being made to the software settings. This only adds to the frustration of assuming the settings for a particular software installation are secure. It is almost impossible to prevent new security holes from appearing as software gets changed.

Complexity of software combinations between the various e-business systems, CRM suites, and other ERP components makes it practically impossible to evaluate the overall systems software in sufficient detail to discover and resolve all potential security exposures. In some cases, one has to depend on each software component being well designed from a security standpoint, and strive to minimize exposures resulting from combining and integrating the software. Many times our system administrators must take it on faith that the components enforce acceptable security.

Sizing Up the Situation

In order to set up a system for successfully managing the security risk, a set of management requirements must be put in place. These imperatives may require management adjustment, but these imperatives are in lieu of an accepted industrywide measurement system. How do companies judge the risks embedded in their current e-business systems? How do they determine if the investments related to reducing risks are warranted? The essential elements of risk and cost involve the following:

- What resources need to be protected?
- What is the cost of loss or compromise?
- What is the cost of protection?
- What is the likelihood of loss or compromise?

What is the cost to an organization? The *2001 Computer Crime and Security Survey* from the Computer Security Institute reports that, "35 percent (186 respondents) were willing and/or able to quantify their financial losses. These 186 respondents reported $377,828,700 in financial losses. (In contrast, the losses from 249 respondents in 2000 totaled only $265,589,940. The average annual total over the three years prior to 2000 was $120,240,180.)"[1]

There are no proven mechanisms that an IT manager can use to compute the company's vulnerability, as the effectiveness of security countermeasures defy quantification. Unfortunately in the real world we do have to deal with budgetary constraints, so choices have to be made. You need to consider the probability of a security breach versus the expense. IT managers can develop metrics that may not be foolproof, but allow for guidelines as the cost of security measures are evaluated. The following Table 24.1 is hypothetical, but could be a guideline for coming up with a way of answering the above questions.

---

1. Computer Security Institute, "2001 Computer Crime and Security Survey, " March 2001. Found at: *http://www.gosci.com/prelea/000321.html*.

TABLE 24.1
Guidelines that manage risk and cost.

Countermeasure	Cost of Compromise	Cost of Protection	Probability of Compromise
Install firewall	$1,000,000	$25,000	50%
Audit analog lines	$50,000	$2,000	5%
Develop security policy	$1,000,000	$40,000	75%

A company's senior management should, with the approval of the board of directors, decide which risks will receive what level of attention and investment. The decisions must be documented and must guide all implementation plans for e-business. Sometimes problems are dealt with as they arise, by whichever manager is involved at the time. Decisions that these managers make must be aligned with the set security policy.

According to recent reports by Network World, budget allocations for security policies should be set to approximately 5 percent of the company's IT budget. Instead, security budgets are usually embedded in individual projects such as the e-business or CRM project, in effect raising the cost of the e-business or CRM project. A dedicated budget based on the risk assessment should be allocated and reconciled with individual business units budgets.

Developing the Security Policy

First of all, the goals of securing a network can be summarized as ensuring the following:

- Confidentiality
- Integrity
- Availability

Since there is no one technology or process that can be implemented in the name of total security, the aim is to develop a defense through an in-depth strategy. Start with important security principles and corporate security standards and, in so doing, use the following guidelines in this development:

1. Appoint a high-level executive with companywide responsibility to enforce and develop security policies consistently across an organization.

2. Ensure security policies are holistically defined and enforced across the e-business and CRM environment, from applications to networks to physical servers, laptop, and handheld device security. It should be clear that the IT systems belong to the company, and are to be used to further the interests of the organization. Enforcing the policy is essential. Organizations must hold specific individuals accountable for incidents as well as holding managers accountable for risk and budget decisions.

3. Ensure the lines of business are actively involved and supportive of CRM security strategy, e-business, and investments. Since in many organizations, line-of-business executives make the majority of the e-business and CRM funding decisions, not having their "buy-in" can lead to the loss of productivity gains from corporate security investments, as the business units continue to "reinvent" security within their applications in an inconsistent and unpredictable manner. The key to success is not only the dos and don'ts, but giving a sense of the whys is also important.

4. Think and plan ahead. Think at least six to twelve months down the road while giving lines of business the tools they need to build secure the e-business environment, without creating a security infrastructure that will become yet another legacy infrastructure within a few months. This includes deploying Web-only security solutions that will not be able to integrate with existing applications as customer access demands naturally grow with Web site usage.

5. Understand the links between e-business, CRM security, and customer satisfaction. In our business, customer intimacy, loyalty, and satisfaction is imperative. A complex security infrastructure, despite its security-oriented benefits, may impede customer satisfaction. Enforcing policies such as password policies that ensure single sign-on can bring the complexity of security under control to help increase customer satisfaction. We have found organizations that require partners and employees to input 3–7 different passwords. This becomes a burden and your user community will become sloppy when this much effort is required.

Along with the paramount guidelines mentioned above, it is also important to take into consideration the following security policy components:

6. Create a single, well-known focal point for security incident reporting. Even with intrusion detection in place, break-ins will happen, but any hope of containment needs to be acted on quickly. All users can assist with this effort, but a well-designed system will facilitate containment.

7. Enforce good administration practices. Control administration consistently from a central policy, but allow flexibility to delegate certain administrative security tasks to business units, partners, or others based upon the needs of the growing business.

8. Develop authentication rules. The most common method is passwords for user access, but you should look at others (smart cards, security tokens, encryption). But do make sure passwords rules are spelled out and enforced.

9. Implement active content screening tools (i.e., virus protection) and have rules for downloading from Internet sites and e-mail attachments. This could possibly be an education issue, which also includes what types of network traffic should and should not be allowed.

10. Use open standards. Utilizing multivendor, open standards in vendor selection and product choice is a key requirement to current and future flexibility and interoperability.

11. Beware of any vendor promising a complete security solution with only its product portfolio. Strong business partnerships are critical in end-to-end security control and management.

12. Implement an e-business privacy policy. Protecting personally identifiable data is important to maintaining brand equity, as well as to conforming to existing and developing privacy legislation.

13. Don't stop updating the policy and checking security. Review your organization's information protection or information security programs. Get assistance, call on experts, and use available tools. The Computer Security Institute is continually updating their Information Protection Assessment Kit (IPAK). IPAK is an inexpensive tool that will give you a clear view of how comprehensive your program is, as well as a way to gauge its progress over time.

14. Ensure that data is backed up frequently. A good policy might include which systems need to be backed up, how often, who will perform, etc. This can be incorporated into a disaster recovery policy. You want to make sure you can recover quickly from any loss that might be incurred. Create a contingency plan that covers all possible scenarios that would result in a loss of data and property.

15. And finally, educate, educate, educate. Annual or semi-annual security training for end users and administrators is a must. In order to maintain a strong security posture, members of an organization should know what to look for concerning security risks. Knowing how to report problems or incidents is also critical in maintaining that posture. Make sure administrators are educated on current technology and can adequately secure your CRM network.

Summary

The ability to deal with computer security and information privacy assurance is critical to the future of e-business. While the technology community is offering lots of new solutions to security problems, IT managers must put this technology through a systematic risk management process. While most companies do not yet handle the process for managing security well, a focused effort can lead to notable improvement within a year. This focus includes analyzing risks, setting a specific security budget, and of course, creating a security policy. Remember that CRM and e-business security is critical for the success of the CRM system.

The Importance of Data Integrity

Introduction

Data integrity consists of both data cleansing and data management. Data cleansing/data management is a core component of every successful CRM program, and should be developed at the outset of the CRM program. Data integrity should include documenting current data inventory, developing data standards, cleansing existing data, and developing processes to maintain, change and enhance the quality of your data. The justification for data integrity is strong:

- Quality data is a strategic asset that will impact your CRM system success.
- The quality and accuracy of data (i.e., customer, market, competitor, product, supplier data) in the CRM system will impact a consistent, error-free way to enhance the customer experience.

- Data inventory is important to determine the source, location, flow, and extent of existing data in order to understand which data may be used for the CRM system.

- Data cleansing is critical to eliminate duplications of data. For example, eliminating duplicate customer entries will reduce marketing costs (e.g., duplicate marketing mailings, faxes, and e-mails).

- Data cleansing tools (e.g., FirstLogic) cleanse, standardize, and consolidate customer-centric data anywhere that data is touched, stored, or moved. They help to consolidate multiple identities of the same customer across several legacy systems' data sources to create a single, cleansed customer view.

- Data cleansing tools can be integrated into an enterprise application architecture environment. There are several data cleansing tool vendors that have APIs already developed for CRM and ERP applications. Depending on the company's enterprise technical architecture, the APIs should be relatively easy to implement. These data cleansing tools follow business rules that proactively maintain data quality.

- An ongoing plan to maintain data cleanliness and integrity, which includes parsing, correcting, and matching data, can help prevent data degradation over time.

- Quality data can, for example, help to deliver more accurate reports to customer-facing personnel and customers.

- There is also a potential reduction in costs (associated with poor data quality) such as redundancy costs (e.g., storing same data in more than one database) and infrastructure costs (e.g., costs of hardware used for data storage).

Lessons Learned

Cleansing/managing customer relationship management data seems quite logical. To some, it may even sound easy. Those who have gone through the effort, however, know that cleansing/managing data is an ongoing and at times elusive effort within each CRM initiative. A few examples, along with a mini case study may be helpful.

I will never forget my experience helping a global telecommunications company with their data integrity efforts. The company had 36 different data sources, ranging from an Oracle back-office database to a myriad of incompatible legacy systems containing bits and pieces of customer information.

Whereas the CIO was convinced that all 36 data sources needed to be integrated into the emerging CRM data warehouse, the VP of marketing and sales (who was paying for the CRM initiative) was not convinced. This issue became quite a debate, and in the end the CIO got his way. Matters went downhill from there, as the cost and time needed to integrate each of the 36 databases continued to grow. At hand was the fundamental question of cost versus benefit for bringing existing data into the emerging CRM system. In the end, after many months of delay and excuse, the IT department concluded that they had underestimated the complexity of cleaning the data and bringing it across to the new CRM system, and agreed with the VP of marketing and sales to limit the number of data sources to be integrated to 15.

Lesson learned: Carefully determine the cost/benefit of integrating data prior to commencing the integration.

I applied this "lesson learned" shortly thereafter, at one of our assignments with a global postal service. In this case, there were in excess of 150 data sources that the CRM program manager felt needed integration. To address the cost/benefit issue early on, I suggested that the CRM program manager approach each data source owner, inform the owners of the cost to integrate their proposed data, collect this amount of money up front, and then commence the integration work. The CRM program manager followed my advice. In the end, 8 data source owners were prepared to pay the required money and 142 data sources dropped out! Savings to the company amounted to millions of dollars. Loss to the company in terms of not having needed data was minimal, since system users were provided incentives to collect missing data just prior to system launch.

Lesson learned: Be careful to consider that it may be less expensive and less time consuming to recreate or reenter data than it is to integrate all supposedly needed data sources.

A Mini Case Study

In another client assignment, a leading global biotechnology company requested that ISM facilitate the specification and implementation of their global CRM initiative. While this company had global customers, each of the company's geographical locations tended to keep their own customer records in data formats that were often incompatible on a global basis. Some company subsidiaries, faced with bad quality data, opted to use the CRM system initiative as a reason to throw away all their old data and do no record importing. The U.S. subsidiary, rich in valuable historical data, had little choice other than to import considerable amounts of data. In fact, the

U.S. entity imported in excess of 250,000 records from three sources: marketing, sales reps, and their SAP back-office system. As the company's CRM project manager noted, the potential for importing duplicate records was quite high, and detecting and de-duping was quite challenging. We tried to map as many contacts in the CRM system to the contacts currently held in SAP. This mapping process was also extremely time consuming. Here are some of the lessons learned (remember these are specific to this biotech's unique situation):

1. **Understanding the data integrity requirements and process.**
   Data integrity (including both the cleansing and the management aspects) is a BIG, BIG job and the least understood job by everyone except for the people who are closely involved. Be prepared to spend considerable time repeating data integrity explanations and needs to many people. *Recommendation:* Those who will make decisions need to be involved from the beginning of the data integrity process; otherwise, they must learn to trust recommendations from the data team members.

2. **Start early.**
   This company started their data integrity process in Q3 2000. After one year, they still have a lot to do. *Recommendation:* come up with one administrative system to track all data integrity tasks and subtasks that all team members can share and view. The company used both MS Project as well as Excel software to help manage the process. MS Project was useful for general management of the project, but Excel was more useful at the hands-on level (e.g., mapping data from one data source to another) due to its flexibility; also, more people know how to use Excel than Project.

3. **Work hard to secure a cohesive data integrity team.**
   - Skill set needed for this biotech company included:
     - One programmer with SQL knowledge.
     - Someone who knew Excel inside out to set the data in the right format for nontechnical people to use.
     - One dedicated person to manage the project.
     - Someone who understood the internal data to qualify what is good clean data. This company tried to use external temps to clean data but ended up spending an unreasonable amount of time explaining and training them. *Conclusion:* Data cleansing/data integrity for some companies is far too complex for outsiders to understand or implement. Consider data cleansing tools in addition to personnel.

- Team continuity is critical to the success. This company lost three data integrity team members due to other projects in the company. This caused delays in the completion of data integrity/data cleansing since this process requires transferring complex knowledge, which may be too detailed to grasp in a short period of the time.
- There is a need for skilled personnel who are detail oriented. This company had a programmer who just gave up and left the team because he could not handle the level of detail required to successfully implement excellent data integrity procedures.
- All team members should receive software training on the selected CRM software package before starting to implement data integrity efforts. Without the knowledge of the selected CRM package, data integrity team members may have a hard time envisioning how the data would flow and connect to each other. This company also felt that there was a value to having the project leader skilled in computer programming or with reasonable computer knowledge since this helped with understanding what could and could not be done when cleaning up and exporting/importing data.

4. **Communications.**
   - Meet weekly with the data integrity team members. Complement this weekly meeting with a daily walk-around to all team members. This helps to avoid the inevitable situation whereby a data integrity team member or programmer commences to work on a data integrity assignment that may be out of focus.
   - Manage user expectations. For example, the sales reps from this company gave the data integrity team their data. The reps failed to understand that whereas their data may have been clean, other departments' data might not be as clean. When combining the data, the de-duplication process can be great and take considerable time. This company found it valuable to communicate to system users during initial training, the naming conventions to be used in the data integrity process. They also sent out memos on a scheduled basis to system users that explained the status of the data cleansing project.

5. **Project management.**
   - Ensure that you have strong project management skills and a data project manager who budgets 90 percent of project time to managing data-related projects instead of actually participating in the cleansing process. A project manager who does too much data cleansing and importing will get lost among the trees and not see the forest. Moreover, 10 percent of hands-on data cleansing tends to be sufficient to

obtain the needed understanding of likely issues and problems. If not apparent, the data project manager should not be the same person as the CRM project manager.

- Define all data elements (i.e., object by object). Then transfer responsibility for securing needed data elements to the people who ultimately own and use the data. The definition of data elements, which should be consistent with data dictionary rules, should be done at the outset of the data integrity project.

- Ensure that the data project manager keeps a good record of the status of all data. Otherwise, it can become an administrative nightmare to sort out which data has been imported, cleansed, and quality controlled.

6. **Integration with other systems (e.g., SAP).**

- Do not over-integrate! This company integrated products, literature, and sales orders out of the gates. It was too big of a job. *Recommendation:* focus on the most useful/needed data integration; in this company's situation, it was sales orders. Other integrations can wait or be can be done manually for a while until you have achieved a stable system and an educated system user-base.

7. **Technical issues.**

- Test and quality control all imported data every time a data import is done. Import small amounts of data initially, to test out the import, prior to ramping up the import procedure.

- Hire competent consultants who have imported data before. The consultant that this company used, for example, did not know that importing zip codes with a "0" in the beginning would create a problem. Be assured that this is not the only company importing zip codes!

8. **Data integrity.**

- Assign data integrity to one or more individuals in the company. Ensure that they receive proper incentives to care about data quality. *Lesson learned:* Many people use data but few pay a lot of attention to its quality.

- Data integrity implies long-term planning. List all of the tasks that you need to do to clean and to keep data clean. At the outset, define how you intend to identify "bad" records and how you intend to clean such records even if this may mean cleaning the record manually. Ensure that you have an internal data cleansing group whose sole job is to cleanse the data record by record if this is required. This company created a Data Entry group and many of these tasks were given to the group. The mistake was asking them to work on data cleansing while simultaneously maintaining their regular workload.

- In conclusion, data integrity boils down to resources and dedication among data integrity team members. If the data integrity project is not carefully planned and executed, you risk maintaining the team's long-term dedication as well as your CRM program.

Summary _____

I hope that you conclude from the above examples and mini case study that one of the most important aspects of a CRM program is to prepare and keep customer relationship management data clean, and to ensure a proper data quality strategy as your CRM initiative moves forward. Here are the key steps for building a data quality strategy:

- Purchase toolsets and integrate them into the enterprise applications where customer data is utilized.
- Review and check management data for quality on a regular basis.
- Understand the company's customer-facing employee information needs.
- Provide a unified view of customers by setting up a master enterprise data architecture.
- Get a data quality program started to maintain a high-quality data standard.
- Set up a data quality audit task force of employees who use customer data at various levels of your organization.
- Provide local language comprehension by understanding, for example, the local word and abbreviations for "Street" versus "St.", "Avenue" versus "Ave.", etc.
- Implement integrated automated data management tools for accurate address and postal code checking. These tools also contain business logic to make sure that the data follows naming conventions (including product names, etc.).
- Secure executive commitment to make sure that data quality will be supported.

CRM: An International Perspective

26

Are there substantial differences when implementing a CRM system internationally versus implementing a system in the United States? What are the differences and do they need to be taken into account prior to implementation or can they be addressed after implementation?

In this chapter, we respond to these and other important questions/issues associated with implementing CRM on a global basis. We will look at key similarities between an international versus a U.S. implementation, then at key differences, and close with key lessons that should be kept in mind when implementing an international CRM project.

CRM is now very much a global business. While the CRM industry got its start in North America (particularly in the United States), the European CRM marketplace is in the process of a boom. The boom results from North American companies opening up offices overseas, and also from emerging European CRM software vendors and third-party players that specialize in CRM consulting, integration, and training/support. Several of the leading

European CRM companies now have customized their software for the North American market with considerable success.

In today's increasingly global marketplace, more and more companies are specifying an international CRM system from the outset. Whereas the international implementation of CRM used to wait until the U.S. system was up and running, today the U.S. and the international version of the system often get specified, customized, and implemented simultaneously.

Given these two observations, let us now turn attention to key similarities and differences between an international versus a U.S. implementation.

Similarities Between U.S. and International CRM Implementations

Key *similarities* include:

1. **The Use of a Structured Methodology to Prioritize Business Needs**
   ISM has had the pleasure of working with several international CRM projects over the past 17 years. This experience has taught us that whether in North America, Latin America, Europe, Asia, or elsewhere, it is imperative that the company uses a structured methodology to ensure that global business needs, where appropriate, rise to the top of the business prioritization list.

   For example, ISM worked with a European company, which at the time sold mining and construction equipment to North and South America (approximately 50 percent of their global sales), to Europe (approximately 30 percent), and to Asia (the remaining 20 percent). The initiative to implement a CRM system came from the top executive of North and South American sales, and the initiative began with a brainstorming session and field visits with top U.S. and Canadian managers.

   The initiative quickly met with resistance from European managers, who had been planning to implement their own CRM initiative but with the use of a very different methodology. After considerable transatlantic discussions, a decision was taken at the board level to make the CRM initiative a global project. Shortly thereafter ISM met with company managers in Asia, Europe and South America and applied the same methodology to all parts of the company. This was particularly important in that the company had recently launched a global account management project and the proposed CRM initiative played a critical role in ensuring that the global account management project was implemented in a similar manner in all parts of the world.

2. Effective Data Synchronization

Whether the CRM project is U.S. or international, it is imperative that the data synchronization piece of the initiative works effectively. Data synchronization is the exchange of customer files and other information from field personnel with headquarters personnel or systems, and vice versa. The importance of data synchronization cannot be underestimated particularly if the CRM system is to support the sharing of files across borders (i.e., for a global account management system). Remember that all countries do not have similar technical capabilities (i.e., data communications), which may be required to ensure that proper data synchronization takes place in more than one country. Plan this aspect of an international CRM system carefully. Web-based CRM systems to a great extent can eliminate this need for synchronization because the CRM data is centralized and available only when a user is connected to the CRM system via the Web.

3. Proper Training and Support

Regardless of the scope of the CRM initiative, training and support remain an essential ingredient in U.S. as well as international projects. As an example, ISM worked with an American food manufacturer, which at the time did approximately 30 percent of their global sales within Europe. When this company launched its global CRM initiative, the company immediately created a training and support plan for users in the United States as well as in Europe.

During the initial training sessions, it became very clear that although the company sold the same products on both sides of the Atlantic, and that the American and European personnel had similar training and support needs for the new CRM system, there were substantial differences in the levels of computer literacy within the company. This, in turn, implied the need for a consistent global training program for the new CRM system, yet sufficient customization within the training program to support the different levels of computer literacy within the company. Of course, adequate CRM application and hardware support is essential as well. Therefore, it is important to check the support options offered in the country where the CRM systems will be implemented, as the vendors may offer differing levels of support and options depending upon geographic region.

Differences Between U.S. and International CRM Implementations

Key *differences* between an international versus a U.S. implementation include:

1. **Differing Business Needs**

   Not all companies, particularly companies with international operations, are able to implement a similar business strategy. This in turn implies that divisions or regions of the same company may in fact have different business needs as concerns CRM support. As an example, ISM worked with an American high-tech manufacturing company whose distribution channel strategy in Europe differs considerably from that of their distribution channel strategy in the United States. Whereas business strategy in the United States is based around the growing independent reseller distribution channel, the European business strategy is based more around the Value Added Reseller (VAR) distribution channel.

   This difference in distribution channel strategy has considerable impact on what types of information need to be gathered and distributed within this company's proposed CRM system. For example, it is reasonable to gather needed sales and marketing information from VARs since they purchase directly from the European office. It is considerably more difficult, however, to obtain sales and marketing information from independent resellers, who buy from VARs in some cases or from large original equipment manufacturers (OEMs) and who really don't want you to know too much about what they are doing.

   These types of business issues should be discussed long before you embark on an international CRM system, and the differing needs should be identified. Whereas a common business strategy or a common set of business needs may not be possible or even desired, it is important that these differences be understood and taken into account when designing and implementing your CRM system.

2. **Differing Technical Infrastructures**

   Another area of difference that often appears in an international CRM system is that of differing technical infrastructures. As an example, ISM has assisted one of the world's leading international oil companies in their efforts to install their second generation of CRM software.

Whereas the United States technical infrastructure of this company had been based in large part on a client/server infrastructure supported by an emerging data warehouse, the European technical infrastructure had been based on a mainframe computer located in one European country and connected to 16 other European countries via data communications leased lines.

Moreover, the hardware in place for this company's field personnel varied considerably depending on the location. Given that data synchronization across borders in Europe often can be difficult, the company decided to try a Lotus Notes solution using Lotus Notes servers in each European country. This differs considerably from the approach suggested for the U.S., which had little difficulty with data communications or data synchronization. In the case of m-CRM, or mobile CRM, wireless standards in the U.S. differ from other parts of the world and the infrastructure and usage of mobile technologies in Europe is in some ways more advanced than in the U.S. The message is clear: be very careful in assessing the technical infrastructure available in regions where you are considering rollout of a CRM system.

Given that differing technical infrastructures can be very costly in the long term to maintain and support, ISM's oil company client formed a global technical infrastructure team who was tasked with coming up with one global technical infrastructure recommendation.

3. **Issues of Internationalization/Localization**
Given that different countries use different languages, have different currencies, work with different financial statements, have different laws about gathering information on customers and individuals, etc., it becomes critical that an international CRM system take these differences into account. The need for customized offerings has become more critical since the emergence of the Euro, triangulation, and other internationalization/localization realities. For example, ISM has worked with a leading air courier express company which has offices in greater than 100 countries around the world and therefore has many internationalization/localization issues to contend with.

Whereas the manager of their international CRM system would like to have a common core module in all offices around the world (facilitating, for example, global account management or financial reporting), this manager also recognizes quite correctly that different countries do require customization to the program taking into account the unique environment within that country (which hopefully can be made without harming the common core module). The need for customization often poses quite a challenge to an international CRM system, and while it may seem outdated or unreal, it is surprising to know how many of today's CRM software packages simply will not or don't do an adequate job with support for multiple languages, multiple currencies, or multiple date formats.

Summary

So, what should be kept in mind when implementing an international CRM project?

Recommendation #1:   International implementation issues should be considered, if at all possible, prior to initial implementation of your CRM system. If this means delaying the project a few weeks or months, consider this time well spent. Planning upfront will save considerable time in the long run.

Recommendation #2:   While similarities do exist, there are substantial differences between the implementation of an international versus a U.S. CRM system. It is important to acknowledge that although striving for as much similarity as possible stands as a priority, differences do and will exist and some sort of vehicle must be utilized for addressing and hopefully resolving these differences early on in the project.

Recommendation #3:   Plan your international CRM efforts well, and be sure to create and work with one or more international superuser groups throughout the life of the project. In addition to providing the input for addressing and hopefully resolving differences early on, superuser group personnel play a critical role in coordinating the involvement of the different players in an international CRM system, namely top management (the funders), the information technology team (the builders or technical supporters), and field/headquarters personnel (the users).

Those companies who have taken the time to acknowledge and incorporate the above recommendations into their international CRM system have tended to do well. As is always the case, by doing your homework first and automating second, you are increasing your likelihood of success.

The Future Direction of CRM

27

How is CRM likely to evolve in the coming years? In Chapter 1, "Customer Relationship Management (CRM)—An Overview," I suggested that the CRM market is currently in transition. Industry growth has slowed from a 40 percent annual rate but still remains strong at a 20–30 percent annual clip. New players/products/services are abundant leading to an at times overwhelming feeling about which CRM solution(s) are best for them. Butting life cycles between client/server and Web-based e-customer vendors create complexity for the user. Doom and gloom findings from leading IT analysts are misleading but are catching the ear of their busy executives.

In Chapter 6, "CRM Business Application Trends," and Chapter 7, "CRM Technology Trends," I described a total of 23 trends that will impact the future direction of CRM. On the business side, there are eight business application trends that range from increased consolidations and mergers to increased availability of lead incubation and supply chain management functionality. On the technical side, there are 15 technical trends that range from the growing role of XML to increased use of EAI tools, portals, and Web services software infrastructure.

Here are an additional 12 CRM trends that are likely to shape the future the industry. Each of these trends are detailed below.

1. Increased executive attention
2. Customer contact centers and self-service
3. E-customers (B2B)
4. Supply chain integration
5. The real-time enterprise
6. XML, wireless, voice recognition technologies
7. Integration of CRM, e-CRM, and m-CRM applications
8. Thin client applications
9. Metrics
10. Implementation
11. Security and privacy
12. People, process, and technology

Increased Executive Attention

There has been a noticeable change among top management over the past year vis-à-vis their desire to get or keep CRM initiatives going within their company, to engage their customers in the process, and to extend their efforts out to both partners and suppliers. I have done a lot of thinking as to why this has been the case and have come up with a few reasons:

- The CRM value proposition (described in Chapter 10, "Creating Your CRM Business Case") is strong, relevant, and convincing.
- There are many "best-in-class" companies that have been very successful implementing CRM (e.g., Cisco, Dell) who are telling their stories to public audiences and magazines.
- Executives are feeling the impact of successful CRM initiatives, regrettably not always their own.

For example, ISM recently received a telephone call from a leading global book publisher seeking help in getting their CRM initiative off-the-ground. When I asked about their expected implementation timeframe, the executive responded, "Immediately!" When I asked why the urgency, the publisher explained that they were being negatively impacted by their two largest competitors who were using CRM automation as a way to lock out sales from this publisher and to lock in long-term customer loyalty. In another example, the president of a global pharmaceuticals company desired CRM throughout the U.S. based on his positive experience of implementing CRM successfully throughout their Canadian subsidiary.

Likely impact on CRM: As with so many new initiatives, ongoing education will be a key success factor. Provided executives keep asking questions, and provided they keep getting valuable answers, it is likely that executives will continue to drive the CRM revolution.

Customer Contact Centers and Self-Service

As described in Chapter 20, "Ensuring Consistent Customer Service Across Channels," customer service centers, which currently are largely telephony-based, increasingly are converting over to customer contact centers. The main benefit of a customer contact center is that it allows a customer to call, fax, e-mail, Web chat, etc., to one location and receive near or real-time assistance. A logical next step for companies that have initiated customer contact centers is to extend their centers out to their customers using customer self-service functionality.

The Web provides quick response to customer needs, and may even reduce costs via customer self-servicing. Customers are able to easily access a company's Web site, obtain needed information, place an order, check on the status of an order, initiate a complaint, check on the status of a complaint, look into their credit status, make a recommendation, or even schedule an appointment with a company representative via an interactive calendar. If during the session the customer becomes unhappy with the self-service option, he/she can request assisted service options like a "call-me-now" button on the Web screen that alerts a customer service agent to call the customer back immediately. Additional assisted service options such as interactive text chat can be initiated via a "lets-chat-now" button on the Web screen; a customer service agent will initiate dialogue with the customer either reactively or proactively, if the customer agent has been monitoring the Web site for customers who may be having trouble. Not only will customers get better and quicker service, but companies can indeed save significant costs in their customer servicing efforts (see Chapter 19, "E-Service and CRM").

CRM vendors increasingly are adding customer self-service features to their software offerings. These vendors include Nortel, eGain, Firstwave, Interact Commerce, KANA, Pivotal, Staffware, PeopleSoft, Worldtrak, and many others.

Likely Impact on CRM: E-customers are driving the move towards the customer contact center, and CRM vendors are responding with increasingly sophisticated tool sets. Customer self-service functionality not only can enhance customer loyalty, but also can provide cost savings over more traditional means of customer service.

E-Customers (B2B)

The Web allows smarter, more powerful customers to access your company's information at any time and from any place. E-customers are an identifiable market segment who wish to interact with a company at any time, using whatever media channel (e.g., cell phone, e-mail, etc.) the customer has available. The onus is on the company to provide all interaction capability that the e-customer demands and to "know" the customer by not only tracking and remembering all interactions across multiple touch points, but also to be able to analyze customer interaction information and to learn the profile of the e-customer in order to better serve the needs of that customer. This is particularly relevant for B2B companies, because the vast majority of e-commerce revenues are being generated in B2B rather than B2C exchanges. While the e-customer may currently be a select market segment, the growth of the e-customer seems inevitable (see Figure 27.1).

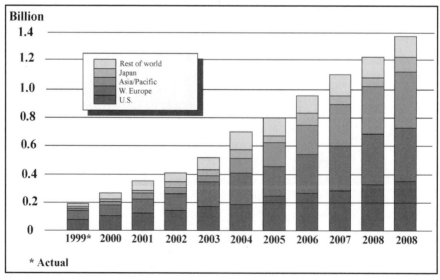

FIGURE 27.1
Global Internet users.

Likely impact on CRM: E-customers will continue to grow in numbers. CRM automation software must accommodate e-customers' choices of media (e.g., phone, fax, e-mail, Web chat, etc.) and offer additional services such as personalization, security, and communities of interest to attract and keep e-customers. Moreover, CRM software vendors will need to build into their software offering the ability to track, analyze, and deliver content to e-customers.

Supply Chain Integration

This trend impacts companies seeking to create partnerships within the supply chain by locking together suppliers, manufacturers, or other distribution channel members including customers. Supply chain integration includes both business-in-business functionality (offered by companies such as i2 Technologies) as well as business-to-business functionality (offered by companies such as SeeCommerce).

Wal-Mart was an early leader in the area of supply chain integration as it created partnerships with a limited number of suppliers and worked closely with their selected suppliers to drive distribution costs down at Wal-Mart while agreeing to long-term business contracts with selected suppliers. Besides linking directly to supply chain members, companies are finding ways to link their CRM systems to Web-based supplier exchanges for e-procurement; these links are more common because of development of new technologies (e.g., XML) that have open architectures which facilitate linkages of various systems.

Likely impact on CRM: CRM automation software will need to accommodate simple, direct links to and from the different supply chain members engaged in a company's efforts. This can benefit the company as well as the e-customer.

The Real-Time Enterprise

A new business model is poised to emerge among companies that recognized the value of true customer loyalty and guaranteed long-term profitability: the real-time enterprise. This represents a fundamental paradigm shift in the way companies conduct business. Call it "business in an instant." It will be a world in which the words "please hold while I check on that" and "let me get back to you with that information" will virtually disappear from the vocabulary of service reps and salespeople.

In a real-time enterprise all company departments, customers, suppliers, and partners are electronically connected via internal and Internet applications (i.e., the e-enablement of all business functions). This allows the company's information systems to function like a 24-hour live video cam on its operations, instantly alerting managers to changes in customer demand, competitive situations, inventory, availability of supplies, and profitability. Real-time enterprises will benefit from recent technological advancements such as real-time computing and e-business. These technologies will allow companies to streamline business processes and manage customer relationships with such proficiency that they will achieve sustainable productivity gains, decreased costs, and long-term profitability. The result will be a fundamental and permanent economic change in the companies' operations.

Consider the following scenarios:

- Customers will have 24×7 access to their suppliers. They can place and check on orders, pay bills or check their account information, check inventory and availability, etc. For example, a customer trying to purchase a widget discovers that it is out of stock, but is able to track exactly when it will be available. In some cases this might include knowing when the manufacturer's own suppliers will have raw materials available to build the widget and when the manufacturer is planning to build it, and when it can then be shipped.

- All employees within an organization will have access to the same, comprehensive information on each and every customer in real time, because all functions and departments are linked electronically. In this scenario a customer purchases a widget online. At the moment the order is placed, accounting is notified to send a bill, manufacturing is notified of the change in inventory, and shipping is notified to send the product. Another scenario might have the customer lodging a complaint with customer service. At that same moment the sales account executive is notified of both the problem and the resolution.

A real-time enterprise strategy is so comprehensive that every function and department within the company will have one view of customers and operations. This is a strategy so irresistible to customers that it will cement their loyalty by allowing them to communicate and conduct business deep within companies however and whenever they want. It will examine how the triumvirate of people, process, and technology are integral to the success of creating a real-time enterprise and show how some companies that have successfully implemented customer relationship management are well on their way to becoming real-time enterprises so powerful that competitors will have no choice but to do the same.

Likely impact on CRM: Assuming the real-time enterprise gains traction—and I and many other leading authorities strongly believe it will—CRM will serve as the foundation for developing a real-time enterprise strategy. This means that companies will need to experience CRM prior to moving onto creating their real-time enterprise.

XML, Wireless, and Voice Recognition Technologies

The expanded use of XML, wireless, and voice recognition technologies within CRM has been documented in many CRM-related publications and is manifested in the most recent releases of many CRM software applications. As detailed in Chapter 7 "CRM Technology Trends," XML is playing a growing role within the CRM industry. XML is very flexible in that it provides a data standard that can encode the content, semantics, and schemata for a wide variety of cases. The functionality can be as simple as a document definition or as complex as a stand-alone applet that operates in a disconnected mode.

The growing role of wireless in CRM also has been described in Chapter 7. Wireless technology is available today. Vendors such as Microsoft, OracleMobile, Sun Microsystems, Palm, Ericsson, AvantGo, ThinAirApps, Openwave, and Broadbeam, among others, are investing large amounts of R&D funds to bring wireless application architectures to market. Numerous CRM vendors offer wireless applications. In fact, based on ISM surveys with CRM vendors, 50 percent of all CRM software applications will work in a wireless environment by the end of 2002. This figure should increase to 75 percent by the end of 2003, and 90 percent by the end of 2004.

Voice recognition technology will occur at a slower pace. Again, based on ISM surveys with CRM vendors, 50 percent of all CRM software applications will work using voice recognition by the end of 2003. This figure should increase to 70 percent by the end of 2003, and 80 percent by the end of 2004. IDC estimates that by 2004, there will be a $16 billion market for voice recognition applications that enhance customer relationships.

Voice recognition technologies provide the ability to identify customers by their "voiceprints," eliminating the need for them to enter personal identification numbers or other passwords to access account information, pay bills, etc. Voice recognition technologies make customer self-service applications easier to use and provide stronger security than passwords since a person cannot easily duplicate another customer's voice. Good examples of voice recognition technologies used in the CRM industry include that of Sound Advantage and JustTalk. Sound Advantage's voice recognition technologies can be integrated with FrontRange's CRM software products. Using Sound Advantage's voice recognition technologies in GoldMine PLUS Voice, users can access information from the GoldMine CRM software application over the telephone simply by voice commands. JustTalk is another company offering voice recognition technologies which can currently be integrated with PeopleSoft's CRM product offering.

I have always been impressed by voice recognition. Imagine a world where voice recognition is the main way of giving and getting needed CRM information. No more keyboards. No more typing. Imagine the impact this will have on today's CRM skeptics!

Here is an interesting example of wireless and voice recognition together. In 2000, Jiffy Lube created a program called "My Jiffy Lube Reminder" which was tested in 49 stores in Houston and is now being extended to a number of nationwide franchises. The program allows customers to choose the particular media channel to be reminded of the need to change their oil. For example, under one option, a voice reminder about a scheduled oil change is delivered to a customer's cell phone via ShopTalk Networks voice-enabled CRM application, provided that the customer has opted-in to the program.

Likely impact on CRM: CRM software will need to incorporate/access the latest information technology applications/tools from within the CRM automation software application.

Integration of CRM, E-CRM, and M-CRM Applications _____

Traditional CRM systems are company employee-centric. E-CRM applications as well as m-CRM applications (the "m" stands for "mobile," as in mobile telephone), on the other hand, tend to be more customer-centric. CRM, e-CRM, and m-CRM applications have some overlapping functionality, but the architecture and delivery mechanisms currently vary considerably. For example, a traditional CRM customer service application tends to be designed to enable company customer service agents to record primarily inbound customer requests, issues, etc.; its underlying architecture may not be Web-based. A typical e-CRM or m-CRM application like a customer contact center or an inquiry form has its foundation in Web architecture, and is set up so the customer can help themselves to customer service information, request assistance from a company agent, or the customer may receive proactive support (e.g., assisted browsing) from the agent that has been monitoring the actions of the customer on the company Web site.

Web-based e-CRM and m-CRM applications enable the customer to engage with a company using familiar Web technology such as a Web browser. This greatly enhances user acceptance and allows for increased use of creative Web-based applications.

Likely impact on CRM: Today's consumer is demanding comprehensive, integrated CRM environments with various implementation and delivery options. As more and more CRM software packages adopt a Web-based architecture, expect to see integration between CRM, e-CRM, and m-CRM applications.

Thin Client Applications _____

ISM's CRM Software Testing Laboratory is witnessing a definite movement among CRM software vendors towards thin client applications, while continuing to retain support for thick client products. Over the last few years, CRM software vendors have had to come up with new architectures to accommodate increased Internet traffic and other related demands. Several CRM vendors have embraced new technological directions such as moving to an N-tiered, Web-centric, XML-enabled architecture and used this as a marketing message. Many other vendors have remained back in the client/server era, but bolted a few Web interfaces onto their product in order to remain competitive. Thin client technology that requires little more than a Web browser on the client workstation is becoming much more prevalent. Thick clients, while still offered and/or supported by some CRM vendors, are being replaced with thin client offerings. CRM vendors that have introduced thin client applications are nonetheless still providing support for their clients using their thick client products. For example, PeopleSoft, which recently offered a CRM system with a completely Web-based architecture, still currently provides support for its Web-enabled Vantive CRM applications.

Likely impact on CRM: As a result of thin client applications, CRM will become available to more people in more places using many new computer devices. Thin client–only applications do have their drawbacks especially for the occasionally connected user. For this reason, expect to see more thin-client CRM applications in conjunction that retain thick client options. As Web services take hold, and wireless CRM applications become the norm, the continued need for thick client applications is likely to come under attack.

Metrics

Executives have been exposed to the CRM acronym for several years now and they are increasingly understanding what CRM means and what it can offer. Nonetheless, executives who will be funding a CRM system may not understand how the benefits of the CRM system will be realized. Executives therefore increasingly demand evidence that the CRM system will deliver on the promises espoused by CRM system proponents. In other words, it is increasingly important to devise metrics for the CRM system in the form of a CRM Business Case, in order that the CRM system will be sufficiently funded and supported over the course of the project. As described in the Chapter 10, "Creating Your CRM Business Case," the CRM Business Case typically determines baselines as well as sets the measurements for the goals of the CRM project. For instance, one goal of the CRM system might be to reduce customer response time in the customer contact center. Another goal might be to increase win rates by a certain percentage. These metrics must be defined, documented, and measured on a regular basis.

Likely impact on CRM: Executives responsible for funding CRM projects will increasingly require distinct metrics and measurement plans as justification for a CRM initiative. This should be seen as a positive development in the CRM industry, where, to date the success/failure of too many CRM initiatives has been measured on subjective rather than objective criteria.

Implementation

Without a doubt, the weakest link in the CRM industry has been and continues to be implementation excellence. With implementation costs typically running anywhere from .5 to 2.5 times the cost of software, the time is ripe to help companies better understand whether their implementation money is being well spent. Being pragmatic for a moment, for obvious reasons it is not always in the interest of implementation firms to take the most cost-effective route. What is the best way to avoid having implementation firms blame CRM software vendors and vice versa while the company is forced to spend more and more money to get to a resolution? In defense of the implementation firms, how do implementation firms hold fickle customers to a signed specification?

Likely impact on CRM: The CRM industry as a whole is paying increased attention to implementation issues to ensure that implementation gets properly monitored and quality controlled. While this is potentially good news for the CRM industry, it requires and will depend on increased professionalism on behalf of the implementation firms.

Security and Privacy

Security and privacy remain a top issue for most computer users, especially CRM users whose applications may contain sensitive company, customer, and competitive data. There are issues of access to systems, access to data, security of e-mail transmissions, risk management, etc. Moreover, these issues may extend to members of a company's supply/demand chain (e.g., distributors, suppliers) as well as customers. Implementing a CRM/e-business security program is complex and can be expensive (see Chapter 24, "Addressing CRM System Security Risks"). Nonetheless, when you compare the cost of security to the cost of doing nothing (a potential problem), remember that according to industry surveys and the Federal Bureau of Investigation, organizations are experiencing more attacks than ever before.

Think about this: If your CRM and e-business systems are compromised, what might be the damage done in terms of lost revenue? What adverse affect on customer loyalty would you incur if your systems went off-line for an extended period? Managing the security risk rather than avoiding it is the top priority for business executives.

Likely impact on CRM: CRM automation software will likely be enhanced with security features that go beyond the security functionality of the underlying tools and technologies. Managing rather than eliminating security risk should be the goal.

People, Process, and Technology _____

Many companies that attempt to implement CRM within their organizations fall short of the expectations that are created. Why does this happen? All too often, CRM is seen as a panacea—a way to make an organization more productive and more responsive to customers using software. Unfortunately, if the organization does not have good, strong, time-tested customer-facing business processes, automation will only make bad processes worse quicker! In addition, there is inevitably resistance to change within an organization, which can inhibit a CRM initiative. Therefore, it is imperative that change management issues associated with the CRM system, as well as other people issues like training, communication of CRM system objectives, schedules, and progress be addressed throughout the CRM project.

The success of the CRM system depends on how well people, process, and technology integration is achieved (see Chapter 3, "Successful CRM: Getting the People, Process, and Technology Mix Right"). This is complicated since the people, process and technology mix changes over the course of the implementation. For example, people and process issues are very important in the initial planning stages, while the technology component becomes much more important in the implementation stages of the project.

Likely impact on CRM: Failure to address people, process, and technology as an integrated set of issues will compromise the CRM initiative. The good news is that software vendors, implementation firms, users and advisors all have come to realize the importance of getting the people, process, and technology mix right throughout a CRM program. This should translate into increasingly more successful CRM initiatives.

Summary _____

As in the theater, timing is everything. I believe that now is the time to understand the impact that these twelve CRM industry trends will have on your existing or planned CRM efforts. Carefully consider these trends as a part of your overall planning process and you will likely see the benefit of your foresight as you implement your CRM efforts.

Understand the importance of technology, but be careful not to get caught up in the technology game. As the founder of American Airlines' Sabre reservations systems, Max Hopper, already warned us many years back, because changes in information technology happen so quickly, and the consequences of falling behind are so devastating, companies will either master the technology or die. Companies will have to run harder just to stay in place—a technology treadmill. As indicated in this chapter as well as throughout the text, remember however that technological wizardry on its own produces very few, if any, practical business results. In short, think of CRM as a three-step process:

1. Determine the prioritized, CRM business functions to automate.
2. Ensure user buy-in.
3. Use CRM technology to help you accomplish prioritized business functions.

After 17 years in the CRM industry, having helped greater than 300 best-in-class companies to automate their CRM programs, I still am a great believer in CRM's bright future. I sincerely hope that you and your company can apply some of the knowledge from this book to your current or planned CRM efforts, and that your journey is safe, successful, and fun.

ISM's Top 30 CRM Software Selections

Clarify eFrontOffice v. 10.2 — by Amdocs Limited

Applix iEnterprise v. 8.3.0 — by Applix, Inc.

Ardexus MODE v. 2.2b — by Ardexus Corporation

Connect-Care v. 7.0 — by Connect-Care, LLC.

E.piphany E.5 — by E.piphany, Inc.

Firstwave eCRM v. 6.1 — by Firstwave Technologies, Inc.

GoldMine FrontOffice v. 5.5 — by FrontRange Solutions, Inc.

Abalon CRM 2001 SP6 — by Industri Matematik International Corporation

SalesLogix.net v. 5.2 — by Interact Commerce Corporation

J.D. Edwards CRM v. 1.0 — by J.D. Edwards & Company

CMS 5.0 — by Oncontact Software Corporation

ONYX Enterprise 2001 — by ONYX Software

ExSellence v. 4.0 — by Optima Technologies, Inc.

Oracle CRM Suite 11i v. 5.5 — by Oracle Corporation

PeopleSoft 8.1 CRM — by PeopleSoft, Inc.

Pivotal eRelationship — by Pivotal Corporation

e-point 5.2 — by Point Information Systems Ltd.

PowerCerv CRM v. 9.0 — by PowerCerv Technologies

Salesforce.com — by Salesforce.com

SalesPage open.space 3.5 — by SalesPage Technologies, Inc.

mySAP CRM 3.0 — by SAP America, Inc.

iAvenue 6.0 — by Saratoga Systems, Inc.

Siebel 2001 — by Siebel Systems, Inc.

Enterprise SalesMaker v. 6.4 — by Software Innovation, Inc.

Staffware Process Suite v. 9.0 — by Staffware plc

Visual Elk 8.1 — by StayinFront, Inc.

SimpleRM v. 2.1 — by TriVium Systems, Inc.

marketing.manager 5.0 — by update.com software AG

Upshot — by Upshot Corporation

Worldtrak v. 5.3 — by Worldtrak Corporation

Sources to Assist in CRM Software Selection

Although we feel that *CRM Automation* is a very comprehensive resource on CRM issues, there may be additional CRM industry information that you desire, as described below.

Publications

Many magazines feature CRM-related information, provide articles about CRM software and issues that are specific to an area such as e-business, lead tracking, sales force automation, etc. The magazines that have regular coverage of CRM issues are *Sales & Marketing Management* and *CRM*. Other publications feature material about CRM, as well as computer and software issues, and sometimes provide both software reviews and analysis. These publications include: *Customer Support Management*, *Field Force Automation*, *Intelligent Enterprise*, *ComputerWorld*, *Selling Power*, *Sales & Marketing News and Strategies*, *Wireless Review*, *PC Magazine*, and *The Industry Standard*.

A word of caution here: articles found in these publications may be based solely on vendor input, whereby vendors fill out and return the magazine's standard form along with promotional literature and brochures. You should note whether the magazine has actually tested and analyzed the software in question.

Trade Shows/Conferences

For those who have the time, trade shows and conferences can be an excellent way to find out more about CRM automation. Speakers with expertise in this field can provide useful information. Also, trade shows and conferences often have a vendor exhibition attached to the show or conference, where you can view CRM software.

To decide which trade show or conference you should attend, we recommend asking the vendors. Many vendors will provide trade show or conference brochures along with free passes to the exhibition. Among the most prominent trade shows pertaining to CRM are the CRM Conference and Exposition put on by DCI (DCI is headquartered in Andover, MA, 978-470-3870, *www.dci.com*), and several local events put on by chapters of Sales & Marketing Executives (SMEI). The American Marketing Association also has conferences where sales and marketing automation is a regular topic. More information on dates and locations of the trade shows can be obtained by searching the Web.

Attending a CRM conference can provide you with a wealth of knowledge about industry trends, vendors, and products. In addition, these shows typically offer excellent seminars conducted by leading experts who can help direct you in your CRM quest. But because there's much information available and you have only a few days to take it all in, you need to prepare a game plan. Here are some guidelines:

Assess the show—Start by learning what the show has to offer. Ask the conference promoter to send a show guide with information on the technical seminars and special presentations, as well as an exhibitor listing and exhibition hall floor plan. Study the brochure and use it to schedule your activities. To avoid any scheduling conflicts, be sure to list the seminars you want to attend, including date, time, and room number. Once you get to the show, prepare a list of potential vendors to visit.

Determine your goals—To ensure that all of your company's CRM issues are addressed, make a list of goals you want to accomplish at the conference. If you're the only person from your company attending the show, ask colleagues for their input.

Develop a specific plan for seeking expert advice—Plan to meet with seminar speakers. Be prepared with a list of questions about your project and issues that you want addressed. Set up a time to meet with experts when they have more time to discuss your project. If that isn't an option, keep a list in hand and talk to important speakers immediately following the seminar. Speakers are interested in furthering the industry and helping CRM projects succeed—so don't be shy.

Research show exhibitors—Use the Web to gain preliminary information about a company's niche, products, and customers. If you need more in-depth information, talk to a representative. You'll save valuable time at the show by focusing only on those companies capable of matching your project's technical and business requirements. Be sure to take advantage of all these vendors being located in the same place by arranging a demonstration of each promising CRM software package.

Talk to the show promoter—Conference promoters can usually provide additional tips and information to help take the stress out of attending an out-of-town conference. For instance, many provide shuttle bus service to and from the conference center through selected hotels. Also, ask about hotel and airfare discounts that might be available.

Remember: Attending a conference is an investment in time, as well as money. By devising a strategy before embarking on your journey, you'll get more value out of the price of attendance.

Web Sites and Web Forums

There are now numerous Web sites that provide CRM-related information, resources, and links to other CRM Web sites. If you want to find background information about CRM industry topics and software, we suggest that you peruse the following Web sites:

- IT Toolbox CRM, *www.crmassist.com*
- Destination CRM, *www.destinationcrm.com*
- CRMCommunity.com, *www.crmcommunity.com*
- CRM Forum, *www.crm-forum.com*

- searchCRM, *www.searchcrm.com*
- CRMDAILY, *www.crmdaily.com*
- Information Week, *www.informationweek.com*
- Computer World, *www.computerworld.com*
- CNET.com, *www.cnet.com*
- ISM, *www.ismguide.com*

Research Companies

There are also a number of organizations that publish research about information systems technology, sometimes CRM technology, CRM industry statistics, etc. Those organizations include:

- ISM
- IDC
- Aberdeen
- Forrester
- Cahner's In-Stat
- Yankee Group
- AMR Research

Although the quality and price of these directories and publications can vary considerably, they do provide analyses that can be useful.

Support/Training References

The following companies can provide support/training for members of your organization. Some also provide integration services for selected CRM software products:

- **Cambridge Technology Partners Headquarters**
  8 Cambridge Center
  Cambridge, MA 02142
  Tel: 617-374-9800
  Web: *www.ctp.com*

- **C3i Inc.**
  Four Silicon Alley, 83 Maiden Ln., 8th Floor
  New York, NY 10038
  Tel: 800-310-3606 x509
  Web: *www.c3i-inc.com*

- **Productivity Point International, Inc.**
  4515 Falls of Neuse Rd., Suite 150
  Raleigh, NC 27609
  Tel: 919-326-6300
  Web: *www.propoint.com*

- **Tech Resource Group, Inc**
  3301 Benson Dr.
  Raleigh, NC 27609
  Tel: 800-874-0062
  Web: *www.trginc.com*

- **Clarkston Potomac**
  2605 Meridian Parkway, Suite 100
  Durham, NC 27713-2294
  Tel: 800-652-4274
  Web: *www.clarkstonpotomac.com*

- **AnswerThink Consulting Group**
  1400 Fashion Island Blvd., Suite 1050
  San Mateo, CA 94404
  Tel: 650-356-0421d
  Web: *www.answerthink.com*

- **Extraprise Group**
  27 Melcher St.
  Boston, MA 02210
  Tel: 617-880-4001
  Web: *www.extraprise.com*

- **Breakaway Solutions, Inc.**
  50 Rowes Wharf
  Boston, MA 02110
  Tel: 617-960-3400
  Web: *www.breakaway.com*

- **KPMG Consulting**
  (Many global locations)
  Web: *www.kpmgconsulting.com*

Software Categories, Vendors, and Pricing

CRM Software Applications

The goal of most customer relationship management software vendors is to help users increase sales productivity. Despite this common objective, vendors differ greatly in terms of the software functions they feel are most important to help enhance customer relationships. Based on our research, we have been able to identify three main software categories:

1. *Software applications that primarily perform business functions particular to one area of the overall customer relationship model.* ISM refers to these software packages as "point solutions." These software packages are offered by the development company as stand-alone solutions, or through partnering arrangements with other CRM vendors. Examples of some point solutions are portals, product/price configurators and proposal generators, marketing encyclopedia or collaboration tools, and marketing automation and lead enhancement. Matrix Technology Group is a company that offers excellent marketing automation software solutions, which manage marketing campaigns and provide for

lead enhancement. Norkom Technologies offers a robust business intelligence tool in the form of a portal, which performs comprehensive data analysis. An example of a software package that is specific to graphical territory assignment/alignment is BusinessMap PRO from ESRI.

2. *Enhanced contact management software that offers basic enterprise account/ contact management, activity tracking, and scheduling, as well as some sales force automation and marketing capabilities (e.g., sales cycle analysis, opportunity management).* Within this group, it should be noted that the complexity, functionality, and customization of these packages vary considerably. Many sales and marketing automation software packages fall into this category. An example of a basic contact management package is ACT! (Interact Commerce Corporation). The more sophisticated contact management packages offer features such as telesales and campaign management capabilities. An example of a sophisticated contact management package is Entice! by the Multiactive Corporation.

3. *CRM software "systems" that offer comprehensive enterprise-wide customer relationship management solutions.* These systems are typically modular and highly customizable, and support major databases and operating systems. Many of these vendors offer sales force automation, marketing automation, customer service and support modules. Examples include Clarify eFrontOffice v. 10.2 by Amdocs, Siebel 2001 by Siebel Systems, Pivotal eRelationship by Pivotal, and Applix iEnterprise v. 8.3.0 by Applix. Many of our Top 30 software packages fall into this category.

CRM Software Vendors

The CRM industry is comprised of a diverse group of vendors that vary in size, but more importantly in specialty and product offering. When selecting a CRM software vendor, attention should be given not only to the product characteristics, but also to the expertise of the vendor. Post-sales support and adequate training are critical to the overall success of your customer relationship management system.

Some vendors offer very comprehensive training and support programs, with 24-hour telephone support, on-site support, Internet/Web forums with news and updates, fax on demand service for technical and marketing documents, online training, etc. This is particularly relevant to companies who subscribe to an ASP (application service provider) service for their automation system.

Most low- and mid-tier vendors who market out-of-the-box CRM software solutions will support and train large clients directly, but typically rely on value added resellers (VARs) or partners for training and support of smaller clients. On the other hand, vendors who sell high-end systems usually handle training, customization, and support themselves.

The expertise, support, and training options offered by vendors vary extensively, based in part on the number of personnel these vendors can assign to customer support and training. Among the Top 30 software vendors, there were no companies with less than 16 employees, and four companies had over 5,000 employees. Interestingly, 40 percent of the Top 30 vendors have more than 500 employees. Figures C.1 and C.2 below depict the number of employees and years in business for the Top 30 vendors, respectively.

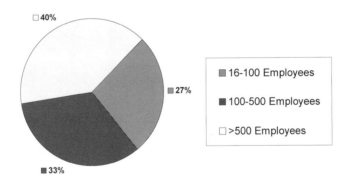

FIGURE C.1
The number of employees in the Top 30 CRM vendor companies.

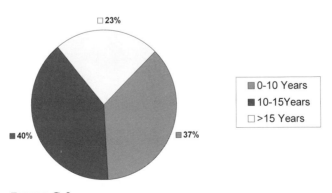

FIGURE C.2
The number of years in business of the Top 30 CRM vendor companies.

Pricing

While the search for the right customer relationship management software should not be based primarily on software prices, price is and will always be an important factor in deciding which system to buy. The ideal way to select software is to find a number of software packages suited for your current (and future) needs, and then compare those packages by price as well as performance. When comparing prices of customer relationship management software, the following points should be addressed:

- **Software functionality and features**—It is very true that you get what you pay for. There are a variety of reasons why some CRM software packages are priced higher than others (e.g., comprehensiveness of functions, ability to customize, databases supported, etc.). Thus, when you look at software prices, be careful to examine exactly what each software vendor is offering for the stated price.

- **Sophistication of the functions included in the software**—While the software package may appear to offer a business function, it is worthwhile to examine the sophistication of each business function. The sophistication within a telemarketing, customer service, or sales forecasting function can be quite diverse, even though most software packages have all of the "neat" features, such as customer self-service, call reporting, etc. An example is forecasting, which can be based on advanced statistical calculations of extensive opportunity/sales information, or simply an estimated forecast value that is entered by sales reps in the field.

- **Ability to customize software**—The ability to customize a software package varies greatly from one package to the other. Some CRM packages come with a customization toolkit that allows the end user to customize the system extensively, e.g., modify and create new fields/screens, alter screen flows and menu options, etc. Other, less expensive packages offer only limited customization options, e.g., a few user-definable fields.

- **Price coverage**—Prior to comparing prices for different packages, it is extremely important to look at all the supplemental costs related to implementing a system. Does the price include training, support, source code, and upgrades? Are report generators included in the price? If not, how much do these add-ons cost? These expenses may in many cases exceed the price of the software itself, making comparisons difficult. Therefore, decide which additional services are needed and get accurate prices for these services before comparing system prices.

Until you have clearly defined your needs with respect to business functionality, technical features, and user friendliness/support, as well as the potential for each package to meet these needs, it will be difficult to fully compare prices. If possible, make sure that you also calculate the cost of training, support, and customization in your price comparison, because these services often form a critical proportion of your overall systems costs.

Figures C.3 and C.4 below depict the pricing of the software packages listed in Appendix A, and are a reasonable indication for the market as a whole. The high-end customer relationship management software such as Siebel 2001 by Siebel Systems may cost several hundred thousand dollars for a customized, multi-user system with 100 licensed users. On the other hand, an enhanced contact management package such as Entice! by Multiactive Software, Inc. can be purchased for around $15,000 for 25 users.

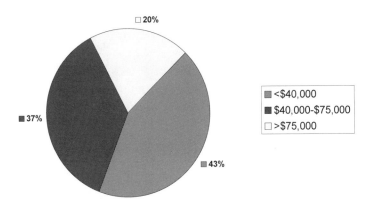

FIGURE C. 3
List prices for the Top 30 CRM software packages for a 25-user system.

Figure C.4 below depicts the server price range of the software packages selected for ISM's Top 30.

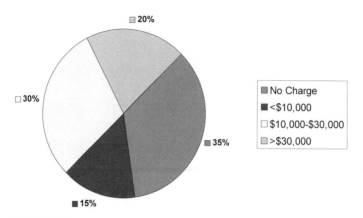

FIGURE C.4
Server prices for the Top 30 CRM softwarepackages.

Glossary
of Terms

ActiveX	A loosely defined set of technologies developed by Microsoft. ActiveX, formerly known as Network OLE control, is a segment of binary codes that can run only on the platform for which it was compiled. ActiveX is an outgrowth of two other Microsoft technologies called OLE (Object Linking and Embedding) and COM (Component Object Model). Understanding the entire ActiveX environment can be very confusing because it applies to a whole set of COM-based technologies.

ADSL	Asymmetric Digital Subscriber Line	A method of sending high-speed data (fast enough to carry digitized movies, for example) over the existing pair of wires from a telephone company's central office to most residences. A line-encoding scheme (that uses both carrier amplitude and carrier phase modulation) provides the following: • A high-speed, one-way data channel at up to 6 Mbits/s (enough for MPEG-compressed full-motion, full-color movies). • A full-duplex data channel at up to 576 Mbits/s, which can be subdivided in many ways to provide several simultaneous services. • Support for the existing analog POTS (e.g., voice, Group 3 Fax, etc.) even if the ADSL part fails. • Runs over a single copper twisted pair (ideally, the one that already exists between the user's home and the central office), up to 23,000 feet long.
AppCenter Server		AppCenter provides a variety of features for managing a large cluster of Web servers and application servers, including load balancing, fault tolerance, replication and testing tools. AppCenter Server is a product from Microsoft.
Applets		Software components that work with other software components to create or make up a full application. All components work within a GUI framework. Components can also work individually or within a Web browser.

Application Server		In local area networks, a node dedicated to hosting a networked application. This server usually does not host database applications, e-mail, or any other enterprise application. However, the application server usually seamlessly integrates with these or servers and services. Application servers are used most often in an "N-tiered" architecture.
API	Application Program Interface	A set of formalized software calls and routines that can be referenced by an application program to access underlying network services.
ASP	Application Service Provider	An application service provider uses the Internet or private extranet to host, manage, and support applications for companies. ASPs make it possible for enterprises to access enterprise class software solutions without deep investments in the software, hardware, and personnel to support those solutions.
Authentication		The function of ensuring that the receiver can positively identify the sender. Authentication is the process of forcing users to prove their identity before they can gain access to network resources.
Authorization		Authorization, or access control, is a method of establishing access privileges for users. Access can be granted to all network resources or restricted to specific LAN segments, network servers, devices, or applications. This task can be accomplished via password or encryption key.
Backbone		A transmission facility designed to interconnect low-speed distribution channels or clusters of dispersed user devices.

Bandwidth	The data-carrying capacity of a communications channel; measured (in Hertz) as the difference between the highest and lowest frequencies of the channel. Bandwidth varies depending on the transmission method.
Baud	Unit of signaling speed. The speed in baud is the number of line changes (in frequency, amplitude, etc.) or events per second. At low speeds, each event represents only one bit condition, and baud equals bps. As speed increases, each event represents more than one bit, and baud rate does not truly equal bps. But in common usage, baud rate and bps are often used interchangeably.
BizTalk	An initiative from Microsoft to spearhead XML usage. The BizTalk Framework provides a special set of XML tags that provide a common transport envelope for wrapping XML documents for business-to-business and application-to-application interoperability.
BizTalk Server	An integration product from Microsoft that combines elements of messaging middleware and Web-based application servers. It provides rules-based routing, conversion between data formats, and serves as a protocol bridge between HTTP, SMTP, MQSeries, and other applications.
BlackBerry	Handheld wireless e-mail device that integrates with e-mail servers and groupware applications such as MS Exchange. Research In Motion Limited (RIM) manufactures the device. The BlackBerry device additionally provides access to contact information, a personalized calendar, and a task list. Developers' toolkits are available for customer applications.

Boolean Logic		The "mathematics of logic," developed by English mathematician George Boole in the mid-19th century. Its rules govern logical functions (true/false). AND, OR, and NOT are the primary operations of Boolean logic. Boolean logic is turned into logic gates on circuit boards.
Bps	Bits Per Second	The basic unit of measurement for serial data transmission capacity; Kbps for kilo (thousands of) bits per second; Mbps for mega (millions of) bits per second; Gbps for giga (billions of) bits per second; Tbps for tera (trillions of) bits per second.
Broadband PCS		The new implementation of Personal Communication Services (PCS) using digital technologies such as GSM, CDMA, and TDMA.
Bulgy Client		A term used for computer clients that maintain more information than "Thin Client" computers such as network computers (NC computers). Bulgy Clients do not carry as much information as "Thick Clients" but can still operate without a network connection. Examples of Bulgy Clients would be portable units that run the Java, Windows CE, Geoworks, or PalmPilot operating systems.
Byte		A unit of information, used mainly in referring to data transfer, semiconductor capacity, and data storage; also referred to as a character; a group of eight (sometimes seven) bits used to represent a character.
C#	C Sharp	An object-oriented programming language from Microsoft that is based on C++ with elements from Visual Basic and Java. For example, like Java, C# provides automatic garbage collection, whereas C++ does not. Geared to Microsoft's .NET platform, C# supports XML and SOAP and has access to the .NET class library.

Cable Modem		A device that enables the user to hook up a PC to a local cable TV line and receive data at about 1.5 Mbps. This data rate far exceeds that of the prevalent 56 Kbps telephone modems and the 128 Kbps of ISDN. The data rate available is comparable to subscribers of Digital Subscriber Line (ADSL) telephone service.
Call Back		A system security procedure that calls back an incoming dial-up caller and verifies the validity of the caller, usually by means of a password, prior to allowing access to the system.
CCITT	Comité Consultatif International Télégraphique et Téléphonique	An international consultative committee that set worldwide communications standards (such as V.21, V.22, and X.25). Replaced by the ITU-TSS.
CDE	Common Desktop Environment	An e-mail platform common to UNIX platforms. This e-mail platform is also becoming a standard platform for Java-based environments.
CDMA	Code Division Multiple Access	An improvement on AMPS and TDMA cellular telephone. Uses a technology called direct-sequence spread-spectrum to provide more conversations for a given amount of bandwidth and digital service. Defines 64 channels (forward direction, transmitted from base station), which support a maximum of 63 simultaneous users, per 1.25-MHz frequency band taken from the standard AMPS allocation (this is 42 standard AMPS channels, which is 10 percent of an operator's 12.5-MHz bandwidth). Data transmission capability has not yet been developed.

CDPD	Cellular Digital Packet Data	An industry standard for data communication at 19,200 bps across unused portions of analog cellular voice channels. 138-byte packets of data are sent at 19,200 bits/s during gaps in conversations or on unused (e.g., no voice conversation established at that time) channels, using the full 30-kHz bandwidth of the channel. Voice always has priority.
Cellular		Based on the use of cells. Cellular telephone and data networks divide an area into regional cells, each of which has its own central transmission facilities; that way, every point in the area is within range of some transmission facility.
Centralized Data Warehouse		A data warehouse implementation in which a single warehouse serves the need of several business units simultaneously with a single data model, which spans the needs of the multiple business divisions.
CGI	Common Gateway Interface	A standard for interfacing external applications with information servers, such as HTTP or Web servers.
Circuit-Switching		A technique in which physical circuits (as opposed to virtual circuits) are transferred (switched) to complete connections. Contrast with a packet-switched network.
Client		A device or entity in a distributed computing architecture that requests services and information.
CO	Central Office	The building in which common telephone carriers terminate customer circuits (also known as Central Exchange).
Collaborative Computing		Software that enables users to set up a workgroup and exchange documents with version control, chat on project issues, and update schedules. Video conferencing is an additional feature that can be added. The industry standard for collaborative computing is the H.323 protocol.

COM	Component Object Model	A model for binary code developed by Microsoft. COM, a broad set of object-oriented technology standards, enables programmers to develop objects that can be accessed by any COM-compliant application. Both OLE and ActiveX are based on COM. COM does specify an object model and programming requirements that enable COM objects (also called OLE components, or sometimes simply objects) to interact with other objects. These objects can be within a single process, in other processes, even on remote machines. They have been written in other languages, and may be structurally quite dissimilar. COM is referred to as a binary standard—it is a standard that applies after a program has been translated to binary machine code.
Communication Protocol		The rules governing the exchange of information between devices on a data link (such as TCP/IP, IPX/SPX, NFS, X.25 and others).
Communication Server		An intelligent device (e.g., a computer) providing communications functions; an intelligent, specially configured node on a LAN, designed to enable remote communications access and exit for LAN users.
CORBA	Common Object Request Broker Architecture	A standardized blueprint worked out by the OMG (Object Management Group) defining how application objects and ORBs can co-operate to deliver services or perform processes independent of platform, network, or location.
Corporate Data		All the databases of the company. This includes legacy systems, old and new transaction systems, general business systems, client/server databases, data warehouses, and data marts.

CRM	Customer Relationship Management	CRM is an enterprise integration of the following 10 components: • Sales/sales management • Time management • Telemarketing/telesales • Customer interaction center • E-marketing • Business intelligence • Multimodal access • Data sharing tools • E-business • Field service support
CTI	Computer Telephony Integration	Enables computers to know about and control telephony functions such as making and receiving voice, fax, and data calls, telephone directory services, and caller identification. It also includes functions such as making and receiving calls, forwarding and conferencing; call and data association —provision of information about the caller from databases or other applications automatically before the call is answered or transferred are some basic functions of CTI enabled applications.
Data Cleansing		Cleansing refers to the elimination of anomalies or outright mistakes in data that will otherwise impede with its intended usage. These include the discovery and elimination of homonyms, "fake" entries such as 999-99-9999 in a social security field, and so on.
Data Completeness		An indication of whether all the data necessary to meet the current and future business information demand are available in the data resource. It deals with determining the data needed to meet the business information demand and ensuring those data are captured and maintained in the data resource so they are available when needed.

Data Extract	Data which normally resides on an operational system and which is removed from that system for loading into a data warehouse.
Data Loading	Once the data is mapped and cleansed, it must be periodically updated and loaded into a single repository where it will be used by the organization.
Data Mapping	Not all databases capture exactly the same information in the same way, and so merging databases into single consistent structure requires transformations, calculations, and other "mappings" from one context to the other. For example, one database may capture a client's age in years, while another captures the date of birth, and a third captures the age in terms of defined ranges (20–35, 35–50, etc.).
Data Mining	(1) A process of analyzing large amounts of data to identify hidden relationships, patterns, and associations. This is often called "discovery-driven" data analysis. (2) The process of utilizing the results of data exploration to adjust or enhance business strategies. It builds on the patterns, trends, and exceptions found through data exploration to support the business. It is also known as data harvesting. (3) A technique using software tools geared for the user who typically does not know exactly what he's searching for, but is looking for particular patterns or trends. Data mining is the process of sifting through large amounts of data to produce data content relationships. This is also known as data surfing.

Data Rate, Data Signaling Rate		A measure of how quickly data is transmitted, expressed in bps. It is commonly, but often incorrectly, expressed in baud.
Database Marketing		A term used to describe the art/science of selecting a database of a potential set of customers for a given product or need. For example, defining a target mailing list for people likely to acquire a new mutual fund product.
Database Server		In local area networks, a node dedicated to providing mass data storage services to the other stations on the network.
DCOM	Distributed Component Object Model	An extension of COM which provides for support of objects distributed across a network. DCOM was developed by Microsoft and submitted to standards bodies. DCOM has been part of MS Windows 95 and NT since 1996. The protocol is based on ActiveX technology that enables software components to communicate directly with each other across a network in a reliable, secure, and efficient manner.
DES	Data Encryption Standard	A scheme approved by the National Bureau of Standards that encrypts data for security purposes. DES is the data-communications encryption standard specified by Federal Information Processing Systems (FIPS) Publication 46. Standard for encryption chips used in devices such as smart cards and PCs.
DHTML	Dynamic HTML	HTML documents with dynamic content; the three components of DHTML pages are HTML, JavaScript, and cascading style sheets. The three components are tied together with DOM, the Document Object Model.

Digital Certificate		An electronic "credit card" that establishes the user's credentials when doing business or other transactions on the Web. It is issued by a certification authority (CA). It contains the user's name, a serial number, expiration dates, a copy of the certificate holder's public key (used for encrypting and decrypting messages and digital signatures), and the digital signature of the certificate-issuing authority so that a recipient can verify that the certificate is real. Some digital certificates conform to a standard, X.509.
Digital Data		Information transmitted in a coded form from a computer, represented by discrete signal elements.
Digital Service		High-speed digital data-transmission services offered for lease by telecommunication service providers. Services include ADSL, HDSL, ISDN, Frame Relay, T1, and dedicated or switched 56-Kbps transmission lines.
DNS	Domain Name Services	Directory naming convention used for IP addresses, network user names, locations, etc.
DOM	Document Object Model	A programming interface specification developed by the World Wide Web Consortium (W3C), that lets a programmer create and modify HTML pages and XML documents as full-fledged program objects.
DS-3		North American data transmission line that runs at the rate of 45 Mbit/sec.
E-1		European digital data circuit transmission line that runs at 2.048 Mbps.
E-3		European digital data circuit transmission line that runs at the rate of 34 Mbps.

EAI	Enterprise Application Integration	Translating data and commands from the format of one application into the format of another. It is essentially data and command conversion on an ongoing basis between two or more incompatible systems using connectivity tools.
E-Business		Electronic business (derived from such terms as "e-mail" and "e-commerce") is the conduct of business on the Internet or extranet, not only buying and selling but also servicing customers and collaborating with business partners.
E-Commerce		The buying and selling of goods and services on the Internet, especially the World Wide Web. E-commerce is performed via EDI or secure servers that use public key encryption.
EDI	Electronic Data Interchange	The intercompany computer-to-computer transmission of business data in a standard format. For pure EDI, "computer-to-computer" means originating application program to processing application program. To the purist, EDI consists only of business data (not verbiage or freeform messages) in a standard format, approved by a national or international organization.
EIP	Enterprise Integration Portals	Web-based portals that use the features of a consumer information portal to distribute mission-critical enterprise data, applications, and processes to employees and partners connected to the Internet.
EJB	Enterprise JavaBeans	A component software architecture from Sun that is used to build Java applications that run in the server. It uses a "container" layer that provides common functions such as security and transaction support and delivers a consistent interface to the applications regardless of the type of server.

Encryption		The function of ensuring that data in transit may only be read by the intended recipient. Encryption disguises/scrambles the contents of a message as it travels over a network, making it unintelligible to hackers who may wish to monitor or copy it. Encryption uses a mathematical algorithm and a digital key (series of bits) based on the algorithm to code a message at one end of a transmission and then decode it at the other end.
Enterprise Data		Data that is defined for use across a corporate environment.
ERM	Enterprise Relationship Management	An integrated information system that serves the "front office" departments within an organization, which are sales, marketing, and customer service.
ERP	Enterprise Resource Planning	Enterprise Resource Planning is a business management system which integrates all the back office business functions of a business, e.g., inventory, sales, marketing, planning, manufacturing, finance, etc.
Ethernet		A network standard first developed by Xerox, and refined by DEC and Intel. Ethernet interconnects personal computers and transmits at 10 megabits per second. It uses a bus topology that can connect up to 1,024 PCs and workstations within each main branch. Ethernet is codified as the IEEE 802.3 standard.
Exchange		A unit established by a common carrier for the administration of communications services in a specified geographic area such as a city. It consists of one or more central offices together with the equipment used in providing the communications services. Frequently used as a synonym for central office.

Extranet		A new buzzword that refers to an intranet that is partially accessible to authorized outsiders. Whereas an intranet resides behind a firewall and is accessible only to people who are members of the same company or organization, an extranet provides various levels of accessibility to outsiders. Users can access an extranet only if they have a valid password and username, and the user's identity determines which parts of the extranet the user can view. Extranets are becoming a very popular means for business partners to exchange information. Sales Channel Automation is one form of extranet.
Fast Ethernet		Any 100-Mbps Ethernet-based networking scheme.
Fat Client		A term used for PCs (Personal Computers) that have internal storage and are connected or occasionally connected to the network. Both laptops and desktops are included in this category.
Fax	Facsimile	A device for transmitting copies of documents by wire or radio; also, a document transmitted by fax.
FDDI	Fiber Distributed Data Interface	An American National Standards Institute (ANSI)-specified standard for fiberoptic links with data rates up to 100 Mbps. The standard specifies: multimode fiber; 50/125, 62.5/125, or 85/125 core cladding; an LED or laser light source; and 2 km for unrepeated data transmission at 40 Mbps.
FFA	Field Force Automation	Term for applications and devices that allow mobile employees easy access to inventory management data, work orders, dispatch components, history, limited access to a knowledge base, skill and location based routing, SLA management and other multiple features.

Fiber Optics	A technology that uses light as a digital information carrier. The transmission medium is made up of small strands of glass, each of which provides a path for light rays that carry the data signal. Fiber optic technology offers large bandwidth, very high security, and immunity to electrical interference. The glass-based transmission facilities also occupy far less space than other high-bandwidth media, which is a major advantage in crowded underground ducts.
File Server	In local area networks, a node dedicated to providing file- and mass data-storage services to the other stations on the network.
Filtering	In LAN technology, discarding packets that do not meet the criteria for forwarding.
Firewall	The shielding mechanism, or gatekeeper, used to qualify users or limit access to files. Firewalls can either be hardware applications or software applications. In either form, the application is a secured entry to corporate networks via an outside connection.
FireWire	A high-speed serial peripheral interface invented by Apple to replace SCSI.
FLEX	A digital transmission protocol developed by Motorola that allows better control both one-way and two-way of the paging network.
Follow-The-Sun Support	Support options are available to users worldwide, regardless of time zone.
Fractional T1	A service aimed at customers who don't need or can't afford all 24 channels of a full T1 line. Fractional T1 service offers the use of one or more channels. The customers then pay only for the channels they use.

Frame Relay		A packet network service, relying on the data integrity inherent in digital transmissions to speed up transmission. Unlike old X.25 networks, frame relay "assumes" the data is correct and starts checking as soon as it receives the header, in a half-dozen error-checking steps. Frame-relay services are offered with T1 and DDS connections. Current packet data at speeds up to 45 Mbit/sec.
FTAM	File Transfer, Access, and Management	An OSI application utility that provides transparent access to files stored on dissimilar systems.
FTP	File Transfer Protocol	An upper-level TCP/IP service that allows copying of files across a network.
G3	Third Generation	The latest generation of cellular services. G3 is based on larger bandwidth thereby allowing the transmission of data, voice, and limited video. G3 is in testing modes in the U.S. and Europe and limited deployment in Japan.
Gateway		A hardware-software combination that connects two LANs (or a LAN and a host computer) that run different protocols, for example, a TCP/IP LAN and an SNA mainframe. The gateway provides the protocol conversion. Gateways, because they operate on the top three layers of the OSI model, are much more complex than bridges.
GPS	Global Positioning System	A system of 24 satellites, each of which orbits the earth every 12 hours at a height of 20,200 km. Four satellites are located in each of six planes inclined at 55° to the plane of the earth's equator. When receivers "see" three satellites simultaneously, they can calculate their latitude and longitude. When a fourth satellite is in view, altitude information is also available.

Group III Fax		The standard for current facsimile devices. Most facsimile systems marketed today are digital devices offering operating speeds of one minute or less.
Groupware		Software designed for network use by a group of users working on a related project. Applications might include, but are not limited to, sales team selling, calendaring, bulletin boards, project management, and other global software application environments.
GSM	Global System for Mobile Communications (previously Groupe Spécial Mobile)	The current and rapidly gaining acceptance, Pan-European (also Pacific Rim and South African) digital cellular telephone standard developed by the European Telecommunications Standards Institute's (ETSI) Groupe Spécial Mobile. Also used in some Middle Eastern countries, parts of Australia, and limited U.S. regions. The frequencies allocated to the service are divided into 200-kHz blocks, each of which supports eight simultaneous users per channel.
GSTN	General Switched Telephone Network	Same as PSTN.
GUI	Graphical User Interface	A graphics-based user interface that incorporates icons, pull-down menus and a mouse. The GUI has become the standard way users interact with a computer.
H.323		An International Telecommunications Union (ITU) industry standard manner for providing video, audio, and data conferencing over nonguaranteed bandwidth packet-switched networks, such as the Internet or other IP-based networks.

Handshaking		Exchange of predetermined signals between two devices, establishing a connection, or providing flow control. Handshaking is usually part of a communications protocol.
HDSL	High-Bit-Rate Digital Subscriber Line	A technology developed by Bellcore that provides full-duplex T1 service (using two twisted pairs of cable) over greater distances than the alternate mark inversion encoding that is traditionally used by T1.
Header		The control information added to the beginning of a message; contains the destination address, source address, and message number.
HTML	Hypertext Mark-up Language	HTML is developing into a platform-independent resource definition language to specify interfaces and graphic representations, and assemble applications from components.
HTTP	Hypertext Transfer Protocol	Protocol that enables Web browsers to interact with other applications or applets.
Hz	Hertz	A measure of frequency or bandwidth; 1 Hz equals one cycle per second.
IDL	Interface Definition Language	A descriptive language that is independent of any programming language; the IDL defines object interfaces. It lets an object reveal to potential clients what operations it can do.
IEEE	Institute of Electrical and Electronic Engineers	An international society of professional engineers that issues widely used networking standards.
IETF	International Engineering Task Force	The IETF is a large, open, international community of network designers, operators, vendors, and researchers concerned with the evolution of the Internet architecture and the smooth operation of the Internet.

IFC	Internet Foundation Classes	A set of Java classes that help speed the development of complex, robust, network-based applications. They introduce new functionality to the developers of network applications, and they expose existing functionality via a unified Java interface.
IIOP	Internet Inter-ORB Protocol	An open industry standard for distributing objects. IIOP will allow the browsers to interact with enterprisewide legacy systems based on the CORBA distributed objects standard.
IMAP	Internet Mail Access Protocol	An Internet mail access protocol that provides robust messaging. Many vendors feel IMAP may replace POP as a more robust, scaleable and manageable messaging protocol.
IMAP4	Internet Message Access Protocol, Version 4	Allows a client to access and manipulate electronic mail messages on a server. IMAP4 permits manipulation of remote message folders, called "mailboxes," in a way that is functionally equivalent to local mailboxes. IMAP4 also provides the capability for an offline client to resynchronize with the server.
Intranet		Intranet is widely used to describe the application of Internet technologies in internal corporate networks. Sometimes referred to as the Internet behind the firewall.
IP	Internet Protocol	The protocol used in gateways to connect networks at the OSI Network Level (Layer 3) and above.
IPX	Internet Packet eXchange	A communication protocol in Novell NetWare that creates, maintains, and terminates connections between network devices, such as workstations and servers. This was an early competitor to TCP/IP.

ISAPI	Internet Server API	A replaceable, dynamic-link library (DLL) that the server calls whenever there is an HTTP (Hypertext Transfer Protocol) request. ISAPI can be used to create applications that run as DLLs on the user's Web server.
ISDN	Integrated Services Digital Network	A CCITT standard for a network that accommodates a variety of mixed digital-transmission services; the access channels are basic rate (144 Kbps) and primary rate (1.544 Mbps).
ISDN BRI	ISDN Basic Rate Interface	An ISDN service referred to as 2B+D. BRI provides two 64-Kbps digital channels to the user's desktop. It is capable of simultaneously transmitting or receiving any digital signal—voice, video, or data. ISDN Terminal Adapters replace modems as the customer-premise connection to this service, enabling the user to make direct connections of data terminals and telephones. Service is also referred to as Narrowband ISDN.
ISDN PRI	ISDN Primary Rate Interface	An ISDN service that provides: • 23 B channels plus one D channel (but sometimes 24 B channels and no D channels if the D channel information can be carried over another circuit) in North America and Japan. In North America, PRI is implemented using a standard T1 circuit. • 30 B channels plus one D channel in Europe and Australia. Also referred to as Wideband ISDN.
ISP	Internet Service Provider	A company that provides end users and companies access to the Internet via POPs (points of presence).
Integrity		The function of ensuring the receiver that the data has not been tampered with by a third party en route.

IVR	Interactive Voice Response	An automated telephone answering system that responds with a voice menu and allows the user to make choices and enter information via the keypad. IVR systems are widely used in call centers as well as a replacement for human switchboard operators.
J2ME	Java 2 Micro Edition	SUN's Java programming environment for mobile devices such as smart phones. The program is made up of components that operate on the mobile device and components that operate on the application server.
Java		A platform independent programming language similar in nature to C++ developed by Sun Microsystems. Java applications, or applets, are different from ordinary applications in that they reside on the network in centralized servers. The network delivers the applets to the user's system when the user requests the applets.
JavaBeans API		An application programming interface which integrates Java, ActiveX, OpenDoc, and Live Connect objects into a new cross-platform framework.
Java OS		A highly compact operating system that runs Java applications on devices such as network computers, cellular phones, PDAs, and other devices.
Java Servers		Server software designed to support Java applications and clients.
Java Virtual Machine		A layer of software, embedded in computer operating systems such as UNIX or Windows, that enables the computer to run Java applications.
JDBC	Java Database Connectivity	A protocol which provides SQL-oriented connectivity to databases.

Jini		A programming language Sun Microsystems calls "spontaneous networking." Using the Jini architecture, users are able to plug printers, storage devices, speakers, and any kind of device directly into a network and every other computer, device, and user on the network knows that the new device has been added and is available. Each pluggable device defines itself immediately to a network device registry. Jini can be viewed as the next step after the Java programming language.
JIT	Just-in-time compilation	This technique is used in the Java computing environment. Java application code is dynamically downloaded from server to client on demand and compiled upon arrival at the client.
Kbps	Kilobits per second	Standard measurement of data rate and transmission capacity. One Kbps equals 1000 bits per second.
Kerberos		Security system developed by MIT and in use by several vendors.
Kilobyte		A standard quantity measurement for disk and diskette storage and semiconductor circuit capacity: one kilobyte of memory equals 1024 bytes (8-bit characters) of computer memory.
L2F	Layer 2 Forwarding	A protocol created by Cisco Systems. It is designed to tunnel the link level of higher level protocols over the Internet. Specifically, it is designed to tunnel PPP and SLIP sessions over the Internet. Competes with PPTP.

LAN	Local Area Network	A data communications system confined to a limited geographic area (up to 6 miles or about 10 kilometers) with moderate to high data rates (100 Kbps to 50 Mbps). The area served may consist of a single building, a cluster of buildings, or a campus type of arrangement. The network uses some type of switching technology and does not use common-carrier circuits, although it may have gateways or bridges to other public or private networks.
Language Mappings		Rules that specify how IDL is translated into a programming language, such as Java, C++, or Inferno, by following the rules defined in the IDL mapping for that programming language.
Latency		The time interval between when a network station seeks access to a transmission channel and when access is granted or received; equivalent to waiting time.
Layer		In the OSI reference model, one of seven basic layers, referring to a collection of related network processing functions; one level of a hierarchy of functions.
LDAP	Lightweight Directory Access Protocol	A protocol used to access a directory listing. LDAP services are seamless across all operating environments and applications on the Intranet and Internet. End users can discover information about people, including e-mail addresses, security keys, and phone numbers. Administrators can centrally manage access control and server configuration parameters across the entire enterprise. It is expected that LDAP will provide a common method for searching e-mail addresses on the Internet, eventually leading to a global White Pages.

LDPA	Lightweight Document Printing Application	Proposed IETF standard for printing across the Internet and corporate intranets.
Leased Line		A telephone line reserved for the exclusive use of a leasing customer without interexchange switching arrangements. A leased line may be point-to-point or multipoint.
LEC	Local exchange, local central office	The exchange or central office in which the subscriber's lines terminate.
Link Layer		Layer 2 of the OSI reference model, also known as the Data Link Layer (preferred usage).
MAN	Municipal Area Network	An extended network or cluster of networks serving a city, an academic or business campus, or any site featuring several widely separated buildings.
MAP	Manufacturing Automation Protocol	A suite of networking protocols that track the seven layers of the OSI model. Originated by General Motors.
MAPI	Messaging API	Messaging transport layer developed and promoted by Microsoft.
Mbps		Millions of bits per second (bps).
Megabyte, Mbyte, MB, Meg, or M		1,048,576 bytes, equal to 1024 kilobytes; basic unit of measurement of mass storage. *See* Byte.
Metadata		Data that describes other data. Data dictionaries and repositories are examples of metadata. The meta tag that describes the content of a Web page is called metadata. The term may also refer to any file or database that holds information about another database's structure, attributes, processing, or changes.

MHS	Message Handling System	The standard defined by the CCITT as X.400 and by the ISO as Message Oriented Text Interchange Standard (MOTIS).
MHz	Megahertz	A unit of frequency equal to 1,000,000 cycles per second.
MIME	Multipart Internet Mail Encoding	SMTP extension that allows audio, binary and visual data to be included as part of a mail message.
MNP	Microcom Networking Protocol	Networking protocols that include standards for error correction and data compression. MNP is used primarily in modems.
Modem	MOdulator-DEModulator	A device used to convert serial digital data from a transmitting terminal to an analog signal suitable for transmission over a telephone channel, or to reconvert the transmitted analog signal to serial digital data for acceptance by a receiving terminal.
MPEG	Motion Picture Experts Group	A standard for lossy compression of full-motion video.
MSMQ	Microsoft Message Queue Server	MSMQ provides the messaging services to support online transactions between users and programs and between programs.
MTBF	Mean Time Between Failures	A stated or published period of time for which a user may expect a device to operate before a failure occurs.
MTS	Microsoft Transaction Server	MTS provides the transaction services to support online transactions between users and programs and between programs.
Multicast bit		A bit in the Ethernet addressing structure used to indicate a broadcast message (a message to be sent to all stations). This is used in electronic meetings.
NAMPS		A Motorola initiative to digitize the AMPS infrastructure so more channels would be available for cellular communications

NC	Network Computer	The Network Computer represents a different approach to desktop computers. It is based on the Java language and Web protocols, and has no permanent local storage. The operating system, applications, and data are centrally stored and loaded over the network as needed. Unlike terminals connected to a shared central computer, however, much of the application processing takes place on the local NC client, and therefore NCs do not have the scaling problems of X-Terminals where all the processing occurs on the central computer and bulky screen-display commands tend to clog the network.
NDIS	Network Driver Interface Specification	A standard established by Microsoft for writing hardware-independent drivers.
NDMP	Network Data Management Protocol	Proposed IETF protocol that ensures interoperability between different file servers, tape drives and management software.
.NET		A Web-based development platform from Microsoft. It includes tools to develop and deploy Web-based applications that can be accessed from anywhere (e.g., browsers, handhelds, cellphones, etc.). Microsoft will also .NET enable its own applications such as its popular Office suite.

(continued)

.NET *(continued)*		.NET provides a complete development infrastructure that enables programming languages to be compiled into a Common Intermediate Language (CIL) that is executed on the fly or compiled into machine language by the Common Language Runtime (CLR) software in the target computer. This is similar to Java's intermediate bytecode, except that Java is one programming language, whereas Microsoft is allowing all programming languages to be compiled into the intermediate code.
		.NET applications can run on intranets as well as public Web sites, thus .NET is an all-inclusive software platform for internal and external use. Microsoft browsers and upcoming versions of Windows are expected to include .NET code which takes more advantage of .NET-based applications. Microsoft has enhanced its programming languages to support the .NET platform (e.g., Visual Studio.NET, Visual Basic.NET, etc.). It also introduced the .NET-enabled C Sharp (C#) programming language. .NET also supports existing Windows components (e.g., DLLs, COM objects, etc.).
NetWare		A LAN operating system from Novell.
NFS	Network File System	A method of mapping (technically called "mounting") shared remote disk drives so that they appear to be local. Developed and licensed by Sun Microsystems. NFS uses UDP, not TCP.
NFS	Network File Server	An extension of TCP/IP that allows files on remote nodes of a network to appear locally connected.

NI-1	National ISDN-1	While ISDN is a great idea, the many incompatible implementations have adversely affected its acceptance. The national ISDN effort is a successful effort to have a common implementation standard.
NNTP	Network News Transport Protocol	An open protocol that allows Internet and intranet servers to interact with ongoing newsgroups.
Notebook		A small portable computer, usually about the size of a standard letter-size notebook.
N-PCS	Narrowband PCS	Often referred to as two-way paging or enhanced paging.
Object Interface		Defines an object's boundaries and all the operations performed on that object.
Objects		A reusable packet that contains related data (called variables) and procedures (called methods) that can operate on the data. Generally, any item that can be individually selected and manipulated. This can include shapes and pictures that appear on a display screen as well as less tangible software entities. In object-oriented programming, for example, an object is a self-contained entity that consists of both data and procedures to manipulate the data.
OC-1		Synchronous data carried over optical fiber networks with data rates of 51.8 Mbits/s.
OC-3		Synchronous data carried over optical fiber networks with data rates of 155 or 311 Mbits/s.
OC-12		Synchronous data carried over optical fiber networks with data rates of 622 Mbits/s.
OC-48		Synchronous data carried over optical fiber networks with data rates of 2,488 Mbits/s.
OC-192		Synchronous data carried over optical fiber networks with data rates of 9.6 Gbits/s.

ODBC	Open Database Connectivity	Microsoft's effort to provide a single API for database (called data sources) access. Most database vendors have adopted the ODBC as a standard.
OLAP	OnLine Analytical Processing	Decision support software that allows the user to quickly analyze information that has been summarized into multidimensional views and hierarchies.
OMG	Object Management Group	An organization with over 600 members formed in 1989 by vendors and users, whose mission is "establishing industry guidelines and object management specifications to provide a common framework for distributed application development."
ORB	Object Request Broker	Acts as a middleman, connecting objects that request services or functions with objects that can satisfy the request. Application programmers do not have to know locations of remote objects.
OSI		An ISO standard for worldwide data communications. The standard is a framework for implementing communication protocols in seven layers. During the communication session control is passed from one layer to another, in a hierarchical approach. Both X.400 and X.500 e-mail and directory standards are OSI-compliant. As Internet communication protocols mature, the OSI standard is becoming less relevant.
Packet-Switched Network		A data-communications network that transmits packets. Packets from different sources are interleaved and sent to their destination over virtual circuits.

Palm		Handheld electronic organizer from Palm Computing, Inc., Santa Clara, CA. The first Palm was the PalmPilot introduced in April 1996, which sold more than 350,000 units by year end. Later renamed simply the "Palm," these devices fit into a shirt pocket, contain an address book, scheduler and to-do list, and newer versions can download e-mail.
		The Palm uses a pen interface and "Graffiti" handwriting recognition for entering data. Its HotSync technology lets the user synchronize the Palm and a PC with the touch of a button. Palm Computing supports an open architecture for its Palm operating system, and third-party developers have created a huge variety of software for it.
PAN	Personal Area Newtork	Refers to a wireless network that operates in the one to five foot area. Either RF or infrared technology is used in this environment. The new Bluetooth wireless technologies are in the PAN category.
PBX	Private Branch eXchange	An in-house telephone switching system that interconnects telephone extensions to each other, as well as to the outside telephone network. It may include functions such as least cost routing for outside calls, call forwarding, conference calling, and call accounting.
PCMCIA	Personal Computer Memory Card International Association	The name of the group that produced the specification for the credit card-sized plug-in boards known as PC cards (initially) for laptop computers.

PCS	Personal Communication Services	The name for a new wireless voice and data communications system. Lower transmit power (than standard AMPS cellular telephones) is to be used, so the telephones can be smaller and lower-cost (since smaller batteries and less-powerful components are needed).
PDA	Personal Digital Assistant	A small, handheld, battery-operated, microprocessor-based device that: • Stores telephone numbers, addresses, and reminders • Sends and receive e-mail and faxes (wirelessly) • Receives pages (just like an alphanumeric pager) • Recognizes handwriting
Pocket PC		A handheld Windows-based computer that runs the Pocket PC operating system (formerly Windows CE). The Pocket PC operating system (Version 3.0 of Windows CE) adds a new interface along with greater stability, Pocket Office applications (Internet Explorer, Word, and Excel), handwriting recognition, an e-book reader, wireless Internet and longer battery life. The Pocket PC was designed to compete more directly with Palm devices.
POP	Point of Presence	An Internet service providers (ISP) point of entrance into the Internet.
POP	Post Office Protocol	Internet mail server protocol that provides basic message transfer capabilities using SMTP.

POTS	Plain Ordinary Telephone Service	The only type of telephone service available 20 years ago. A simple analog telephone (and the corresponding service from the phone company) on which the user can dial and receive calls. The lowest common telephone service available everywhere. A pair of copper conductors (a twisted pair of wires, called the local loop) connects a telephone to the nearest central office. It is estimated that there are about 560 million such local loops in the world.
PPP	Point to Point Protocol	Standardized dial-in protocol for Internet access from client to Internet Point of Presence (POP) equipment
PPTP	Point to Point Tunnel Protocol	The specification was developed by the PPTP forum, a collaboration between Microsoft Corporation and a group of several leading manufacturers of Internet Service Provider (ISP) equipment. PPTP enables implementation of secure, multi-protocol Virtual Private Networks (VPNs) through public data networks such as the Internet.
PRM	Partner Relationship Management	Allows for a more seamless relationship with partners through the management of channel programs, opportunities, sales, marketing, and leads.
PSDN	Packet-Switched Data Network	Provides connections to computers in other parts of the world using the X.25 protocol. The interface between a PSDN and a PSDN user normally operates over a data communications link (e.g., an ISDN link). Each PSDN interface is capable of supporting multiple virtual circuits. A virtual circuit is a logical connection between two PSDN users. Data is exchanged across virtual circuits as packets. A packet is the smallest unit of data transfer supported by the PSDN.

PSTN	Public Switched Telephone Network	The telephone system over which calls may be dialed.
Push	Server-push	The delivery of information from the Internet, an intranet, or news server that appears to be initiated by the information server rather than by the information user or client, as it usually is.
QoS	Quality of Service	The ability to define a level of performance in a data communications system. For example, ATM networks specify modes of service that ensure optimum performance for traffic such as real-time voice and video. QoS has become a major issue on the Internet as well as in enterprise networks, because voice and video are increasingly traveling over IP-based data networks that were not designed for continuous speech or viewing. The protocols of the Internet were designed for the military with exactly the opposite in mind: to withstand an enemy attack. Thus, transmissions are broken into packets that can travel different routes and arrive at different times.
RAID	Redundant (or Reliable) Array of Inexpensive Disks	A disk subsystem (that appears as a single large, fast, super-reliable disk drive) composed of more than one (usually equal-sized) disk drives (called an array) to provide improved reliability, response time, and/or storage capacity.
RAS	Remote Access Services	A method used to allow remote computing users to access multiple computing environments from a dial-up connection.
RBOC	Regional Bell Operating Company	One of the regional Bell telephone companies that were created when AT&T was dismantled in 1984.

Real-Time Enterprise		A new business model for the 21st century. In a real-time enterprise all company departments, customers, suppliers, and partners are electronically connected via internal and Internet applications (i.e., the e-enablement of all business functions). This allows the company's information systems to function like a 24-hour live video cam on its operations, instantly alerting managers to changes in customer demand, competitive situations, inventory, availability of supplies, and profitability. Real-time enterprises will benefit from recent technological advancements such as real-time computing and e-business. These technologies will allow companies to streamline business processes and manage customer relationships with such proficiency that they will achieve sustainable productivity gains, decreased costs, and long-term profitability. The result will be a fundamental and permanent economic change in the companies' operations.
Remote Access		The ability of a computer in one location to reach a device that is some distance away, perhaps at another site.
RF	Radio-Frequency Modulation	The electromagnetic format in which broadcast and cable TV signals are transmitted.
Router		A network device that examines the network addresses within a given protocol, determines the most efficient pathway to the destination, and routes the data accordingly. Operates at the Network Layer of the OSI model.
RSA		A de-facto standard for untappable public-key encryption developed by RSA Data Security Inc.

RSVP	Resource Reservation Protocol	A standard for reserving resources required in each network (there could be many networking technologies involved) along an end-to-end path so that an application (likely multimedia) receives the required quality of service.
RTSP	Real-Time Streaming Protocol	A proposed standard that was submitted to the IETF for delivery of real-time media over the Internet. RTSP is a communications protocol for control and delivery of real-time media. It defines the connection between streaming media client and server software, and provides a standard way for clients and servers from multiple vendors to stream multimedia content. Audio, video, and other content can be streamed in real-time using this protocol. It incorporates aspects of the International Telecommunications Unions H.323 specification.
SET	Secure Electronic Transactions	MasterCard, VISA, and several other technology vendors have developed a single method that consumers and merchants will use to conduct bankcard transactions in cyberspace as securely and easily as done in retail stores today.
SFA	Sales Force Automation	The first generation of automating the sales force with contact management, forecasting, sales management, and team selling. SFA has evolved into CRM.
S-HTTP	Secure Hypertext Transfer Protocol	A method that is used to support the encryption and decryption of specific WWW documents sent over the Internet. S-HTTP uses RSA public-key encryption. A main use is expected to be for commerce (payments). An alternative method is SSL, which encrypts all traffic for specific TCP/IP ports.

Smart Phone		A telephone with advanced information access features. It is typically a digital cellular telephone that provides normal voice service as well as any combination of e-mail, text messaging, pager, Web access and voice recognition. Smart phones emerged in the late 1990s and are expected to become widespread.
S/MIME	Secure Multipurpose Internet Mail Encoding	A standard way to send and receive secure electronic mail. Based on the popular Internet MIME standard, S/MIME provides the following cryptographic security services for electronic messaging applications: authentication, message integrity and nonrepudiation of origin (using digital signatures), and privacy and data security (using encryption).
SMS	Short Message Service	A text message service that enables short messages of generally no more than 140-160 characters in length to be sent and transmitted from a cellphone. SMS is supported by GSM and other mobile communications systems.
SMTP	Simple Mail Transfer Protocol	Dominant e-mail messaging protocol for use on TCP/IP networks.
SNA	Systems Network Architecture	IBM's proprietary data communication protocols. Original SNA (introduced in 1974) is now sometimes called Subarea SNA. SNA was mainframe-centric, since all communications were directly from a dumb 3270-type terminal to a mainframe (running Advanced Communication Facilities/Virtual Telecommunications Access Method--ACF/VTAM).
SNMP	Simple Network Management Protocol	SNMP services allow centralized, replicated, secure management of user information, access control parameters, and server configuration information.

SOAP	Simple Object Access Protocol	A protocol from Microsoft, IBM, and others for accessing services on the Web. It employs XML syntax to send text commands across the Internet using HTTP. Similar in purpose to the COM and CORBA distributed object systems, but lighter weight and less programming intensive (at least initially), SOAP is expected to become widely used to invoke services throughout the Web. Because of its simple exchange mechanism, SOAP can also be used to implement a messaging system. SOAP is supported in COM, DCOM, Internet Explorer, and Microsoft's Java implementation.
SONet	Synchronous Optical Network	A synchronous data framing and transmission scheme for (usually single-mode) fiber optic cable. Based on multiples of a base rate of 51.84 Mbits/s. This base rate (called OC-1) can carry 672 DS-0s, or 28 T1s, or 21 E1s, or 7 T2s, or 7 digitized television channels (typical for submarine fiber optic cables), or 1 T3, or combinations of these. It has additional capacity for an order-wire (a digitized-voice intercom for technicians to use), error detection, and framing and bit-rate matching. The 51.84 Mbits/s comes from the basic frame of 810 bytes (nine rows of 90 columns of bytes each), which is sent 8,000 times per second.
		Speeds up to OC-192 are currently standardized. An equivalent scheme for copper media (called STS-1) has identical rates, formats, and features.
		SONet can be used to carry ATM traffic as well as any other type of traffic (for example, it can be a "faster point-to-point T1").

SQL	Structured Query Language	An English-like, ASCII text, standardized language that is used to define and manipulate data in a database server.
SSL	Secure Sockets Layer	A security protocol that provides communications privacy over the Internet. The protocol allows client/server applications to communicate in a way that is designed to prevent eavesdropping, tampering, or message forgery.
STS-1		Synchronous data carried over copper networks with data rates of 51.8 Mbits/s.
STS-3		Synchronous data carried over copper networks with data rates of 155.5 or 311 Mbits/s.
STS-12		Synchronous data carried over copper networks with data rates of 622 Mbits/s.
STS-48		Synchronous data carried over copper networks with data rates of 2,488 Mbits/s.
Sub-notebook		A small portable computer, usually smaller than the size of a standard letter-size notebook. Size is less than 5 lbs.
T-1		A digital carrier facility used to transmit a DS-1 formatted digital signal at 1.544 Mbps. A T1 carrier can transmit large volumes of information across great distances at high speeds at a (potentially) lower cost than that provided by traditional analog service. A T1 carrier uses time-division multiplexing to manipulate and move digital information. It consists of one four-wire circuit providing 24 separate 64-Kbps logical channels; the aggregate data rate equals 1.544 Mbps. T-1 lines are asynchronous.
T-3		28 T1 lines in one; the aggregate data rate is 44.746 Mbps. T-3 lines are asynchronous.

T.120		An International Telecommunications Union (ITU) industry standard for multipoint data conferencing.
TAPI	Telephony Application Programming Interface	Microsoft's and Intel's method of integrating telephone services and computers so that the user's computer can control the user's telephone.
TCP	Transmission Control Protocol	UNIX's connection-oriented layer 4 protocol (also called transport), which provides an error-free connection between two cooperating programs, which are typically on different computers.
TCP/IP	Transmission Control Protocol/Internet Protocol	A layered set of protocols that allows sharing of applications among PCs, hosts, or workstations in a high-speed communications environment. Because TCP/IP's protocols are standardized across all its layers, including those that provide terminal emulation and file transfer, different vendors' computing devices (all running TCP/IP) can exist on the same cable and communicate with one another across that cable. TCP/IP corresponds to Layers 4 (Transport) and 3 (Network) of the OSI reference model.
TDMA	Time-Division Multiple Access	A high-speed, burst mode of operation that can be used to interconnect LANs; TDMA was first used as a multiplexing technique on shared communications satellites.
Thin Client		*See* NC or Network Computer.
TSAPI	Telephony Services Application Programming Interface	AT&T's and Novell's method of integrating telephone services and computers.

Tunneling		Tunneling is a technology that allows a network transport protocol to carry information for other protocols within its own packets. For example, IPX data packets can be encapsulated in IP packets for transport across the Internet, which isn't normally possible. The packets are delivered unmodified to a remote device that has been set up to handle them. The packets may be secured using data encryption, authentication or integrity functions. A VPN can be created by using tunneling.
Unicode Character Set		A character coding scheme designed to be an extension to ASCII. By using 16 bits for each character (rather than ASCII's 7), virtually every character of every language, as well as many symbols (such as "&"), can be represented in an internationally standard way, and the current complexity of incompatible extended character sets and code pages should be eliminated. The first 128 codes of Unicode correspond to standard ASCII.
URL	Uniform Resource Locator	The "address" that is used to specify a WWW server and home page. For example, *http://www.yourcompany.com*, which indicates that the host's address is *www.yourcompany.com*.
vCalendar		An industry standard format developed by the Versit Consortium for exchanging scheduling and activity-recording information electronically. If a person sends the user a week's schedule in a vCalendar attachment to an e-mail note, the user can drag-and-drop it to a personal information manager (PIM) type of application program and integrate it with or relate it to the user's own schedule. Several CRM and SFA vendors are developing to this standard.

vCard		An industry standard format developed by the Versit Consortium for the exchange of an electronic business (or personal) card. Many people are beginning to attach vCards to e-mail notes. Software application developers can create programs that process vCards by letting the user view them, or drag-and-drop them to an address book or some other application. vCards can include images and sound as well as text.
VCS	Version Control System	A software management scheme that keeps software up to date on clients connected to the server.
VoIP	Voice Over IP	The two-way transmission of audio over a TCP/IP channel. VoIP can be transmitted over the Internet, private intranet, or WAN. QoS issues must be taken into account.
VPN	Virtual Private Network	A virtual private network utilizes a public network such as the Internet as a secure channel for communicating private data. VPN technology allows the creation a of secure link between a corporate LAN (local area network) and a remote user's PC. Encryption and other security mechanisms are utilized to ensure that only authorized users can access the network and that the data cannot be intercepted.
VRML	Virtual Reality Modeling Language	An extension of HTML to support 3D views, simulation and modeling.
VXML	Voice XML	An extension to XML that defines voice segments and enables access to the Internet via telephones and other voice-activated devices.
W3C	World Wide Web Consortium	An organization that is dedicated to keeping open standards as part of the Internet infrastructure.

WAN	Wide Area Network	A data communications network that spans any distance and is usually provided by a public carrier. In contrast, a LAN typically has a diameter (the maximum distance between any two stations) limited to less than a few kilometers and is entirely owned by the user.
WAP	Wireless Application Protocol	The Wireless Application Protocol is an open, global specification that allows mobile users to use handheld wireless devices to instantly obtain and make use of real-time information.
Web Services		Self-contained, self-describing, modular application that can be published, located, and invoked across the Web. Web services perform functions, which can be anything from simple requests to complicated business processes. Once a Web service is deployed, other applications (and other Web services) can discover and invoke the deployed service
Webtop		Refers to a desktop environment that can run Java or Windows CE applications. This may be either a Java-enabled browser on an existing desktop platform, or a Java device desktop.
Wideband		A system in which multiple channels access a medium (usually coaxial cable) that has a large bandwidth, greater than that of a voice-grade channel; typically offers higher-speed data-transmission capability.
Windows CE		A streamlined version of Windows from Microsoft for handheld PCs (HPCs) and consumer electronics devices. It runs "Pocket" versions of popular applications such as Microsoft Word and Excel, as well as many applications that are geared specifically for the smaller platform. As of Version 3.0, Windows CE was changed substantially and renamed Pocket PC.

Windows DNA	Distributed InterNet Architecture	Microsoft's umbrella term for its enterprise network architecture built into Windows 2000. It includes all the following components, which collectively provide a Web-enabled infrastructure for an organization. • Web Server and ASP (Active Server Pages) • COM Objects • MTS and MSMQ • AppCenter Server
WWW	World Wide Web	The network of servers on the Internet, each of which has one or more home pages, which provide information and hypertext links to other documents on that and (usually) other servers. Servers communicate with clients by using the Hypertext Transfer Protocol (HTTP). WWW server addresses (Uniform Resource Locators or URLs) are typically of the form *http://www.orgname.com* where *orgname.com* is the DNS name of the organization running the server.
X.25		The standard interface for packet-switched data communications networks, as designated by the CCITT.
X.400		International standard for message transmission, used for e-mail and EDI data.
X.435		International standard within the X.400 family for EDI messaging. Offers improved ability for EDI and e-mail to travel together, a purchase order and an e-mail plea for meeting the schedule mentioned in the PO, as an example. The PO and e-mail plea are called "body parts."
X.500		A CCITT directory services standard.
X.509		Public key encryption protocol. A certificate is the digital equivalent of an employee badge, passport, or driver's license.

| **XML** | eXtensible Markup Language | A new Internet language that will make the World Wide Web smarter, an ISO-compliant subset of SGML, HTML is a markup language, consisting of text interspersed with a few basic formatting tags. XML is a meta-language, containing a set of rules for constructing other markup languages. With XML, people can make up their own tags, which expands the amount and kinds of information that can be provided about the data held in documents. |
| **XSL** | eXtensible Stylesheet Language | A style sheet format for XML documents. It is the XML counterpart to the Cascading Style Sheet (CSS) language in HTML, although XML supports CSS1 and CSS2 as well. XSLT (XSL Transformations) are extensions to XSL for converting XML documents into XML or other document types and may be used independently of XSL. |

Index

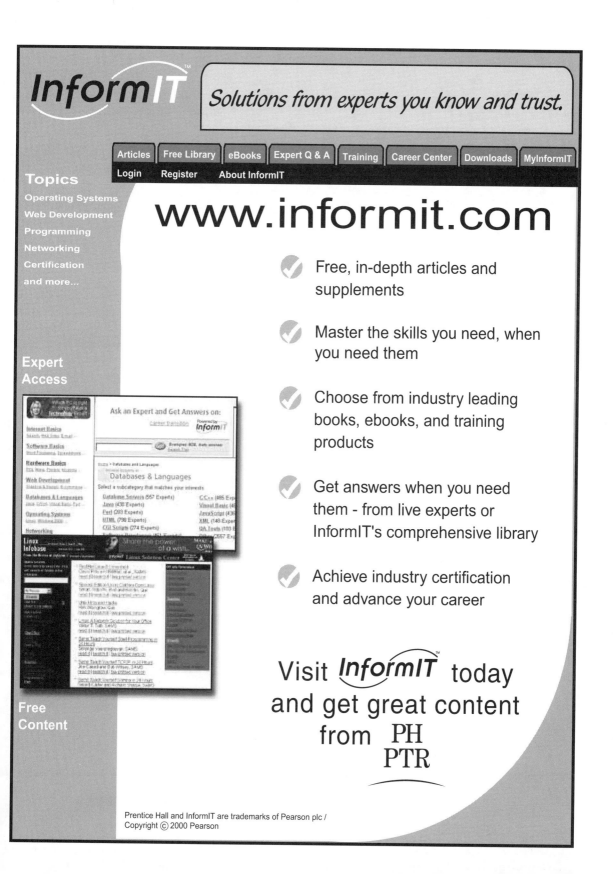

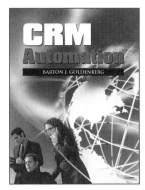